AN INTRODUCTION TO
HUSSERLIAN PHENOMENOLOGY

Northwestern University
Studies in Phenomenology
and
Existential Philosophy

AN INTRODUCTION TO HUSSERLIAN PHENOMENOLOGY

Rudolf Bernet
Iso Kern
Eduard Marbach

With a Foreword by Lester Embree

Northwestern University Press
Evanston, Illinois

Northwestern University Press
Evanston, Illinois 60208-4210

First published 1989 as *Edmund Husserl: Darstellung seines Denkens* by Felix Meiner
Verlag, Hamburg. Copyright © 1989 by Felix Meiner Verlag. English translation
and foreword copyright © 1993 by Northwestern University Press. First published
1993. All rights reserved.

Second paperback printing 1995
Third paperback printing 1999

Printed in the United States of America

ISBN 0-8101-1030-X

Library of Congress Cataloging-in-Publication Data

Bernet, Rudolf.
    [Edmund Husserl. English]
    An introduction to Husserlian phenomenology / Rudolf Bernet, Iso
Kern, Eduard Marbach.
        p.   cm.—(Northwestern University studies in phenomenology
and existential philosophy)
    Includes bibliographical references and index.
    ISBN 0-8101-1030-X (pbk.)
    1. Husserl, Edmund, 1859–1938. 2. Phenomenology. 3. Knowledge,
Theory of. I. Kern, Iso. II. Marbach, Eduard. III. Title.
IV. Series.
B3279.H94B4513 1993
193—dc20   93-16547
                                                            CIP

Contents

Foreword

This masterful volume will be the standard overview in English of Edmund Husserl's philosophy for at least a generation. Of course, an enormous amount has now been written about phenomenology. One can have mixed feelings about the fact that the vast bulk of it is interpretive when the phenomenologist himself hoped so hard that there would be generations of research, not on what he had written, but rather into the matters themselves, that is, investigations for which his own crude results would provide only points of departure and inspiration. The first generation of phenomenologists understood this, and perhaps the third will remember it. This is not to say that there is no place for scholarship on texts, for such invaluable research makes finding points of departure and drawing inspiration easier. From that perspective, then, the present work simply raises Husserl scholarship to a new plateau. Future investigators will appreciate this great leg up.

A few words on earlier Husserl scholarship, especially in America. First there was a literature in what may be called the "report genre." In English that begins with Marvin Farber's *Foundation of Phenomenology* (1943), which summarizes Husserl's *Logische Untersuchungen* of 1900–1901, includes a forgotten analysis by Dorion Cairns of the "Die Frage nach dem Ursprung der Geometrie" in the first volume of *Philosophy and Phenomenological Research* (1940), and is continued in reports on other works, such as that on *Ideen II* reprinted in Schutz's *Collected Papers*, vol. 3 (1966), and above all those by Gurwitsch on *Krisis*, reprinted in his *Studies in Phenomenology and Psychology* (1966), and on *Phänomenologische Psychologie*, reprinted in his *Phenomenology and the Theory of Science* (1974). The master of this genre is

Paul Ricoeur, whose reports were gathered and translated by Edward Goodwin Ballard and myself in 1967 as *Husserl: An Analysis of His Phenomenology* (with the present translation, that work, which in many thousands of mostly paperback copies was long the sole road for Anglomonoglots to an overview of Husserl, now becomes chiefly an access to an aspect of Ricoeur's own thought). Except for the Schutz—and of course the journal *PPR*—the mentioned works were brought out by James Edie in the great Northwestern University Press series, Studies in Phenomenology and Existential Philosophy, up through the early 1970s in an effort at professional leadership that deserves a prize.

In part on the foundation of that earlier literature, there are now many outstanding books in English on Husserl by such researchers as David Carr, Fred Kersten, J. N. Mohanty, Robert Sokolowski, Elizabeth Ströker, William McKenna, and others, studies better called critical interpretations. Yet those works—for example, Mohanty's *Edmund Husserl's Theory of Meaning* (1969) or Sokolowski's *The Formation of Husserls's Concept of Constitution* (1970) (currently the article literature gravitates toward *Husserl Studies*)—focus on aspects. The first and for long the only attempt at an overview was Alwin Diemer's *Edmund Husserl: Versuch einer systematischen Darstellung seiner Phänomenologie* (2d ed., 1965), which was never translated and is far from being as well grounded or objective as this volume, which, in retrospect, appears the long-awaited as well as authoritative synoptic presentation.

Why have we had to wait so long? There seem to be two reasons. Husserl was astonishingly productive; and, as his last assistant, Eugen Fink, and his closest American student, Dorion Cairns, always emphasized, his philosophy actually lies in the over 45,000 shorthand pages of *Nachlass* (accordingly, the seven substantial publications of Husserl's lifetime are only an iceberg's tip). Thus the *Nachlass* has had to be transcribed, analyzed, and, at least to some extent, published. (The Summer 1991 catalog from Kluwer Academic Publishers lists twenty-seven volumes of *Husserliana* edited by the Husserl Archives in Louvain, Freiburg, and Cologne, which, with [Nijhoff] Kluwer, ought also to receive medals for their dedication, for a total of merely 14,698 pages!) Somehow one is confi-

dent that—between them at least—the three authors of
this work have not only deeply studied all of that (among
them they edited several volumes of *Hua*), but are also
deeply familiar with vast quantities of the still-unpublished
materials.

The other reason that we have had to wait so long is that
Husserl's thought and especially expression take consider-
ably more effort to master than, say, Kant's. The team of
authors here shows itself not only to have mastered all the
material but to have been masterful in selecting and ar-
ranging the thought in the exposition, which—as it
should—takes the form of successively shorter chapters in
a series where the later ones assume what the earlier have
established. To be sure, while Husserl's indissoluble difficulties are not dissolved, the needless difficulties are reduced.

It is daunting to recall the historical era in the American
phenomenology of our youth that is best called "Phenomenology and Existentialism" if only because, in that great
upsurge of energy, Husserl was, incredibly, read by so
many as the father of existential phenomenology, a pater-
nity that still needs challenging. That was challenged
chiefly on the basis of what Merleau-Ponty confected in
reference to a book whose English title actually is *The Crisis of the European Sciences and Transcendental Phenomenology*. No competent reader can study the present work and
fail to comprehend (a) that Husserl's was from about 1905
through to the end of his life a transcendental philosophy,
and (b) that Husserl's focus was in the philosophy of science. Existential phenomenology is not transcendental
and, although not lacking in interest in science theory, is
more concerned with human existence.

(In the present work's emphasis on Husserl as philosopher of science, one could wish that there were more
about the human sciences. But, again correctly, the emphasis follows Husserl's own emphasis primarily on the so-
called formal sciences, i.e., logic and mathematics [which
the phenomenologist considered "positive sciences," at
least until they were grounded in transcendental intersub-
jectivity], secondly on the natural sciences [essentially
physics, naturally, with which he kept up at least during his
Göttingen period and through students including Alexan-

der Koyré and Aron Gurwitsch], and finally the human sciences, in which he had been interested since his encounter with Wilhelm Dilthey before World War I.)

Positively speaking, existential phenomenology was chiefly a reflective-descriptive philosophical preoccupation with concrete individual human subjectivity. That philosophical project has great continuing merit, but not the Husserl "reading" it spawned, which can be objected to in three further respects. First, there was opposition from the friends of Being to Husserl's alleged intellectualism. That is what the concern with the concrete was about; constitutive phenomenology was thought oblivious to passion and action. Now, however, with the recent publication of the phenomenologist's lectures on ethics and value theory from 1908 to 1914, the illusion that his thematization of the intellect was essentially exclusionary rather than a matter of emphasis can fade. The chronology of Husserl's life, work, and teaching in the Appendix of this work shows that he actually taught ethics (and for him that included value theory) not only during 1908–14 at Göttingen but also annually at Halle between 1891 and 1901 and again at Freiburg in 1919, 1920, and 1929, all told about a score of times. (But of course sections are devoted to evaluation and volition from the *Prolegomena* through the *Ideen* to *Formal and Transcendental Logic*; one need only scan tables of contents to find them, if, that is, one is interested and thus is beyond one's own albeit "anti"-intellectualism. The authors of the present work are well aware of this aspect but explicitly deemphasize it.)

The existentializing thinkers seem, second, tacitly to have made specifically *human* subjectivity or consciousness their topic (even overlooking Merleau-Ponty's discussions of insects and other nonhuman animals). From his lifetime publications, Husserl could also be assimilated to such a scheme, but the authors of the present work offer the contrary view on the basis of the manuscripts.

Finally, Husserl explores the question concerning the *a priori* grounding of the possibility of diverse kinds of unitary surrounding-worlds in correlation with diverse kinds of "personal" subjects. Summarizing his efforts in a very general fashion, we may say that he investigates the surrounding-worlds

belonging to humans—among them the world of early childhood, the world of the "mature" person as "normal," the
world of "primitive" peoples, the world of the abnormal, the
world of the sick—over against the surrounding-world belonging to animals. From the 1930s in particular, one finds notes in
which Husserl is seeking to grasp the specific difference of the
surrounding world belonging to humans, or of the person, as
against the animal world. [see below, chap. 8]

It is not insignificant that, as his review of Husserl's
"Nachwort" in 1932 shows, Aron Gurwitsch may have con-
tributed to that intensification of the Husserlian concern,
which goes back at least to *Ideas II*. If this broadening did
not include gender differences on all levels and for all species, it was no more unusual for the time than it is acceptable
today. However, clearly the potential for such a further expansion of the problematics is possible and right.

Finally, decades of discussion of Husserl on intersubjectivity ought finally to have eliminated illusions about the ontological (but not methodological) priority of *individual*
subjectivity for Husserl, although the preoccupation with
the lone individual in our current wider intellectual culture
and its relation to the science of psychology remain interesting. Perhaps it is time to move from the question of how the
collective precedes the individual to whether Husserl may
actually have been a transcendental animist, which these
ecological times may be prepared to hear. In short, some
emphases in Husserl's lifetime publications ought not to be
considered essences.

Let us return now to the interpretation and its expression
in the work here being prefaced. The stated and achieved goal
is to bring out the dynamic of Husserl's constantly growing
thought. Many interpreters proceed on the assumption of a
great sea-change between the *Logical Investigations* and the
Ideas; after all, Husserl's philosophy became transcendental
then. The present work, in contrast, shows the continuity of
development in which a philosophical emergence reached its
broad outlines before World War I and then filled in some
spaces during the Freiburg period. Except for one chapter,
where a need was felt to respond to the Derridian preoccupation (and it is a very interesting chapter), the interpretation is
objective, which is not to say naive but rather that a balanced

and well-grounded text about texts was skillfully striven for and essentially attained by fairly classical philological or hermeneutical methods (but, happily, there was no felt need to explicate that). Husserlian views are not analyzed in order to be attacked. As stated, it will be quite some while before sufficient reasons can be found for transcending this presentation.

Regarding the problem of Husserl's expression, it bears remembering that he was trained as a scientist, specifically as a mathematician. He seemed to have thought he could simply take over the words of other thinkers to express new significations that his readers would learn because they were engaged in attempting to verify the accounts he offered. Perhaps the worse case is the word pair, "transcendental/ empirical" he took from Kant. (Incidentally, the list of Husserl's courses included here shows much teaching of Kant, but then the dominant school of thought before phenomenology was neo-Kantianism in France as well as in Germany—but not in America, where a positivism cum logical empiricism has replaced pragmatism before phenomenology was imported.) Even so, Husserl's chief source of inspiration is in Locke, Berkeley, Hume, Stuart Mill, the author of *Psychology from the Empirical Standpoint*, and the Brentano school, no surprise in an Austrian philosopher formed in the late nineteenth century—which should also be remembered if he is to be properly understood as a reflective theoretical observer and describer of phenomena rather than a transcendental deducer of unobservable conditions of possibility.)

Since some advanced thinkers today still cannot grasp how Husserl's transcendental is observable (but they have heard that he saw essences), perhaps a small chart and a few comments will help (see table 1).

Table 1

	worldly	transcendental
eidetic	(2)	(4)
factual	(1)	(3)

As is quite clear in *Cartesian Meditations* and *Formal and Transcendental Logic*, Husserl recognizes four bideterminate types of phenomenological cognition. As numbered in the

four cells of table 1, number (1) would be a factual inquiry
into worldly subjectivity; this is what occurs in the experimental (nonbehaviorist) psychology of Husserl's time and
might be somewhat empirical in Kant's sense. Number (2)
would be an eidetic phenomenological psychology in which
now the essences pertaining to the intelligibility of worldly
subjectivity can be ascertained, for example, perception,
empathy, recollection, and reflection. Number (3) would be
a factual inquiry into conscious life as nonworldly and would
be capable of asserting, for example, that a transcendental
human intersubjectivity called Husserl Scholarship exists on
Earth late in the twentieth century and has reached a new
plateau. And number (4) is something like Kant's transcendental in its function, for it is concerned with what is universal and necessary in nonworldly subjectivity for any world
and positive science whatever. But, again, and against Kant-
ianism, neo- or paleo-, this transcendental intersubjectivity
is in the broad signification observed, not factually, to be
sure, but eidetically; from the transcendental rather than
the natural standpoint; and, to repeat, not transcendentally
deduced as a set of conditions of possibility.

The above exercise is offered to demonstrate how Husserl's terminology thus can mislead and also to show how
complex is the thought expressed in it. It may be added that
his terminology changed. For example, early on "real" signified "spatiotemporal" and later just "temporal," so that,
at Freiburg, transcendental subjectivities are realities; and
"sense" [*Sinn*] early expressed the concept that "signification" [*Bedeutung*] later specifically expressed when *sense* was
broadened for a generic role. But the authors of this interpretation know all that and much more. In sum, the ultimate virtue of this work is that it systematically guides the
reader through the conceptual as well as linguistic thickets
of practically the entire knowable philosophy of Edmund
Husserl, a leading candidate for the title of the most influ-
ential philosopher in the twentieth century. It is difficult to
see what more it would take to make a masterpiece of
scholarship.

LESTER EMBREE

Introduction

This presentation of Edmund Husserl's phenomenological philosophy proceeds *developmentally* (chronologically); however, it is also divided according to *systematic connections*, which become evident in the progression of Husserl's thinking. The development of his thinking is traced by returning to the sources, that is, Husserl's *Nachlass* and the critical edition of his work. It is his work which stands in the foreground and neither its philosophical-historical origins nor Husserl's influence on other thinkers.[1]

In first approaching the very extensive collection of Husserl's work, a kind of splitting into two parts can be made out. Viewed chronologically, the split can be said to begin in the last years at Göttingen (around 1915–1917), but is only clearly seen in the early years of Husserl's teaching at Freiburg (around 1917–21) (see "Chronology of Husserl's Life" in the Appendix). Considered systematically, the partition relates to the consistent extension of the research program of phenomenological philosophy towards a *genetic-explanatory* phenomenology as a supplement to the hitherto carried-out *static-descriptive* phenomenology. Roughly speaking, this development can be outlined as follows.

In the early phases of his thinking, Husserl was concerned chiefly with the phenomenological-descriptive analysis of specific types of experiences and their correlates (experiences of thinking and knowing and their products) as well as with describing general structures of consciousness; he also aimed at the foundation and elaboration of the corresponding methodology (phenomenological reflection, reduction, and eidetics).

In the later phases, along with further refinements and some essential supplements to those problem areas, there appears in the foreground ever more intensely the attempt by means of genetic phenomenology to elucidate the concrete unification of experiencing in the personal ego and in the transcendental community of egos, or monads, as well as in the constitution of the correlative surrounding worlds and of the one world common to all.

Our introduction reflects the systematic connections in this movement of thought through its various chapters. In so doing there resulted a certain reduction of the importance of crucial points which occur in the sources. This is because large parts of the publications Husserl produced in his lifetime (above all, the *Logical Investigations* [1900/ 01], the *Ideas* [1913], and *Formal and Transcendental Logic* [1929]) look like purely momentary states of rest, or "condensations," of a thought-movement that was constantly in flux and which can be followed precisely only in the manuscripts. According to Husserl's own testimony, the *Ideas* and *Formal and Transcendental Logic* were composed, on the basis of many years of preparatory work, as if he were in a "trance." What became "fixed" in such publications has been time and time again pondered in the manuscripts and often, in accordance with his progressive thinking, put into novel connections. This presentation orients itself in important respects on these partly still unpublished research manuscripts (see "Note on Husserl's *Nachlass*" in the Appendix). It must be clearly stated, however, that topics whose textual basis consists almost entirely of unpublished manuscripts have not been taken into account in this text. Thus, in particular, Husserl's work on ethics, practical philosophy, intentional anthropology, and also his later treatment of the universal time problems, as well as the realm of feeling and willing, all of these are not considered here.

Structure of the Presentation

The first chapter, "Mathematics, Logic, and Phenomenology," focuses on fundamental ideas in Husserl's philosophical beginnings, paying attention to their logical connection and especially to their prefiguration of his later thought. Coming from mathematics (see "Chronology of Husserl's Life" in the Appendix), Husserl raises questions in his first work, *Philosophy of Arithmetic* (1891), regarding the psychological origin of basic arithmetical concepts such as unity, multiplicity, and number (as permanently determined number—the cardinal numbers). In the first place, we will discuss Husserl's analysis of the origin of the *authentic* concept of number, that is, number to be conceived of intuitionally (§ 1). Act-performances of collecting and reflection upon them stand at the center here. Special attention is paid to the question of the foundation of abstraction for the basic arithmetical concepts. The answer given to this question is of great importance in connection with so-called logical psychologism. The discussion also makes it possible to characterize the epistemologically motivated point of departure of the critique of the foundations of arithmetic and logic that is specific to Husserl and distinguishes him from Frege. The description of the subjective origins of authentic concepts of number is complemented by some remarks on Husserl's view of the *inauthentic*, that is, the purely *symbolic* representations of number, and of the construction of the infinite series of natural numbers by means of permanently determined number-symbols and rules of construction.

At the heart of the presentation of the development of thought subsequently followed by the early Husserl, there is a series of questions pertaining to the working out of the idea of *pure logic* and to the outline of its tasks (§ 2). Husserl's refutation of logical "psychologism," which was to become famous, was required for the idea of pure logic and cannot be separated from its positive counterpart. This positive companion consists in a novel, eidetic-descriptive "psychology" of the experiences of thinking and knowing, which Husserl introduced in the six "Investigations towards a Phenomenology and Theory of Knowledge" in the second volume of the *Logical Investigations* (1901). The "purification" of the objects and laws of formal logic from psychological determinations, which is accomplished in the *Prolegomena* (1900), was not Husserl's final aim. Rather, it is preliminary work paving the way for an understanding of the connection between pure logic and concrete acts of thinking, between ideal conditions of cognition and temporally individuated experiences of cognition. In this perspective, the *Prolegomena* appears as a continuation of questions previously raised in the *Philosophy of Arithmetic*.

The discussion at the end of the first chapter focuses on Husserl's early and continuous interest in a specifically phenomenological theory of knowledge, one that goes back to the "performing activities" (§ 3). The original task of providing a subjective complement to objective logic led Husserl to investigate the general *a priori* of correlation of cognition, of the sense of cognition and the object of cognition, and to conceive an absolute science designed as universal analysis of constitution in which the origins of objectivity in transcendental subjectivity are elucidated.

The second chapter is dedicated to the "methodological founda-tion" of phenomenology as the science of pure and transcendental con-sciousness, in which the constitution of objectivities is accomplished. In this chapter, the internal connections between reflection, reduction, and eidetic inquiry are set out in such a way as to show how they gradually appeared to Husserl himself in his returning "to the matters themselves [*zu den Sachen selbst*]." The fundamental achievement of *phenomenological reduction*, which Husserl only began to understand clearly around 1905, consists in its making it possible to secure a methodically *pure* grasp of consciousness as an object of reflective research. The *motivation* for per-forming phenomenological reduction is closely related to Husserl's mo-tives for practicing philosophy in general and his idea of philosophy, which mainly took shape in arguments with philosophical skepticism. Husserl adopted "different, equally possible ways" in his works, in order to move by means of phenomenological reduction from the natural to the philosophical attitude. He distinguished essentially three types of path. These paths are sketched here by tracing Husserl's position with respect to Descartes, to Kant, and to the English Empiricism of Locke, Berkeley, and Hume. Husserl's idea of philosophy is determined by the thought of a revival of the Socratic-Platonic idea of philosophy as abso-lute knowledge in its connection with self-knowledge. As such an idea, philosophy is only to be realized in Husserl's view in an infinite historical process, and not as the work of one man and his "system."

The subsequent discussion of the method of *eidetics* or, as Husserl also put it, of *eidetic reduction*, provides a clearer picture of the kind of science that Husserl strove for with his pure or transcendental phenome-nology. Our presentation draws attention to the connections between Husserl's theory of eidetics, the science of consciousness in respect of its essence, his view of the meaning of the *a priori*, and the exemplary nature of the mathematical way of thinking. Against this background, we com-ment on the "new" descriptive eidetics of transcendentally pure con-sciousness that Husserl conceived as parallel to, and contrasted with, the "old" eidetic disciplines of geometry and arithmetic. Husserl's under-standing of the relationships between sciences of fact (empirical sci-ences) and sciences of essence (eidetic sciences) is also sketched here, as well as his idea of the *application* of *a priori* knowledge to matters of fact as a rationalization of the empirical sciences.

The discussion in the following chapters (3–6) centers on Hus-serl's analyses of the activity of consciousness that forms the genuine object of phenomenological investigations, methodically clarified along the lines of chapter 2. Activities of consciousness are clarified according to their general structures and functions as well as to particular basic forms and modalities.

In chapter 3, we discuss the structures and functions of *intentionality* and immanent *temporality* which universally mark out consciousness in general. In his *Logical Investigations*, Husserl had established the variety of intentional relations to objects, considered to be proper to "psychic phenomena," primarily in the essential structures of the intentional *act* (*noesis*), and not in those of its objects (§ 1). From 1906 onwards, however, Husserl began to include the intentional correlate, that is, the *noematic* forms of givenness and function, within the field of the phenomenologically pure given. This step was decisive for the further development of his intentional analysis towards the realization of the program of constitutional analysis, as is shown by reference in the *Ideas* (1913) to the earlier discussion. More specific questions regarding the theory of the relation of noematic sense to the actual object are pursued further in chapters 4 and 6.

Time-consciousness (§ 2) was understood by Husserl as the most fundamental consciousness and as presupposed in all other structures and forms of consciousness. Husserl followed two main directions in his analyses of time-consciousness. On the one hand, and in critical discussion of Brentano's theory of time, Husserl answered the question of how it is possible to grasp a temporal object (a duration or a temporal flow) by means of his doctrine of the three moments of present consciousness (primordial impression, retention, and protention). In contrast to the originary, perceived temporal field, recollection is to a certain extent a reiteration of the whole temporal fringe as "presentiated present." As such, recollection or presentation is radically different from mere retention. The idea of *objective* time is explained by Husserl as achievement of presentation and identification.

On the other hand, Husserl pursues the question whether time-constituting consciousness is itself within time. Husserl moved in the course of his thinking from the view that time-constituting consciousness was itself within time, to the opposite view according to which time-constituting consciousness itself was to be designated as nontemporal, as "absolute, primordially constituting consciousness." Finally the question is addressed of how it is at all possible, according to Husserl, to grasp this "true and ultimate absolute." We consider here Husserl's suggested solution of the self-appearance of the flow of consciousness through the so-called longitudinal intentionality of retention.

With chapter 4, the presentation of Husserl's analyses of basic forms and modalities of consciousness begins. Consciousness of *percep-*

tion plays a paradigmatic role for Husserl; it is thus handled first and in detail. To begin with, we discuss the phenomenological finding that spatial perceptual objects are never fully given in intuition with respect to all their sides and characteristics, and yet, in the simple performance of a perception of a thing a unified *thing* is seen, and not merely, say, its front side (§ 1). The position that Husserl held in the *Logical Investigations* regarding mixed forms of awareness (i.e., both signitive and intuitive) as a clarification of the full act of perception is critically discussed. Next, we comment upon the concrete continuum of appearances as perceptual process and its constitutional achievement (§ 2). The continuous synthesis of perception is defined more precisely as a process of fulfillment (see also chapter 6). Finally, Husserl's doctrine of the bodily conception of the perceiving subject is outlined (§ 3). The central question here is directed at the constitutional achievement of the kinaestheses by means of which Husserl made the various stages of the constitution of thing and space in perceptual processes phenomenologically intelligible.

The fifth chapter exhibits Husserl's analyses of basic forms of *intuitional presentations* [*anschaulicher Vergegenwärtigung*]. First, acts of phantasy, picture-consciousness, and memory are explained according to their essential intentional characteristics (§ 1). As acts of *intuition,* they are contrasted to conceptual presentations [*begrifflichen Vorstellungen*]. As intuitional *presentations,* they are distinguished as modifications of simple sensuous perceptions or presentations. A sketch is presented of how Husserl, beginning with the inspiration he received from Brentano's account of *inauthentic* presentations, gradually developed his doctrine of intuitional presentations. Speaking quite generally, Husserl's analysis of presentation deals on the one side with the moment of *intuitiveness* in presentation and presentation, respectively; on the other side it treats the moment of *positing* and attempts descriptively to grasp the partially intertwined distinctions of the two sides. More precisely outlined are the doctrines of the eidetic law of intentional implication or modification and of the neutralizing modification; the phenomenon of the overlapping or the conflict of intuitions; and finally the phenomenon of the "permeation" or "interpenetration with conflict" of intuitions, which Husserl sees actualized in ordinary picture-consciousness.

We then turn to Husserl's analysis of the form of presentation called empathy [*Einfühlung*] which exhibits special complications (§ 2). Before 1910 and then primarily in discussions of the doctrines of Th. Lipps, Husserl took his departure in the analysis of the experience of other psychical beings from the dilemma that this experience can be understood neither as an authentic perception, nor as an authentic, logical inference founded in categorial acts. As regards the more detailed discussion, our presentation is guided along the lines of Husserl's exposition of the problem of the experience of the other in the fifth of the *Cartesian Meditations* (1929). In the first place, an ambiguity in Husserl's reflections on the sphere of ownness or the primordial sphere [*Eigenheitssphäre*] is clarified. On the one hand, Husserl takes this concept to mean the sphere of the most primordial [*ursprünglichst*] self-givenness imaginable, which is by no means a solipsistic sphere. On the other hand, however, Husserl sometimes means by "sphere of ownness" something like a solipsistic sphere in the sense of a stratum of experience *prior to* our experience of the other, a stratum of experience which is supposed to underlie and found the higher stratum, our experience of the other.

We then explain more precisely how Husserl's concrete analysis of the presentiating experiences of empathy shows them to exhibit a structure of mediate apperceptive transference. Fundamental for the motivation of this transference is the similarity between a perceived external body [*Körper*] and my own bodily organism [*Leib*]. This section then closes by mentioning several further distinctions and extensions of the analysis of empathy within the discussion of the intersubjectivity of the world as well as of authentic social acts.

The sixth chapter, "Judgement and Truth," looks at the phenomenological elucidation of acts of thought and knowledge in the pregnant sense of authentic acts of thinking and of true judging, respectively. The chapter begins with a close examination of Husserl's theory of language, as expressed in particular in the first of the *Logical Investigations*. The focus here is on the concept of the intentional act of significant speech (§ 1). In a further step, Husserl's account of the connection of the identical expression or the identical signification and the individual semantical intention is critically discussed. It becomes evident how Husserl moved to a noematic understanding of the concept of signification, an understanding first brought out in lectures of 1908 and similar to Frege's position on "thought [*Gedanke*]." In this connection, we discuss problems concerning the relation of (noematic) signification and object of reference, which result from the quasi-objective interpretation of signification.

We then turn to the question of how Husserl is able to account for the difference between true and false speech within the framework of his theory of signification and judgement (§ 2). The key to Husserl's theory of truth is his concept of intuitive fulfillment, which is discussed in the sixth of the *Logical Investigations* in particular. More specifically, we explicate what is to be understood by founded "categorial acts" and their "ideal" objects, and above all what is meant by the intuitively fulfilling act of "categorial intuition." Afterwards, we point out how knowledge, and primarily scientific knowledge, as a complex act of satisfied cognitive interest or justified cognitive pretension is able to be distinguished by Husserl according to levels of completeness as regards its evidence and how the connection between evidence and truth is made. Finally in this chapter, we take into account Husserl's doctrine that sensuous acts of cognition are necessary as a basis for categorial acts of thinking and true judging which are acts of cognition in the pregnant sense.

In the remaining chapters (7–10), we consider those problem areas, in particular, that come into view with Husserl's turn towards including genetic-explanatory phenomenology alongside the fundamental static-descriptive one.

We first discuss in chapter 7 what Husserl meant by *genetic phenomenology,* the idea of which was outlined during the period of 1917 to 1921. This is done in contrast to its counter-concept, static phenomenology. Static phenomenology or constitutional analysis has a fixed "ontology" as guide, and it inquires into experiences [*Erlebnisse*]. With regard to genetic phenomenology it is first shown that even before the actual breakthrough of this idea, Husserl had occasion to use the term "genetic" within three topic areas (constitutional phenomenology versus ontology; constitutional systems as hierarchical structure; and time-consciousness). The basic insight that characterizes the idea of authentically genetic phenomenology is then brought forward. This insight is that Husserl no longer speaks of the "I" as empty pole of identity—a position he still held in *Ideas* (1913)—but rather elaborates a concept of "I" which possesses capabilities, takes positions, has convictions, etc., and to which the world is pregiven as the horizon of an "I can" do this and that. The task of genetic phenomenology will be one of investigating into the history of the "I," one of inquiring into the very origin of constitutional systems and the objects constituted within these systems. We then sketch the two basic forms of genesis, active and passive genesis, which were distinguished by Husserl. Regarding passive genesis, its universal principle of *association* is outlined according to two main forms. Husserl's idea of genetic phenomenology also implies his view of the self-constitution of the "I" as a determinate personality as well as the task of elucidating the genesis of any concrete monad in its communalization with other monads. At the end of the chapter, attention is given to Husserl's understanding of his philosophy as *transcendental idealism* in connection to the idea of genesis.

In chapter 8, the *concepts of the pure "I" and the personal "I,"* which have just been mentioned in characterizing genetic phenomenology, are discussed at greater length. "Pure I" and "personal I" denote two aspects of a uniform problem which became increasingly important only after the *Logical Investigations.* Two completely different contexts within the static analysis of experiences motivated Husserl to take the pure "I," which he had first regarded as a fiction, into consideration. As a result, there arises an ambiguity in the concept of the pure "I" within Husserl's work as a whole. On the one hand, Husserl advanced the pure "I" shortly before the *Ideas* (1913) as the principle of unity delimiting one stream of consciousness over against other streams of consciousness. A brief look at Husserl's later work is given in order to show that this intersubjective context of the function of the pure "I" is to be found time and again. On the other hand, and again shortly before the *Ideas*, Husserl introduced the concept of the pure "I" for defining the act of consciousness in the pregnant sense of the *cogito.* This occurred in connection with the phenomenon of attention. In his later work, Husserl went on to conceive the notion of the "I" as the pole of the affections, as the center of reception, in correspondence with the notion of the pure "I" as the center of radiation of intentional experiences. Husserl's conception of the personal "I" is very closely related to the turn to a genetic understanding of the problem of constitution. Through thematizing the relation between the personal "I" and the surrounding world, Husserl arrived during his Freiburg period at a theory, linked to Kant, of transcendental subjectivity and intersubjectivity in correlation to the objective world of experience. The chapter ends with a reference to Husserl's determination of the relationship between pure "I" and personal "I."

Chapter 9 is devoted to the exposition of Husserl's definition of the *lifeworld* [*Lebenswelt*]. Following a preliminary remark on Husserl's use of the word "lifeworld," the theme is more closely explicated in three stages. First, the lifeworld is discussed as a problem concerning the foundation of the objective sciences. It was only in the 1920s that—in opposition to his being oriented initially toward the multitude of the special sciences—the question concerning the *unity* and fundamental organization of the sciences stepped into the foreground of Husserl's discussions in the theory of science. This new question arose for Husserl principally with respect to the unity and the inner structure of the *world* to which the special sciences refer. This question of unity is related to the ideal of a universal science resting upon an ultimate philosophical ground. The motivation for Husserl's development of the problem of the "natural concept of the world," or the "lifeworld," grew out of his attempt to come to terms with the dualism of nature and spirit of the Cartesian tradition. In a further step, we look more closely at Husserl's account of the relation between the scientific world and the lifeworld. It will be explained why what at first was for Husserl a grounding problem in the theory of science developed in his considerations into a universal problem of Being and truth, such that, in his last work, the *Crisis* of 1936, "lifeworld" has come to designate a "universal problem." In the final step of this chapter, we discuss Husserl's scheme for an ontology of the lifeworld. Its establishment requires an epoché in respect of all the objective sciences as well as in respect of all interests directed toward an aim which remain related to special horizons. We clarify the attitude here demanded by contrasting it with the so-called "personalistic" attitude. After some remarks on Husserl's vision of an "*a priori* of the lifeworld," the chapter ends by relating the ontology of the lifeworld to the problem of a transcendental-phenomenological reflection on subjectivity.

In the final chapter, we briefly comment on Husserl's overall conception of philosophy. This consists basically of an explication of the titles "*transcendental phenomenology*" and "*metaphysics*." Transcendental phenomenology in its systematic execution forms in Husserl's eyes the complete eidetic foundation and hence the decisive condition of the possibility of a scientific philosophy and metaphysics. Husserl also speaks of eidetic phenomenology as *first philosophy*; in this conception, empirical philosophy of factual actuality is taken to be *second philosophy* or metaphysics. Ultimately, however, Husserl's conception of the philosophy of actuality, his metaphysics, does not merely consist in the interpretation of the factual sciences according to transcendental *a priori* principles. Rather, and already in quite early texts, it is the irrational fact of the rationality of the world which is regarded by Husserl as a theme of metaphysics in a new sense, whereby Husserl mainly thinks of ethical and religious problems. Finally, we point out a change in Husserl's account of the relation between First and Second Philosophy. One is tempted in this regard to speak of a "turn [*Kehre*]" in Husserl. Indeed, reminiscent of Heidegger's hermeneutic of facticity, the starting points of Husserl's philosophy now appear to be the primordial fact of the "I" and the fact of its historical world as such. Nevertheless, Husserl held fast to eidetics as the condition of possibility of transcendental knowledge.

The present book is the result of a combined effort of three authors. Structure and content of each chapter have been defined in common and repeatedly discussed. Despite this close collaboration and the many mutual suggestions for revisions of the manuscript, a text has resulted in which each author's individuality has left clear traces. It thus seems appropriate to mention who was chiefly responsible for which parts of the text: R. Bernet: chapters 1, 3/§ 1, 4, and 6; I. Kern: chapters 3/§ 2, 5/§ 2, 7, 9, and 10; E. Marbach: introduction, chapters 2, 5/§ 1, and 8.

1

Mathematics, Logic, and Phenomenology

usserl's entire philosophical work moves within the magnetic field of the concept of *science*. Thinking within this field, Husserl exposes himself to a basic tension in the character of science itself, a tension that may be conceived as an opposition between philosophically and nonphilosophically or "naturally" oriented science. The establishment of phenomenological science thus comes about by way of a critique of the already more or less successfully functioning sciences, philosophical and natural. In the development of Husserl's work, however, this phenomenological critique of science undergoes certain essential alterations. The early Husserl, interested primarily in mathematics and logic, searched for a philosophical, that is, an epistemological, foundation for the most abstract procedures in the formation of logical and mathematical theory. The later Husserl, by contrast, focuses more and more on the epistemological relevance of both sensuous experience and human praxis. This trend should not, however, be overestimated. The *Philosophy of Arithmetic, Crisis, Ideas,* and *Formal and Transcendental Logic,* all indicate the same philosophical interest in the subjective life of cognition. For Husserl, the phenomenological critique of the foundations, validity, and consequences of the natural sciences always leads to the phenomenological science of the subject of cognition. However often and however fundamentally either the determination of this subject or the articulation of its connection with the objects of the sciences may have altered in the development of Husserl's thinking, the science of scientific *activity* retains priority.

In its first phase of development, phenomenology is essentially the science of the subjective "origins" or "sources" of mathematics (especially arithmetic and geometry) and formal logic. A pertinent discussion of this may thus be regarded at once as a representative historical exposition of Husserl's early work. In what follows, we shall therefore lay primary stress on the considerations in the *Philosophy of Arithmetic* (1891) and the *Logical Investigations* (1900–1901). We shall refer to the *Formal and Transcendental Logic* (1929) only where compelled to do so by our central concern with earlier developments.

§ 1. The Psychological Origin of Arithmetical Concepts

The following exposition of certain basic thoughts from Husserl's *Philosophy of Arithmetic* necessarily remains limited and schematic. Above all, our interest is directed toward demonstrating that this first book represents, not a mere youthful transgression stemming from Husserl's psychologistical period, but a highly valuable work of intrinsic and enduring importance. We shall confirm this in our exposition by observing that the *Philosophy of Arithmetic*, in spite of undeniable shortcomings, anticipates certain decisive results not only of the *Logical Investigations* but also of Husserl's later work. The phenomenological analyses of the sixth of the *Logical Investigations* concerning the epistemological grounding of the validity of mathematical and logical objects are a (partial) actualization of the program of research projected in the *Philosophy of Arithmetic*. Their doctrine of the intuitive and the signitively mediated, empty categorial acts and the doctrine of the constitution of ideal objects and formal, universal concepts is an answer to questions that Husserl pursues in the *Philosophy of Arithmetic*. If Husserl later distances himself from the *Philosophy of Arithmetic*, this has nothing to do with the results of those early researches but only with their operative methodological understanding of the subjective direction in the clarification of arithmetic.[1]

The Proper or Authentic [*eigentlich*] Concepts of Number

The initial and most crucial portion of the *Philosophy of Arithmetic*, chapters 1–4, takes over, without substantial alterations, the text of Husserl's habilitation thesis at Halle in 1887, "Concerning the Concept of Number: Psychological Analyses" (*PA*, 289–338). Husserl's analyses of the concept and origin of the cardinal numbers are thoroughly oriented by a preconception according to which number is understood as a complex "objectivity," as a "multiplicity of unities," "a plurality, ensemble, aggregate, collection, set" (297). His primary interest is directed toward the more precise determination of the particular kind of "multiplicity" or "whole" that makes up the concept of number. According to Husserl's plausible argument, it is possible to clarify just what a "numerical whole" is only by describing more precisely both the "unities" involved within the whole and their encompassing "combination" [*Verbindung*]. Moreover, Husserl assumes that both of these tasks may be discharged exclusively by a "reflection" on the "act" that sorts out each of the "unities" and "at the same time holds each together with the others, thus unifying all of them" (337). He justifies this by maintaining that the formation of the formal concept of number would have to support itself in the element common to all the determinate, concrete wholes, namely, in the very act of collecting that is implicit in their formation. Thus, the concept of number can be made clear only in reflection on its "origin" in certain psychical activities. Frege inferred from this that Husserl's theory mixed "psychology and logic" so as to yield an alkali in which "everything becomes a presentation" [*Vorstellung*].[2] Until now, this judgment has scarcely had to justify itself in the light of a close examination of Husserl's actual doctrine. On the contrary, it has become a commonplace that, with this judgement, Frege cured Husserl of "psychologism," the mixture of logic and psychology, and led him onto the path of a clear distinction among "concept," "signification," and "object."[3] We ourselves shall be able to take a position in regard to this question only when we have better understood Husserl's deliberations about the psychological origin of number.

The whole or determinate manifold that forms the intuitional basis for the acquisition of the concept of number is the result of a synoptical view of certain more original unities. The concern here is with a process of inclusion and exclusion, a process of "selective attention" that determines which pregiven unities will be combined into an ensemble. It should be clear that the determination of the content of the unities combined into a whole is entirely irrelevant for the determination of the concept of number.

> Every presentational object [*Vorstellungsobjekt*], whether physical or psychical, abstract of concrete, whether given in sensa-

> tion or phantasy, etc., can be united in a whole together with
> however many other such objects one likes, e.g., . . . a feeling,
> an angel, the moon, Italy. [298]

If, unlike the case of the set in Husserl's example, the concern is no longer with a concrete but rather with an abstract or formal whole, such as that of number, then one may no longer speak of "objects" in reference to the "unities" thus combined. In fact, the concern here is with any "contents whatever," the determination of which is irrelevant, that is, freely variable. These contents come to be "thought . . . as something or other, as one thing or another" (335). Husserl characterizes the "concepts 'something' [*Etwas*] and 'one thing' [*Eins*] . . . as formal concepts or categories" (84). The same holds *a fortiori* for the abstract concepts "multiplicity and number" that are formed from them (ibid.). The "number" thereby comes to be conceived more precisely as a "multiplicity" for which the "how many" of the "something" comprehended by it is "sharply determined" (83). A number, for example "three," is nothing but the determinate multiplicity formed by means of the collective combination of ones.

> Something and something and something . . . or: some such
> one and some such one and some such one . . . or, more
> briefly: one and one and one . . . [335]

The concept of number is thus the concept of an abstract but, in relation to the unities from which it is built up, "sharply determined" multiplicity.

Husserl is primarily concerned "not with a definition of the concept of multiplicity [i.e., of number], but rather with a *psychological characterization* of the phenomena on which the abstraction of this concept rests."[4] It then becomes the task of this "psychological characterization" to trace the formation of the concept of number in the corresponding psychic activities. The formulation of this question about the psychological origin of the concept of number is imprinted with the psychology of Brentano and especially with the investigations of Carl Stumpf (*Über den psychologischen Ursprung der Raumvorstellung*, 1873), under whose supervision Husserl had elaborated his habilitation thesis. The "psychological analyses" concerning the concept of number find their legitimation in the observation that the act of combining represents the only invariant within the compass of all concrete wholes. Where the concern rests with characterizing the determination of the contents of the *concepts* "multiplicity" and "number," the easy, obvious approach is to orient oneself in respect of this psychical invariant. At the same time, with this clarification of the sense of the "formal concepts or categories," "multiplicity and number" (84), by way of describing their formation in a "psychical act of second order," that is, "of higher order" (74, 92), our concern becomes directed toward an initial, still deficient execution of a phenomenological constitutive analysis.[5] It is no accident that this constitutive analysis was carried out for the first time in respect of an object for which there is no equivalent in the realm of the sensuous experience of an empirical thing. Wholes such as multiplicity and number are given only in virtue of the combining activity which mutually relates and synthetically unifies abstract objects such as "anything whatever" or "something-in-general [Etwas-überhaupt]." Translated into the language of the *Logical Investigations*, this means simply that categorial objects are constituted not in sensuous intuition but only in categorial activity (see below, chapter 6, § 2).[6]

There remains, however, a problematical feature in Husserl's discussions of the psychological origin of the concept of number, namely, the function ascribed to *reflection*. Husserl asserts that the concept of number as determinate multiplicity results from reflection on the act of combining. The concept of number is derived, namely, from the concept of collective combination, the collective combination of elements is a distinctive characteristic of all concrete wholes; this characteristic can be gathered by abstractive attention from every concrete whole; this abstractive attention is necessarily linked to reflection because the collective combination originates in the psychical act of collecting. An initial difficulty results from the determination of the activity of collective unification. It is this activity upon which one must reflect in order to gain the concepts of collective combination and multiplicity (330, 333ff.). The act of collecting consists in discerning discrete contents in temporal succession and logically determinate order and at once in comprehending these contents within a comprehensive unity (337). Considered more precisely, the act of collecting directs itself toward contents *given in consciousness*. It is a "psychical act of a second order," that is, "of a higher order," which, collectively unifying them, refers itself to the psychical acts in which the corresponding discrete contents come to be discerned for themselves (74, 92). Translated into the language of the *Logical Investigations*, the collecting act is a founded act of categorial formation, an act bestowing categorial form upon freely variable but, ultimately, sensuously given materials. In the *Philosophy of Arithmetic*, however, this act of categorial formation is still determined quite unclearly as an "act of comprehending *interest* and *discernment*," an act of selective attention (337; cf. also 335).

As concerns the reflection upon this act of combining, such reflection must be prepared not merely to describe the essential characteristics of the psychical performance of this act, but as well, and more decisively, to form the "abstract" "general concepts [*Allgemeinbegriffe*]" of collective combination-in-general and formal multiplicity-in-general.

> In reflection upon that elementary act of selective interest and
> discernment, an act which possesses as its content the presentation of the whole, we acquire the abstract notion [*Vorstellung*]
> of collective combination. It is by means of this notion that we
> form the general concept [*Begriff*] of the multiplicity as a whole
> which combines parts in a merely collective manner. [335]

In this regard, it becomes clear that reflection itself is unable to form the general concept being sought. Rather, the data of reflection form the "bases for the formation of the general concept of multiplicity" (300). One does not learn, however, just how this formation of the general concept on the basis of the reflective datum is itself to be understood. At this stage, Husserl lacks not only a clear understanding of the process of "ideation" implied in the formation of a concept (see below, chapter 2, § 2). He also lacks an understanding of the distinction between the formation of a categorial objectivity and the formation of the concept of this objectivity.

It also remains unclear how and whether reflection upon the act of collecting would be beneficial not only for the formation of the "abstract notion of collective combination," but also, "by means of" this notion, for the formation of the "abstract concept of multiplicity." Is it really true that reflection plays the same, necessary role both in the formation of the relational concept "collective combination" and in that of the concept of objective "multiplicity"? It seems plausible, of course, that "a special reflection" (330) upon the categorially formative act of combining would prove useful for *grasping* a purely formal relation such as collective combination. It is also true that the formation of the general concept "collective combination" must orient itself in respect of the question of how "this unification [comes to be] discerned" (330). Nevertheless, it remains unclear, whether it is the collecting act itself or the logical relation produced by it which should serve as the foundation for this formation of the concept.

The fact that such a question finds no clear answer suggests that in the *Philosophy of Arithmetic* Husserl was not yet fully conscious of the distinction between the categorial act and the correlative categorial objectivity. We encounter an analogous difficulty when we make the transition from the general logical concept "collective combination" to a consideration of the formation of the general concept "multiplicity." In its formation, the concept of the multiplicity should presumably be mediated by the notion of the collective combination and thus by a reflection upon the act of collecting. Nevertheless, for the formation of the concept of this multiplicity one scarcely requires an express reflection upon the act. It would seem more plausible to found this concept in respect of an individual multiplicity of determinate content, that is, in directly regarding the ("sensuously mixed") categorial objectivity, than to appeal to reflection upon the categorial act constitutive of this objectivity. As we shall see, this is precisely the view that Husserl advocates in the *Logical Investigations*.

First of all, however, we wish to discuss the role played by reflection in the formation of the general concept "something," the concept which, together with the concept of collective combination, is supposed to constitute the concept of number. The "formal concept" (84) of "something" is related to the "unities," emptied of content, which function as the "foundations" of the collective combination. "Something or other" (335) can be combined with "one thing or another" (335) so as to yield a formal multiplicity. When the "how many" of this manifold "one thing or another" is determinate, the formal multiplicity is a number (83). According to Husserl, the concept of this "one thing or another" or "something" (335), quite like the concept of collective unification, owes its emergence to reflection. It is his argument that "something" designates an arbitrary content of a presentation-in-general [*Vorstellung-überhaupt*] and is thus to be grasped only in reflection upon this act of presentation.

> "Something" is a name which fits every conceivable content. . . . That wherein all objects . . . agree is in being contents of a presentation. . . . Obviously the concept of the "something" owes its emergence to reflection upon the psychical act of presenting, every determinate object being given precisely as the content of this act. . . . Naturally the concept "something" can never come to be thought except if some content be present in respect of which the reflection may be performed. [335f.]

In any case, what is plausible in this argument is the suggestion that when the "something" comes to be designated as the arbitrary content of a presentation, a regard for the correlative, invariant act of presentation may be of service in epistemologically clarifying this concept "something." One must again ask oneself, however, whether "reflection upon the psychical *act* of presenting" is required *of necessity* for the formation of the formal concept "something" or whether the intentional *object* of presentation should not much rather serve as the foundation of abstraction for the formation of this general concept. In the above quotation, Husserl himself seems already to move in this direction when he says that reflection would be performed in respect of some present content and that this content would be the determinate object. It does not become clear, however, whether this object of presentation is a simple object ("every determinate object," 336) or a categorial object (a "thing of thought," 335). Furthermore, it remains utterly obscure how the formal concept of "anything whatever" or "something" can emerge from the "reflection" upon some (contentually) determinate object of a concrete intentional presentation. In its relation to the "reflection" as well as to the conceptual generalization, just as overall with regard to its proper essence, the process of formalization implicit in this conceptual formation remains fully undetermined.

Looked at more precisely, this problematical doctrine of a *reflection* which constitutes the concepts "collective combination," "multiplicity," "something," and accordingly "number," points to a more fundamental difficulty, namely, to the absence of a lucid doctrine of the categorially formative activity. When Husserl comes to deal with the theory of the intuitional-categorial act and its intentionally correspondent categorial objectivity in the sixth of the *Logical Investigations*, he expressly remarks that the formation of formal universal concepts [*Allgemeinbegriffe*], orienting itself in respect of the givenness of categorial objects, should not be mediated by an explicit reflection upon the corresponding categorial acts.

> We find the foundation of abstraction for the realization of the
> aforesaid concepts not in *reflection* . . . [upon the categorial
> acts, that is,] not in these acts *taken* as *objects*, but *in the objects of*
> *these acts*. . . . For example, a whole is given and can be given
> only in an actual grasping together. . . . But the concept of the
> whole does not arise through reflection upon this act. Instead
> of attending to the giving act, we have rather both to attend to
> that which it gives, to the *whole* which it brings forth *in concreto*,

and to raise the universal form of this whole into universal conceptual consciousness. [*LI* II/2 (VI), § 44]

In addition, the process of abstraction implied in this formation of concepts first comes to a satisfactory clarification in the *Logical Investigations*. While the abstraction that forms concepts was still understood in the *Philosophy of Arithmetic* as an act of selective attention, the *Logical Investigations* speak in this regard already of "ideative abstraction": "Naturally I do not here mean 'abstraction' merely in the sense of a setting-in-relief of some non-independent moment, but its Idea, its Universal, is brought to consciousness, and achieves actual givenness" (§ 52).

The *Logical Investigations* do not find fault with the *Philosophy of Arithmetic* because it appeals to categorial acts such as collecting in order to clarify the psychological, that is, the epistemological origin of categorial objects such as the whole. They merely criticize the fact that it never became clear in the *Philosophy of Arithmetic* that the foundation of abstraction for the ideation of the universal concept of categorial objects like multiplicity, something, and collective combination, is presented not through reflection upon the performance of the categorial *act* but through the *objective* correlate of this performance. There are three distinct reasons for Husserl's continuing to appeal to a *reflection* upon the act in the *Philosophy of Arithmetic*.

1. Husserl oriented himself entirely in respect of the observation that the selfsame, uniform act of combining is implicit in the formation of the manifold, variously determined, concrete wholes. From this he inferred that reflection upon this act must provide the direction for the formation of the concept of the collection [*Kollektivum*] in general.

2. Husserl remained under the influence of the "doctrine, widespread since the time of Locke but fundamentally in error, that . . . the logical categories, such as . . . unity . . . or number . . . spring up in reflection upon certain psychical acts, that is, in the domain of the inner sense, the 'inner perception' " (*LI* II/2 (VI), § 44). We have seen that in the *Philosophy of Arithmetic* Husserl had already begun to distance himself from this influence.

3. Husserl still lacked a lucid concept for the objective correlate of the categorial act and its function as the basis of a further categorial act, namely, the formation of the universal concept. The foundation of the general concept "collective combination in general" is not the view toward the act of collecting itself but the view toward the formal combination of contents that is established by that act. So, too, the concept "something" is to be won in departing not from an arbitrary act of think-

ing but from an arbitrary object of thinking. Passages *can* be found in the *Philosophy of Arithmetic* which point in this direction (e.g., 337). Nevertheless, the adherence there to the necessary function of reflection shows clearly that the subjective and objective determination of the foundation of abstraction and, hence, the categorial act and the categorial objectivity, act and signification are not yet clearly distinguished.

In his review of the *Philosophy of Arithmetic*, Frege clearly exposed this sore point.

> By taking the subjective and the objective together under the heading "presentation," one obliterates the boundary between the two. . . . Thus, the whole (set, multiplicity) . . . appears . . . now as presentation [*Vorstellung*] . . . , now as something objective [*Objektives*]. [Frege, 318]

very much a problem in, e.g. Hume as well

It is not true, however, that Husserl has Frege's review to thank for his later insight into the distinction between categorial objects and formal concepts, on the one hand, and of both of these from the acts which constitute them, on the other hand. Already in the *Schröder-Review*,[7] which appeared in the same year as the *Philosophy of Arithmetic*, that is, three years before Frege's review of the *Philosophy of Arithmetic*, Husserl reproaches Schröder for failing to distinguish clearly enough between signification and presentation as well as between signification and object (cf. *AR*, 11f.). Over against this, Husserl insists both that the oscillation of the subjective presentation of an object may not *eo ipso* be called an oscillating signification and that names without real, corresponding objects are nevertheless not without signification.

In his critique of the *Philosophy of Arithmetic*, Frege went much further, however, even maintaining that with Husserl "everything becomes presentation" (Frege, 316). For Frege, this means that everything becomes a temporally individualized, intramental content of consciousness belonging to an empirical person. Unfortunately, even in the later literature regarding the *Philosophy of Arithmetic*, the opinion has been propagated that precisely this censured identification of arithmetical objects, concepts, and relations, on the one hand, with really immanent contents of consciousness, on the other hand, constitutes the characteristic "psychologism" of this work. But Frege's critique goes too far and the interpretation of Husserl supported by that critique usually goes far astray. It is true that Husserl does not work out clearly enough the relation between the objective-logical collective combination and the act of collecting. Nevertheless, he does not designate the collective combination as a psychical act. Only a superficial reader can fail to grasp that in designating the collective combination as a "psychical combination" Husserl does not employ the term "psychical" in opposition to "objective," "logical," or "ideal," but in opposition to "physical." This terminology is modelled on that of Brentano according to which a "psychical" relation, in opposition to a "physical" relation, is a combination which is not founded in the determination of the content of the connected terms (*PA*, 329ff.).

Husserl does, indeed, maintain that reflection upon psychical activities is required for the formation of the concepts "something" and "collective combination." However, the "formal concept or category" (84) of collective combination is not thereby *eo ipso* identified with the "psychical act of a second order" that serves as the foundation of abstraction for this category. Likewise, Husserl's oscillating determination of the foundation of abstraction for the concept "something" in no way signifies that he identifies the object of a (simple or categorial) presentation with this presentation itself. In consequence of this view, the concepts "multiplicity," "something," and accordingly, "number," result necessarily from an abstractive consideration of corresponding presentations. Nevertheless, they are not essential determinations of these presentations taken as psychic facts; rather, these concepts refer to the "logical content" of the presentations (218, 78). As we will see shortly, the *Philosophy of Arithmetic* is also concerned at great length with the difference between authentic (that is, intuitive) and inauthentic (that is, signitive or symbolic) presentation of numbers. If the same number can be given both in authentic and inauthentic presentation, then it also follows that a number cannot purely and simply coincide with the corresponding presentation to which it is related.

Quite probably because the very point of departure for the Husserlian problematics remained foreign to Frege, these nuances escaped the latter's acumen. The onset of Husserl's problematic is characterized by the subjectively oriented clarification of ideal objects with the aim of carrying out an "epistemological investigation" and "critique" of the "foundations" of arithmetic and logic (5f.). Such a point of departure was further unintelligible for Frege precisely because he grasps the concept of number not in respect of a categorial *objectivity* like whole or multiplicity but as a "concept-word" whose objective referent ["*Bedeutung*"] is to be determined as *concept*.[8]

Nevertheless, Frege's emphasis upon the fundamental separation of the empirically psychical and the ideally logical domains has left clear traces in Husserl's work. Above all, these traces of Frege's influence have to do with the insight into the necessity of a pure-logical foundation for arithmetical and logical operations. Husserl's later self-criticism, in which he charged his early philosophical analysis of arithmetic with psychologism, is not so much related to an alleged identification of number with its psychical presentation, but is concerned above all with the connection of arithmetic and logic.[9] It is the understanding of logic (to which arithmetic belongs as a particular discipline) that is psychologistic. More precisely, the criticism concerns the determination of logic as technique of thinking, a determination showing signs of Brentano's influence (see below, this chapter, "Logical Technology and Its Theoretical Foundation").

In addition to affecting the development of Husserl's idea of an objectively oriented ideal logic, Frege indirectly influenced the development of phenomenology as the subjectively oriented grounding of arithmetic and logic. Husserl did not, in fact, allow himself to be dissuaded by Frege from his project of providing a subjective foundation for the validity of arithmetical operations and logical laws (of thinking) as well as for all assertions as such. He did, however, grasp the necessity of clarifying the methodological status of such an undertaking. The psychological, foundational analyses of the *Philosophy of Arithmetic*, are then transformed into a phenomenological analysis of the intentional consciousness in whose performances the ideal validity of mathematical and logical operations is epistemologically founded, that is, constituted. The execution of this subjectively oriented or epistemological grounding of ideal arithmetical objects remains in the *Philosophy of Arithmetic* psychologistic only insofar as it rests upon empirically and psychologically rather than eidetically and phenomenologically determined acts of cognition.

The Symbolic Concepts of Number and the System of Numbers

The psychological clarification of the "proper or authentic concepts of number" is supplemented in the second part of the *Philosophy of Arithmetic* by the psychological clarification of the "symbolic concepts of number." The distinction of authentic and inauthentic presentations of numbers shows once again that in his analysis of arithmetic, Husserl owes more to his philosophical master Brentano than to his mathematical mentor Weierstrass. The necessity in arithmetic of operating with symbolic concepts of number and graphic signs for numbers results from the fact that, "in the proper sense," that is, intuitively, we can "scarcely count beyond three [1891: 'ten to twelve']" (339). Analogously with the treatment of the intuitionally given concepts of number, Husserl's exposition of the "symbolic presentations of *number*" (chap. 12) rests upon the analysis of the "symbolic presentations of *multiplicity*" (chap. 11).

Our powers of apprehension and memory do not allow us to separate larger sets of objects step by step and then, in a single act of intuitive surveillance, to combine all these objects in a *collective* unity. There are, however, cases in which greater numbers of individual objects are given immediately in *sensuous* intuition. We speak, for example, "of a row of soldiers, a heap of apples, an avenue of trees, a brood of hens, a flight of birds, a flock of geese, etc." (203). "Row," "heap," and so on, are qualities of the entirety of the set and not of the individual terms. Husserl therefore names them "quasi-qualities" (202) or, more precisely, "sensuous qualities of a second order" (201). These sets are not, however, categorially articulated wholes. Rather, they are sensuous groups of objects of like content, formed by the comprehension of a "figural moment," a "shape [*Gestalt*]" or a sensuously intuitable type (205).[10] Within these sets, a small number of individual terms can be fixed one after another and categorially-intuitionally collected. Since the entire set is given quasi-sensuously in the form of gestalt-qualities, this rudiment of intuitionally collected terms assures us of the fundamental (but not factual) possibility of intuitionally counting out the entire set. The small multiplicity of the intuitionally collected terms of a set, the set being given at once as a gestalt-quality, functions thereby as a *sign* for the (possible) intuitional givenness of the entire multiplicity.

> The rudiment of the process [of intuitive-collective combination] serves . . . as a sign for the intended full process. Hereby, the uniform figural quality belonging to the intuition of a set assures us of the possibility of advancing the process already begun, all the more so as the intuitional unity of the set of those members that have thus been brought into relief comes to be recognized as a part of the entire intuition of the set. [213]

Hence, the sign and what is designated, the intuitive-collective combination of some individual terms and the entire multiplicity, enter into a relation with one another under the mediation of the sensuous and typical presentation of sets. This mediating function is founded in the experiential and habitual association of the multiplicities that are formed in step-by-step intuitional collection and the immediately, sensuously given shapes or sensuous sets.[11] Since we know that sensuous sets can be collected in their entirety by way of *intuition*, a few rudimentary steps of intuitional collection, coupled with the habitual consciousness of being able to proceed in the same way to a complete counting-up of the terms, actually suffice.

Symbolic presentations of *numbers* arise when, with the symbolic presentation of multiplicities, the "how many" of the multiplicity comes to be determined (222). Here it is a question of conceiving a symbolic system of numbers within which every number no longer capable of intuitional formation can be represented by a graphic symbol and at once conceptually and unequivocally determined.[12] With the intuitionally acquired concepts "more," "less," and "one," it is possible to situate every number from the series of natural numbers unequivocally in respect of its immediate predecessor (−1) and successor (+1). On this same basis, there emerges a "process of successive formation of numbers through the repeated addition of a unit to the already formed number . . . : 1; 2=1+1; 3=2+1; 4=3+1; . . . ; 10=9+1" (226). This process does, indeed, permit the formation of an infinite series of numbers. As for the higher numbers, however, the determination of their systematic position in the series of numbers (and hence every reckoning with them) is highly intricate.

> The concept 50 is given to us by the formation 49+1. But what is 49? 48+1. And what is 48? 47+1, etc. Every answer means pushing the question back a step further. Only when we have arrived in the domain of the proper [*eigentlich*] concepts of number [1, . . . , 12] can we be satisfied. [229]

This difficulty can be overcome when, on the basis of the proper concepts of number, we construct a system of numerical symbols and figurative [*uneigentlich*] numerical concepts, "which provides each determinate number with a suitable, easily distinguishable sign, and sharply demarcates its systematic position in the series of numbers" (228). There is here a possible principle of construction for designating the (intuitionally formed) numbers 1 through 9 as elementary numbers and forming the further numbers by way of a repetition of the series of elementary numbers. A numerical sign placed ahead of one of the elementary numerical signs designates the degree of the repetition. The first repetition = "1": 11, 12, 13, . . . 18, 19; the second repetition = "2": 20, 21, 22, 23, . . . 28, 29; the fifth repetition = "5": 50, 51, 52, 53, . . . 58, 59, and so on. Thus, the system of numerical symbols rests upon the series of intuitionally given numerical concepts. According to Husserl, there are merely factual reasons that only the first ten members of this series function as elementary numbers, namely our natural endowment of ten fingers (cf. 246).

§ 2. Pure Logic and Psychology

The first volume of the *Logical Investigations*, which appeared in 1900 under the title "Prolegomena to Pure Logic," is probably the one work of which Husserl's contemporaries took the greatest notice. Indeed, the mere circumstance that a nearly unknown *Privatdozent* would not shrink from confronting established and well-recognized philosophers, logicians, and psychologists of his time[13] with the charge of perpetrating nonsensical modes of thought, may have directed attention to this work. When, upon closer examination, it became clear that the *Prolegomena* was no mere polemical treatise but a careful and serious investigation of a problematic central to the contemporary philosophical discussion, this work was assured a broad and deep influence upon the philosophical world. Husserl thus succeeded in breaking the spell cast upon his contemporaries by the swift development of scientific psychology. With the introduction of a pure logic, philosophy regained not only its own domain of research independent of psychology and natural science but as well a domain of the "highest dignity."

Only with the emancipation of philosophy from the modes of thought of natural science was a vista opened upon the full range of a philosophical theory of science, upon pure logic as *mathesis universalis*. Many readers of the *Prolegomena* failed to see the paradoxical character of this achievement. The emancipation of the formal-logical objects and laws from psychological determinations was not Husserl's ultimate goal,[14] but merely the preparatory work for understanding the connection between pure logic and concrete (psychical, or rather phenomenological) processes of thinking, between ideal conditions of cognition and temporally individuated acts of thinking. Hence, the *Prolegomena* are to be understood throughout as the continuation of the problematic already embarked upon in the *Philosophy of Arithmetic*.

The *Prolegomena* investigates two basic forms of logical science: normative logic and pure logic. The common interest of both, however, lies in the *"grounding"* of a possible scientific cognition. Logic is "theory of science," that is, a doctrine of the conditions for true assertions and their orderly arrangement within the systematic connection of a coherent scientific theory. If logic is naturally related to possible acts of thinking, then a precise, reciprocal demarcation of the conformity of such acts with logical as well as with psychological laws is not merely the preparatory task of methodological work, rather it is the central task of logic itself. The rejection of logical "*psychologism*," that is, the emancipation of "pure" logic from its ordination within (empirical-genetic) psychology, may not be separated from its positive counterpart, the cultivation of a novel, eidetic-descriptive "psychology." With a pertinent necessity, the antipsychologistic, pure logic of the *Prolegomena* points forward to the "Investigations Concerning Phenomenology and Epistemology" in the second volume of the *Logical Investigations*.

Logical Technology [*Kunstlehre*] and Its Theoretical Foundation

It is clear that the essential interest of the *Prolegomena*, and thus also the driving force in the polemical controversy with logical psychologism, is determined by the idea of a *pure logic*. Since the projection of the never published second volume of the *Philosophy of Arithmetic*, Husserl's goal had been the elaboration of "a universal theory of formal deductive systems,"[15] a *formal mathesis universalis*. One may not, however, overlook the fact that with the proposal of such a pure logic the "legitimacy" of a practical-normative logic, "logic as a methodology, as a technology of scientific cognition . . . , naturally remains unimpugned."[16] Even if it is not to be denied that in the *Prolegomena* the treatment of this logical technology serves the primary purpose of introducing pure logic as its theoretical foundation (*PPL*, chaps. 2 and 3), one may nevertheless venture the assertion that Husserl's idea of a pure logic remains essentially bound to practical motives. This is so not only because a normative technology requires a theoretical foundation, but also because a theory which treats the conditions of rationality in general must serve the advancement of a rational, concrete *life*.

The technology of scientific cognition consists in precepts stipulating the conditions under which scientific cognition can be attained. These precepts fall into normative propositions and practical directives for their concrete realization. The normative propositions concern correct thinking, judging, and inferring, as well as the systematic ordering of propositions within the internal coherence of a theory. The practical

PPL ~ / F4,

directives concern particularly the psychological conditions for the realization of the normative precepts. A normative proposition can be exemplified by the following precept: "A judgement ought to be accepted only under the condition of full insight into the state of affairs in question!" The practical directive for the realization of this precept demands concentration, attentiveness, and so forth, by the judging subject. It is clear that later precepts refer to earlier ones, but also that earlier precepts do not rest upon themselves. Normative propositions require a grounding, and an essential moment of this grounding is the thematization of a *basic norm* to which all the propositions of a determinate normative science are bound.[17] The basic norm of normative logic, which states why one "ought" to judge insightfully, derives from the goal of scientific cognition. The basic norm designates the basic value aspired to by science, namely, the uniform basic goal of a determinate normative science. Every normative proposition of normative logic regulates a concrete state of affairs while itself remaining subordinate to the basic norm. This revelation of "measuring" the normative propositions "against the basic norm" and the concrete states of affairs against various normative propositions implies a *theoretical* "relation between the condition and the conditioned." "Thus, for example, every normative proposition of the form 'An A should be B' includes the theoretical proposition 'Only an A which is B has the property [= value] C.' " (48 / F, 87f.) Like every other normative science, a normative logic requires a theoretical "foundation," that is, a theoretical investigation of the "innermost theoretical content" of the "relations between the state of affairs to be regulated and the basic norm" (49 / F, 88). The question now is, in the case of the technology of thinking, which science will carry out this investigation or, more precisely, which science studies the basic theoretical laws of thinking that are implied in normative logic.

We shall be able to answer the latter question, however, only when we know what is meant by "basic laws of thinking." A possible answer to the question was offered by the "economy of thinking" [*"Denkökonomik"*] developed principally by H. Cornelius in connection with the work of R. Avenarius and E. Mach and contested by Husserl in chapter 19 of the *Prolegomena*. According to this doctrine, the "basic laws of the understanding" concern the "economy of thinking," roughly in the form of the "principle of the smallest quantum of force" as developed by Avenarius. The basic norm, to which every thinking and judging is ultimately subordinated, is the most sparing possible engagement of the energy of thinking, the goal being the most effective possible accommodation of thinking to the phenomenal domain under investigation and finally to the world of experience pure and simple. Thinking serves man toward the end of his accommodating himself not only reactively but prospectively to external reality and maintaining himself successfully in the struggle of life. The "economy of thinking" occupies itself with the task of optimally shaping this concrete human reality. The exploration of this connection between norm and regulated matters of fact occasions the development of "measure in accordance with the economy of thinking." In his critical controversy with this theory, Husserl does not dispute that thinking is factually determined by biological laws of accommodation and, hence, that the laws of the economy of thinking take their rightful place within a practical-normative logic. His fundamental critique of this form of "biological pragmatism" directs itself much rather against the claim of such a doctrine to supply the theoretical foundation for practical logic. If one abstracts from the specifically practical precepts of the economy of thinking and restricts oneself to its implicit theoretical assertions regarding the essence of human cognitive life, then it becomes clear that this theory rests upon a biologically inspired psychology. The question whether laws of the economy of thinking serve well the end of establishing a theoretical foundation for practical-normative logic, leads us back to the more general question whether and to what extent *psychology* is able to provide a theoretical foundation for practical logic (cf. chap. 3).

Husserl's answer to this latter question runs as follows: The psychological description of the processes of thinking is a necessary but insufficient theoretical condition for a logical technology. It is a necessary condition simply because the logical technology regulates processes of thinking and thereby presupposes a theory concerning the nature of these psychical processes. Yet such knowledge concerning the nature of human thinking, that is, concerning the psychical activities, factors, and causes implicit in human thinking, is not sufficient to formulate not only all the laws that make thinking possible, but also a practical science of correct scientific thinking. For thinking is a psychical process that is at the same time regulated by universal logical laws, and these laws are not derivative from the factual nature of thinking. The exploration of such universal laws of thinking forms the task of a *pure logic*, which is to be sharply distinguished from psychology.

Logical psychologism is nothing other than the failure to recognize this distinction. It consists in assigning to the domain of psychological research the most universal, pure-logical laws of possible thinking. The refutation of this psychologistic "metabasis" [= transition, transformation, alteration] (145 / F, 161; 169 / F, 179) from a pure, that is, an at once formal and *a priori* logic, into an empirical-genetic psychology, is the actual motor for the deliberations of the *Prolegomena*. Behind this negative task and with increasing lucidity there is profiled the proper essence of pure logic as a universal-objective science not only of *ideal* laws of thinking, but of ideal-logical truths or, respectively, ideal being-in-itself. The subtle antipsychologistic arguments of the *Prolegomena* all lead to this same fixation-point in the theory of pure logic as an ideal science. They move again and again, in painstaking discussion with a multitude of philosophical schools and their representatives, along the same path, leading from the consideration of a delimited empirical science to the recognition of an encompassing formal-logical ideal science.

The treatment of the question regarding the theoretical foundation of logical technology offers a good opportunity to familiarize ourselves, by way of an initial overview, with the essential points in Husserl's struggle against psychologism. As appears in this encounter, logic is not necessarily practical-normative logic. Rather, there is also a pure logic which founds practical logic. At the same time, however, not only pure logic but psychology, too, belongs to the theoretical foundation of practical logic. Hence, the task arises of clarifying both the reciprocal relation between these two disciplines and their common relation to practical logic. Husserl thus clarifies matters by *opposing* the psychologistical claim to be able to found the possibility of thinking (and hence of a normative logic) by psychological explanations alone. While psychology is a science which investigates a delimited domain of matters of fact, practical logic is a universal theory of science, that is, it concerns every possible form of scientific cognition. Is it not contradictory, so runs an argument employed by Husserl again and again, to seek the universal conditions for any possible science within a particular science, that is, within the individual case of a science that deals with a particular range of facts? As is seen upon more attentive analysis, this logical contradiction (the part-whole fallacy) rests upon a failure to recognize the radical distinction between the laws of a particular science and the laws of science in general. The laws of a particular science, such as those of psychology, are applicable to a restricted domain of matters of fact, that domain from which they have been acquired by means of inductive generalization. Conversely, universal laws concern the possibility of every cognition, whether empirical or *a priori*. They concern the ideal-objective conditions of rational thinking in general. The "essential theoretical foundation" of decisive importance "for rendering possible" the technology which regulates *every* correct thinking is not psychology but "pure logic" (§§ 16, 20).

The Refutation of Logical Psychologism

The psychologistic logicians fail to recognize the fundamentally
essential and eternally unbridgeable distinctions between ideal
law and real law, between normative regulation and causal regulation, between logical necessity and real necessity, and between logical ground and real ground. [68 / F, 104]

We now wish to consider, in a schematic exposition, a series of Husserl's antipsychologistic arguments. These concern, on the one hand,
the absurd consequences and, on the other hand, the false presuppositions of logical psychologism. Chapters 4 and 7 of the *Prolegomena* are
devoted respectively to the "empiricistic" and "skeptical" *consequences*
of logical psychologism. The former consequences serve Husserl to
demonstrate that psychologism is unable to found the absolute necessity of logical laws. It is the next stroke, however, that delivers the *coup
de grâce* to psychologism. Here Husserl shows that the form of psychologism that embraces the empiricist consequence, that is, the relativity
of logical laws, will find itself compelled to deny the most universal
conditions for possible cognition in general and will thus end in skepticism. Chapter 8 then brings together systematically the *presuppositions*
that nourish psychologism. There it is essentially a question of repeat-
ing the results of the foregoing critical discussion from a somewhat
altered point of view.

"Up to now," *psychological laws* have remained vague "laws of nature, vague generalizations of experience . . . , assertions concerning
approximate regularities in the coexistence or succession" of matters of
fact and for which a strict conceptuality has been wanting (61 / F, 98).
Yet even the development of a strictly scientific psychology would not
alter the fact that laws concerning the psychical dimension of nature can
never attain more than a *probable* validity. A natural science that investigates the causal connections of *matters of fact* rests upon the inductive
generalization of empirical data. Its laws hold only under certain factual
conditions and never absolutely. Even in the very best case, namely, the
development of an exact natural science of psychology, to designate logical laws as psychological laws of nature would be to ascribe to them a
"probability of the highest dignity" (72 / F, 106), without, however, being able to exclude their possible falsification. But the logical principle of
contradiction claims an absolute validity under all circumstances or,
more precisely, independent of all matter-of-factual circumstances.

The claim on the part of the laws of logic to be absolute, that is, to

Overview of PPL argument [?]

be valid at all times, for every person, under all circumstances, thus excludes their possible determination as laws of nature. They are not to be
acquired by way of the inductive generalization of matters of fact. Conversely, they do not regulate thinking as the laws of nature regulate natural phenomena, that is, they do not refer to matters of fact.[18] But do the
logical laws not refer essentially to thinking, and is thinking not a matter
of fact that concerns "psychical beings," "judging beings rather than
stones" (142 / F, 159)? Do not logical laws, therefore, exhibit a necessary
relation to psychological matters of fact, after all, even if they "spring"
(§ 24) from pure logical concepts rather than from experience? What
Frege and others failed to see was that this question plays a central role
in the battle against psychologism. Husserl himself answers this question
only indirectly. He compares the (psychological) performance of thinking with the functioning of a "calculator [*Rechenmaschine*]" (§ 22). It is,
of course, correct that the mechanical production of results "is regulated by laws of nature in a manner that accords with the arithmetical
principles. . . . Nevertheless, in order to explain the functioning of the
machine in physical terms, no one will appeal to the arithmetical rather
than the mechanical laws" (68 / F, 103). May not the functioning of the
human "thought-machine [*Denkmaschine*]" be quite similar, even so that
every operation of thinking is a psychological performance whose cor-
rectness is regulated but never caused by logical laws?

Before we pursue this question of the justifiable sense of the connection between logic and psychology further, we wish to deepen our
insight into the consequences of their unjustifiable identification. We
shall attempt to do so by studying Husserl's discussion of B. Erdmann's
Logik, I, Logische Elementarlehre (1892), in § 30, chapter 7 of the *Prolegomena*. Erdmann especially interested Husserl because he was the only
one among the contemporary psychologists criticized by Husserl—these
included, among others, Sigwart, Wundt, Th. Lipps—who professed the
extreme consequences of "relativism" with "instructive consistency"
(137 / F, 155). The logical relativism represented by Erdmann is a "specific" relativism. It refers the validity of cognition and the logical laws to
the existence of a particular species of living creatures, namely, the human being. In this regard, therefore, Husserl speaks about an "anthropologism" (§ 34). Anthropologism asserts a radical dependence of the
logical laws upon the make-up of human nature. Such an assertion implies a further one, namely, that the assumption of some other kind of
thinking, for which the laws governing "our" thinking would not hold, is
not absurd but rather the expression of a real possibility. The central
motivation for Erdmann's style of anthropologism is the emphasis upon

the *limitedness* both of human beings as such and of the achievements of their thinking. For him, the logical laws hold good as *human* "laws of thinking." Logical absolutism, which "supposes itself at this point . . . able . . . to leap over the boundaries of our thinking" and which demands a universally objective validity for these laws, is for him but an expression of human "presumptuousness" (Erdmann, *Logik*, 378f.; also in Husserl's citation, *PPL*, 137 / F, 155). The absolute necessity of logical laws is a mere semblance, according to Erdmann. It stems from the fact that in human thinking one cannot step outside the laws of this thinking, one remains factually subjected to the constraint of these laws and therefore cannot deny them (137, 141 / F, 155, 158f.). Furthermore, as factual laws of specifically human thinking, the logical laws may claim no "eternity," that is, no ideal identity. Should human thinking suffer an alteration "in its make-up," the logical laws would also be altered (146 / F, 161f.; cf. also 137, 139 / F, 155, 156f.).

In Husserl's eyes, the chief objection to anthropologism is that a radical *skepticism* follows from its presuppositions. The anthropological clarification of the laws of logic runs "counter to the self-evident conditions for the possibility of a theory in general" (110 / F, 135). Yet a theory that negates the very conditions for the possibility of a theory in general necessarily entangles itself in "an evident contradiction between the sense of its own thesis and that which cannot with good sense be separated from any thesis as such" (116 / F, 140). Husserl demonstrates this in a series of arguments (§ 36) of which we shall mention only the first.

> The specific relativist makes the following assertion: For every species of judging beings, that will be true which has to count as true according to the specific constitution, or according to the laws of thinking for that species. This doctrine is absurd. It implies that the same content of judgement (proposition) can be true for one, namely, for a subject of the species *homo*, but false for another, namely for a subject of a differently constituted species. Yet the same content of judgement cannot be both true and false. . . . what is true is absolutely and inherently true. [117 / F, 140]

If we pay heed to the fact that skepticism denies what "lies implicit in the very meaning of the words true and false," then the contradiction of skepticism issues immediately from the negation of the "basic principles" of pure logic, principles which express no more "than certain truths grounded in the bare sense . . . of certain concepts such as truth, falsehood, judgement (proposition), and the like" (139 / F, 156; cf. also 122 / F, 144f.).

Against this, the proponent of anthropologism will point to the fact that the demonstration of the absurdity of his position can be furnished only on the assumption of the absolute validity of the laws of logic and that it is precisely this assumption which he disputes. As long as "the logical absolutist" does not ground his position positively, as long as a nonpsychologistic theory of the connection between logic and psychology remains wanting, the proponent of psychologism will fear neither "empirical" nor "skeptical" consequences. Let us, therefore, return to Husserl's controversy with *Erdmann*, paying particular attention to those elements in the critical discussion which imply a positive grounding of logic as an ideal science.

The necessity in the laws of logic, so emphatically stressed by the logical absolutists, is in Erdmann's eyes nothing other than the factual impossibility for thinking to deny the laws constitutive of its own essence. Husserl's first critical remark refers to the fact that "impossibility" can here mean nothing but "the impossibility of performing such a denial" (141 / F, 158), that is, the *real* [*reale*] impossibility of an assertion which negates a law constitutive of the possibility of thinking. For Husserl, however, what is decisive is the *ideal* impossibility, strictly speaking, the absurdity or countersense [*Widersinn*] concerning not the particular *act* of denial but rather the ideal *content* of this act, namely, the *law* of thinking. Husserl can thus pointedly counter Erdmann by observing that the negation of a law of logic is indeed able to be performed, but that such a negating would be absurd, logically counter to good sense. The "ideal impossibility of the negative proposition does not conflict in the least with the real possibility of the negative act of judgement" (141 / F, 158). Inasmuch as it is now applied to the *distinction between the act of judgement and the content of judgement*, the conceptual duality of "real and ideal" that governs the entire battle over psychologism receives forthwith a new content within this very discussion. The failure to recognize the distinction between the real and the ideal impossibility of negating the laws of logic is only a special case of the more general failure characteristic of psychologism as a whole, namely, the failure to recognize the distinction between the psychological act of judgement and the ideal-logical content of judgement.[19] When Erdmann further assumes a possible alteration of logical laws, the ambiguous designation of the laws of logic as "laws of thinking" lends essential support to his assertion. An alteration in the constitution of human thinking, he argues, cannot be fundamentally excluded and, if it should occur, then the ("hypothetical" [147 / F, 162]) validity of our laws of thinking would not remain unaffected. Over against this, Husserl maintains an "eternal" or ideally "transtemporal"[20] and "absolute" (137 / F, 155) validity for the laws of logic (for example, the principle of noncontradiction). Indeed, one might speak of "hypothetical" and "alterable" validity only in connection with *real* laws. The laws of logic, however, are not real laws. Rather, as "trivial generalities," they are merely "formal" conditions of cognition which, far from expressing "the essence of our human thinking," merely "protect [us] from formal contradiction" (139ff. / F, 156ff.).

For Husserl, the problem of psychologism is essentially a problem in the theory of science. It concerns the lawfully structured conditions of possible scientific cognition. The entire course of Husserl's argumentation is then directed toward persuading the reader of the necessity not of psychological but of pure-logical laws of possible thinking. The means he employs for this is the distinction in the theory of science between a science that concerns itself with facts and an ideal science, or between empirical and ideal laws. Independence from factual contingency, universality, and absolute necessity are the more essential epistemological prerogatives lending distinction to pure-logical laws over and above psychological laws. These prerogatives are grounded, on the one hand, in the purely conceptual (analytical) and formal character of the pure-logical laws,[21] and, on the other hand, in their apodictically evident givenness.[22] For Husserl, pure-logical propositions are deductive derivations from "axioms given in immediate insight" (159 / F, 171). They concern formal concepts applicable to the signification and to the object of scientific statements. Pure logic itself is a hierarchically constructed system of pure-logical propositions and *a priori* truths-in-themselves. Nevertheless, that the being of these truths is not real but "ideal" being, should in no way suggest that such truths "exist in a τόπος οὐράνιος or in the divine spirit" (*LI* II/1 [I], 101 / F, 330). It simply means that they possess *absolute validity*, validity which remains independent of the persons or spatial-temporal circumstances in which cognition occurs.

> every truth-in-itself remains what it is, it retains its ideal being.
> It is not suspended "somewhere in the void," but is, rather,
> a *unity of validity in the atemporal real of ideas.* [*PPL*, 130 / F,
> 149f.][23]

The Psychological Givenness of Pure-Logical Objects

Before we proceed to consider more closely Husserl's sketch of an architectonic of the pure-logical sciences, there remains for us the task of interrogating Husserl in respect of his *positive* views concerning the relationship between pure logic and concrete acts of thinking. Psychologism is radically overcome only when the refutation of the intermingling of the real and the ideal is augmented by a positive exposition of their correctly conceived connection.

> One must arrive at a clear understanding of the ideal, both in itself *and in its relation to the real,* an understanding of how the ideal is related to the real, how it can *inhabit* the real and so *come to be known.* [188 / F, 193]

It must be shown how pure-logical laws regulate concrete acts of cognition without forsaking their ideality. Conversely, it is necessary to grasp how the particular psychological acts are constituted, those acts in which the ideal being of the pure-logical laws comes to be conceived. Both tasks are intimately bound up with one another. They intersect in the question "in what sense [ideal, pure-logical] truth is seated in cognition" (150 / F, 164f.). In fact, it is the task of part two of the *Logical Investigations,* especially of the first and sixth *Investigations,* to answer this question. If, however, in spite of the primarily polemical intentions of the *Prolegomena,* we are able to identify there an anticipation of such an answer, then we shall simultaneously have demonstrated the often doubted systematic continuity between both parts of the *Logical Investigations.*

    The first question concerns the *application* of pure-logical laws to the psychological matters of fact of individual acts of thinking, speaking, and knowing. The first of the *Logical Investigations* pertinently summarizes a basic thought of the *Prolegomena,* when it makes the point that "pure-logical unities . . . form an ideally complete whole of general objects for which actually being thought and expressed is merely incidental" (*LI* II/1 [I], 105 / F, 139). In accordance with their proper sense, the laws of logic are of a purely conceptual order and hence free of every relation to psychological matters of fact. Although one speaks in the context of pure logic about a "particularization" of pure-logical generalities, one means thereby to refer to the stages of generality of ideal being-in-itself. Such "particularities" are not psychological matters of fact but the "lowest specific differences" of a general concept, that is, they are "ideal unities" (178 / F, 185 and 173 / F, 181f.). Thus, for example, the number three is a "particularization" of the general concept of number just as the idea "predicative propositional signification" is the "particularization" of the idea "propositional signification in general."

The pure-logical laws attain an express relation to psychical matters of fact, such as acts of thinking, only by way of a secondary "transformation," for example, in their being "qualified to play a role in the *regulation* of thinking" (140 / F, 157). Pure-logical laws can be equivalently formulated as normative laws without suffering the loss of their ideal validity and without thereby entering into a relationship of dependence upon the psychical nature of thinking (158f. / F, 170f.). In this case, however, they do not belong to a practical technology of thinking (see above, "Logical Technology and Its Theoretical Foundation"). They are "pure-logical norms" and not "technical rules of a specifically human art of thinking" (159 / F, 171). As an example of such a rule grounded exclusively in a pure-logical law, consider the following precept: "Whoever judges that every *A* is also *B* and that a certain *S* is *A*, must (should) also judge that this *S* is *B*" (155 / F, 169). Yet such an equivalent reformulation of pure-logical laws, expressly related to thinking, knowing, and judging, is also thinkable outside of any possible normative transformation. Thus, all logical propositions of laws are able to be formulated as propositions or laws concerning conditions of possible evidence. The proposition "*A* is true," for example, is equivalent to the proposition "it is possible for any one at all to judge with evidence that *A* is the case" (184 / F, 190; cf. also 129 / F, 149). But in all these transformations, how is the assertion of their pure-logical content to be reconciled with the reference to an arbitrary judging subject? Are the judging subject and the respective individual act of judgement not psychological matters of fact? The answer is, yes, they are psychological facts but they do not function as such in the examples we have cited. In other words, the propositions adduced contain no assertions whatsoever concerning the psychological nature of the subject of judgement and its acts. More precisely, in the case of the conditions for the possibility of evidence, the propositions concern exclusively the *ideal* possibility or impossibility of the performance of certain judgements (183 / F, 189f.); and in the case of the normative precepts, they concern simply the *pure-logical* compulsion for the deduction of a syllogistic conclusion. Finally, one may say that neither the conditions for possible evidence nor the normative precepts principally concern the acts of judgement themselves. Rather, they concern the logical "content" (142f. / F, 158f.; and 101 / F, 128), that is, the *ideal signification of the judgement* (179 / F, 186).

We may thus say in *summarizing* that the pure-logical generalities are ideal validities free of every essential reference to subjective, immanent experiences. "A purely ideal and indirect" (183 / F, 189) relation of pure-logical generalities to subjective matters of fact can, however, be established by pointing to the *ideally possible givenness* of the ideal validities. That an ideally true proposition is secondarily to be taken as an ideal condition for the possibility of evident judgements of the same content rests upon the fact that in all these judgements the same true proposition is given, that is, comprehended. Husserl conceives this relation of pure-logical truths to acts of evident judgement in a way analogous to the relation of ideal significations to the multiplicity of judgements in which an ideally identical signification is expressed. And this relation of the ideally identical signification and the momentary act of judgement is determined throughout the *Prolegomena*, as well as in part two of the *Logical Investigations*, as the *particularization* of an ideal species in singular *individual* cases.

> The signification [*Bedeutung*] is thus related to the momentary acts of signifying [*Bedeuten*] (the logical presentation to the acts of presenting, the logical judgement to the acts of judging, the logical conclusion to the acts of concluding), just as the species "redness" is related to the strips of paper lying on the desk, all of which "have" this same redness. In addition to the other constitutive moments, each strip has . . . its individual redness, that is, its own individual instance of this species of color. The species "redness" itself, however, is neither in the strips of paper nor does it really exist anywhere in the world.[24]

Regarded more precisely, an ideally identical signification particularizes itself not in the full psychological content of the acts of judgement in which it is implied, but rather in a "similarly determined psychical character" found throughout all these acts and designated in the fifth of the *Logical Investigations* as the "semantic essence [*bedeutungsmäßiges Wesen*]."[25] If pure-logical significations are particularized in psychological facts, pure-logical laws are likewise related to individual acts of thinking.

> Inasmuch as *ideal* significations are particularized in acts of signifying, so [*sic*] every pure-logical law expresses a generality which is able to be referred *eo ipso* to the ideal extension of the pertinent species of signifying, that is, to possible, *real* acts of thinking.[26]

Even if this doctrine still calls for elucidation, we have found in it an answer to the question about the *application* of pure-logical laws to concrete acts of thinking. Considered more precisely, this doctrine of the particularization of ideal species in singular, psychological individualities, contains an answer to the other question which we posed at the outset. This second question concerned the *cognitive comprehension* of pure-logical generalities. The insight into a pure-logical idea, whether concept or law, beginning from individual acts taken in comparison with one another, that is, beginning from the semantic essence of such acts, is to be understood analogously with the process of particularizing a pure-logical idea in a multiplicity of semantic essences of individual acts. Instead of descending from the ideal generality to its individual givenness, "ideation" ascends from singular individual to the comprehension of the species. The *Prolegomena* already have at their disposal the essential moments of the doctrine of the "intuition of essences [*Wesensschau*]," developed more amply in the sixth of the *Logical Investigations.*

> [J]ust as a species is an ideal identity over against the multiplicity of possible, individual cases (which are themselves, [for example], not colors but instances of *one and the same* color), so, too, the identical meanings or concepts are related to the conceptual presentations of which they are the "contents." The ability ideatively to comprehend the universal in the individual or the concept in the empirical presentation . . . is the presupposition for the possibility of cognition. Just as in the act of *ideation* we intuitively lay hold of a concept—as one species, the unity of which we comprehend insightfully over against the multiplicity of matter-of-factual or matter-of-factually presented individual cases—so, also, we can gain the evidence for the *laws of logic.* . . . The presentations have their "contents," their ideal significations, which we . . . can take possession of in ideating abstraction; and therewith is given, in every case, the possibility for the *application* of the logical laws. The *validity* of these laws is, however, unlimited. It in no way depends upon whether we or any one else . . . is able factually to perform conceptual presentations.[27]

Let us now summarize the deliberations of the *Prolegomena* concerning the relationship between "the ideal and the real." Considered in themselves, pure-logical concepts and laws have no relation to psychological matters of fact. They are ideal validities subsisting in and for themselves. The pure-logical generalities acquire a relation to the psychological acts of thinking, speaking, and knowing only when one inquires into their application to or comprehension in "real" acts of thinking. Both in the matter of application and in that of comprehension, the question is motivated by an *epistemological* interest comprising both the interest in a thinking which conforms with pure-logical thinking and the interest in unequivocal concepts. Husserl understands this psychological givenness of ideal objects by analogy with the particularization of a species of color (redness) in a multiplicity of individual, colored objects (red objects). Such a doctrine calls forth at least two objections.

1. If ideal objects are particularized as moments of psychological acts, is not the radical separation of psychology and pure logic, or of real and ideal being, once again obliterated? Does this doctrine not mean a *relapse into psychologism*?

2. Pure-logical significations are mere forms of signification or formal "essential truths." Must one not, however, distinguish between the significations conceived by pure logic as formal essences and the identical significations of concrete, that is, temporally individuated assertions of determinate content? In consequence of this distinction, must one not further differentiate between the *particularization* [*Vereinzelung*] of formal, essential significations, and the *individuation* [*Individuierung*] of assertorical significations determinate in content?

In the *Prolegomena*, Husserl counters the *charge of psychologism* with the tireless reference to the fact that the application or particularization of pure-logical laws and concepts in empirical-psychological matters of fact is a merely "ideal possibility."

> the being or being-valid of an [ideal] generality . . . possesses
> the value of an *ideal possibility*—namely, in respect of the *possible* being of the *empirical* particularities which would fall within
> the scope of those generalities.[28]

The ideal possibility of the psychological givenness of pure-logical objects is in no way affected by the fact that such givenness, whether because of incidental circumstances or natural laws, is "*in reality* impossible" (129 / F, 149). Thus, the psychological particularities belong to pure logic only *qua* ideal possibilities and never *qua* real matters of fact. Such a position is threatened, however, whenever the psychological matters of fact cease to be understood as merely ideally possible particularizations of pure-logical objects and come to be seen as the epistemological foundation for these logical objects. If, in order to provide an epistemological account of *ideal* being, it is *ideally* necessary to describe the *real* psychological givenness of such being, then we shall find ourselves confronted anew with the basic problem of psychologism. Whoever maintains that the ideal being or ideal validity of pure-logical objects has its epistemological "origin" in empirical-psychological acts of "ideation," is attempting to ground ideal being by means of real matters of fact and is, therefore, a genuine proponent of psychologism.[29]

Upon closer inspection, such a proponent of psychologism turns out to be the very thinker who is at work in part two of the *Logical Investigations*, "Investigations Concerning the Phenomenology . . . of Knowledge." To be sure, *phenomenological epistemology*, especially when it devotes itself in the sixth of the *Logical Investigations* to the determination of "categorial intuition," is explicitly contrasted with empirical-genetical psychology. Nevertheless, as long as it remains unstated that we are dealing here with a science of essences, Husserl's phenomenology lies exposed to the justifiable charge that it constitutes a relapse into psychologism. It is only with the second edition of the *Logical Investigations* that the status of phenomenology as an ideal science comes to be consistently emphasized in a lucid, methodological self-interpretation. At the time of the appearance of the second edition, Husserl asserted the following in regard to the epistemological analyses which had already been executed in the first edition:

> *De facto*, the analyses were *carried out as eidetic analyses* [*Wesens-analysen*]. They were not, however, maintained within a uniformly clear, reflective consciousness. The entire refutation of psychologism rests on these analyses—especially the sixth, but also the other investigations—being taken as eidetic analyses, that is, as apodictically evident analyses of ideal essences.[30]

The deliberations of the *Prolegomena* (and the *Logical Investigations* as a whole) concerning the connection of the ideal and the psychologically real are exposed to a second reproach as well. This involves the inadequate differentiation between the ideality of formal-logical significations and the irreality of assertorical significations. It seems to make little sense to designate even the (identical) significations of concrete assertions as significations "for which being thought and expressed is merely incidental" (*LI* II/1 [I], 105 / F, 333). Long years of investigation brought Husserl to the conviction in later life that one may designate as essences *neither* the *significations* of assertions which refer to matters of fact, *nor* the *significations* of assertions which, as in the case of pure logic, refer to essences. To be sure, even the significations of concrete assertions can be said to be ideal or irreal. They are not essences, however, and hence they cannot be particularized, in the way an essence is particularized, in the really immanent tenor [*Gehalt*] of assertorical acts [*Aussageakten*] or semantical intentions [*Bedeutungsintentionen*]. By contrast, as the objects of pure-logical science, significations are formal essences "for which being thought and expressed is merely incidental." In accordance with the very sense of their own being, these logical-apophantical essences particularize themselves not as psychological individualities but rather, as is quite correctly explained in the *Prolegomena*, as "ideal individualities, . . . genuine species" (*PPL*, 173 / F, 181; cf. also 178 / F, 185). Only when concern turns to the epistemological clarification of the logical-apophantical essences does the comprehension of these essences beginning from the subjective acts of cognition, as well as their application to the subjective acts of cognition, become at all relevant.

We have already seen that the *Prolegomena*, no less than the sixth of the *Logical Investigations*, understands the comprehension of logical essences as an idealizing abstraction which begins with a mutual comparison of the really immanent moments of manifold acts. Nevertheless, if it is true that assertorical significations can not be particularized, in the way an essence is particularized, in the really immanent tenor of the pertinent assertorical acts, then Husserl's characterization of the process of ideation becomes questionable. The same situation prevails here as in the acquisition of the concept "whole." Not reflection upon the act of collecting but rather the object of this act, that is, a concrete whole, forms the foundation for abstraction. One does not comprehend the formal essence "signification-in-general" by beginning from the manifold of semantical intentions. Rather, one begins from the identical (noematic) signification of a concrete act of assertion. The formal essence "signification-in-general" particularizes itself in a concrete, identical, assertorical signification. This concrete signification, however, does not proceed to particularize itself in the really immanent [*reell*] moments of an occasional act of assertion. Instead, it individuates itself temporally. We shall later discuss a second mistake in the doctrine advocated in the *Logical Investigations* regarding the abstractive ideation of formal essences as beginning from the really immanent content of individual acts. This mistake concerns the determination of such ideation as an act of categorial representation [*Repräsentation*].

The Idea and the Tasks of Pure Logic

The doctrine of the ideally possible particularization of pure-logical generalities in subjective acts of thinking is certainly a significant moment in the argumentation of the *Prolegomena*. As long as the question of the possible *application* of pure logic to concrete thinking fails to be treated carefully and consistently, psychologism remains unvanquished. It is characteristic of Husserl's answer to this question that it consists in a limited rehabilitation of the "psychologistical" interest in a "human" logic, that is, a logic which places itself in the service of human thinking and inquiry. Even if the pure-logical concepts and laws are not able to be derived from human experience, they nevertheless are able to be grasped at once and without contradiction as regulative norms, *a priori* conditions for possible scientific cognition. The struggle against psychologism, a struggle which is waged on behalf of the proper essence of pure logic, should not blind us to the fact that Husserl combines the development of this pure logic essentially with an interest in the theory of science.

The final chapter of the *Prolegomena* (chap. 11) is striking proof of this. Here Husserl turns anew to the question concerning the function of pure logic in the theory of science as already sketched out in chapter 1. A comparison of the first and last chapters of the *Prolegomena* is instructive in this regard, for it not only demonstrates the continuity of Husserl's interest in the theory of science, but also brings clearly before our eyes the positive insights and essential advances which Husserl owes to the controversy with psychologism. Thus, a new concept for the function of logic in the theory of science results from the clear separation of real and ideal being or real and ideal possibilities. The theory of science is not a mere matter of the technical utilization of logic. In the proper sense, it does not even concern the application of logic. Rather, in their most proper sense, as *ideal* conditions for possible scientific cognition, the pure-logical concepts and laws are nothing other than the guiding principles for the theory of science.

Pure logic, however, is quite a special kind of theory of science, namely, a *formal and universal theory of science*. It explores the formal structures underlying every (ideally possible) science, as well in respect of its theoretical formation as in respect of its objects and their integration into a particular domain of research. Pure logic explores the most general forms and compositional laws of the *essences* "signification-as-such," pure logic is the formal science of all sciences. *Pure logic is mathesis universalis*. This is at least the goal of pure logic and Husserl is well aware that the attainment of this goal presupposes the previous performance of certain less pretentious tasks. Only when one has clarified what a proposition is as such and how propositions are able to be brought into consequent connection with one another, can one proceed to study the connection of assertions characteristic of a scientific theory. And only when one knows what a theory is, can one investigate the various forms of theory and their possible derivation from a highest form of theory. Thus, the way to the *mathesis universalis* is a long and difficult one. It is the way of an "ascending integration," in which preliminarily independent forms of signification appear as dependent moments of a more encompassing form of signification. One must climb step by step to the highest form of scientific theory as such, without being able to skip a step. Both the *Prolegomena* and the *Formal and Transcendental Logic*[31] agree in designating the most essential "tasks" or "stages" of the ascent as (1) the doctrine of the forms of meaning, (2) the logic of consequence or noncontradictoriness, and (3) the theory of the possible forms of theory.

The leading form of signification for the *first task* of pure logic is that of the proposition or judgement, but at this first stage the appurtenant doctrine of the forms of (propositional) significations, or *pure-logical grammar*, is able to be subdivided into the following three further disciplines: (a) the doctrine of the forms of the primitive semantic categories, (b) the doctrine of the laws of (syntactical) composition, and (c) the doctrine of grammatical operations.[32] The first discipline not only makes an inventory of the fundamental semantic categories, but also systematizes them according to their respective independence and dependence. "Predicative proposition," for example, is an independent semantic category to which "predicate" belongs as a dependent semantic moment. The explicit investigation of the laws of composition that concern the combining of dependent semantic forms toward the end of building up (various kinds of) independent semantic forms, however, is already the task of the second discipline. This discipline investigates the way the same "inferior semantic elements" are able to function as the "stuff" of various forms of syntactical combination. It investigates, for example, the way the same "word" (or, more precisely, the same presyntactically formed "nuclear stuff") inserts itself into the uniform context of predicative, attributive, conjunctive, hypothetical, and other modes of proposition.

The third pure-grammatical discipline joins in with this task and, on a still higher plane of generality, investigates the system of grammatical operations. These operations constitute new syntactical forms on the basis of the fundamental syntactical forms and by means of the laws of syntactical combination. The nominalization in which the subject-form "that *Sp* . . . " is "derived" from the predicative proposition "*S* is *p*" is an example of such an operation. It is thus a question of certain grammatical "laws of complication" which are founded in the syntactical "laws of composition" and in the morphology of the primitive semantic categories. In the present context, what is more important for us is the pure-logical character of this "grammar" as well as its function in the theory of science. Pure-logical grammar is devoted to the morphology and syntactics of *a priori semantical forms*. It is an ideal science which presupposes no matter-of-factual linguistic structures. Not as the science of the grammar of factual languages but as the science of the "grammatical itself," it guides the construction of pure logic (*FTL*, § 22). And as the science of the grammatical itself, its concern is with the ideal conditions of scientific cognition insofar as the latter is seated in the medium of language. Pure-logical grammar "aims at the *concepts* which constitute the idea of theoretical unity" and at their "elementary forms of combination" (*PPL,* § 67). It treats the most primitive conditions of scientific assertions, namely, the formation of significant [*sinnvollen*] propositions and theories and the *avoidance of nonsense* [*Unsinn*].

Building upon this, *the second "task" of pure logic* concerns *the avoidance of countersense* [*Widersinn*] or contradiction in the conjunction of well-formed propositions, that is, in propositional conjunctions that are formed according to the rules of pure grammar. Whereas, for example, the assertorical form "All A are B, but certain A are not B" satisfies the requirements of pure grammar, that is, it is grammatically significant; it is nevertheless in conflict with the requirements of the *logic of consequence*.[33] The logic of consequence or the "logic of noncontradictoriness" concerns the ideal conditions of possible (formal) truth and falsehood, particularly in the case of complex propositional forms. It consists of a number of laws enjoining the avoidance of contradiction and able to be integrated into an encompassing theory. Traditional *syllogistic logic*, for example, is one such theory. The logic of consequence thus selects the grammatically possible, complex propositional or inferential forms, and determines those which "have the value of formal eidetic laws [*Wesensgesetzen*], namely, as general truths concerning the consistent interrelation of judgements, that is, concerning the ('analytical') inclusion of judgements of such and such a form in premises, that is, in prior judgements, of a corresponding form" (*FTL*, § 14). Just as in the case of pure-logical grammar, the basic structure is one of wholes and parts, with the distinction, however, that in addition to grammatical

"possibility" attention is now paid to "compatibility" or noncontradictoriness.[34]

However, this logic of consequence is still not a proper, formal
logic of truth; instead, it is merely one of the most important presuppositions of a logic of truth. This new insight of *Formal and Transcendental
Logic* remained hidden, according to Husserl, not only in the *Prolegomena*, but in the entire tradition of formal logic hitherto. For Husserl, this
distinction between formal logic of consequence and formal logic of
truth (*FTL*, § 15) resulted first from the consideration of the "different
manners of subjective givenness" belonging to judgements (§ 16a), that
is, it resulted from the "subjective-phenomenological" reflection upon
the "attitude involved in judging," or upon the forms of evidence in
judging (§ 70a). It resulted from an "attitude of cognition" which investigates the "forms of judgement" together with "their adequation to the
things themselves" (§ 19), without leaving the framework of the formal-
logical conditions of truth. In this subjective elucidation of formal logic,
judging in the sense of the logic of consequence is understood to be
judging within the "evidence of distinctness [*Deutlichkeit*]"; judging in
the sense of a formal logic of truth demands an "evidence of clarity
[*Klarheit*]" (§ 16). Formal-logical principles of possible judgemental
truth, such as the principle of noncontradiction, can accordingly be formulated within both the framework of a formal logic of truth ("given two
contradictory judgements, it is necessarily the case that one is true and
the other false") (§ 20). The logic of consequence thereby forms a necessary presupposition of formal logic of truth, or formulated in a subjective-phenomenological manner: "The cognitional striving tends . . .
from 'confusion' toward distinctness, . . . it tends further, . . . to clarity" (§ 16c).

Finally, *the third "task" of pure logic* no longer concerns the ideal
presuppositions of a scientific theory (the possibility and compatibility of
the semantic forms), but rather the idea of theory pure and simple and
its possible modifications. The highest task of pure logic is the development of a *"theory of possible forms of theory."*[35] Husserl obviously understands by this a hierarchical system of possible forms of scientific theory,
analogous to the axiomatically and deductively formulated mathematical
theory of multiplicities [*Mannigfaltigkeitslehre*]. For this "last and highest
goal of a theoretical science of theory as such" there are no historical
paradigms and even Husserl contents himself with a rough sketch. Such
a science owes its unequivocal sense mainly to its "objective correlate,"
namely, the objective domain of cognition which corresponds with the
theory of the forms of theory. In mathematical comprehension, strictly

scientific domains of cognition have the form of a *definite multiplicity* [*Mannigfaltigkeit*]. It is this concept of form which lends "a *systematic form of unity* [*Einheitsform*] [to the] entirety of a science's infinitely proceeding propositions, a form of unity that is able to be constructed *a priori* from a finite number of pure forms of axioms [*Axiomenformen*] by means of the logical-categorial concepts" (§ 35b). The theory of the forms of theory is thus more precisely "a theory of the systems of judgement in their entirety" or "a theory of the deductive systems" (§ 28).

Although they are mentioned in the *Prolegomena*, it is the *Formal and Transcendental Logic* that first devotes detailed investigations to the correlations between the conditions and forms of scientific theory, on the one hand, and of the objects of such theory, on the other. Pure-logical grammar, logic of consequence, and theory of the forms of theory all orient themselves thoroughly in respect of the form of *signification*. Husserl names the pure-logical science embracing them "*formal apophantics*" and opposes to this the correlative pure-logical science oriented toward the form of the object. This he calls "*formal ontology.*"[36] Three tasks of formal ontology correspond with the three tasks of formal apophantics. With pure grammar there corresponds a morphology of the formal objective categories such as "object, state of affairs, unity, multiplicity, number, relation, combination [*Verknüpfung*], etc.—all these concepts being kept free of the particularity of the material of cognition" (§ 27b). As the apophantic logic of consequences (and logic of truth) concern the necessary conditions of (formal) truth and falsehood of significations, so the correspondent formal-ontological science concerns the "being and non-being of objects in general, states of affairs in general, etc." (*PPL*, A, 246 / B, 245 / F, 238). As the logic of the syllogism was an example of a theory concerning the apophantic logic of consequence, so the "theory of multiplicities," that is, the "theory of numbers" or arithmetic, is an example of a formal-ontological logic of consequence. Finally, with the apophantical theory of the possible forms of theory there corresponds the formal-ontological, pure theory of multiplicities.

The theory of multiplicities is the theory concerning the form of the "domain of cognition" corresponding with a given form of theory. If we replace this formal description of the domain of cognition with a materially determinate one, that is, with a description of the objective theoretical correlate, a description determinate in content but nevertheless general, there result the so-called "*material ontologies*" (cf., *Id* I, § 10; *PI* I, 125ff.). Unlike formal ontology, the material ontologies are oriented not toward the formal concept "object-as-such" but rather toward the concept of a region of objective being. In traditional terminology, mental and corporeal being are regions of being. The material ontologies related to these regions are then nothing other than *psychologia rationalis* [rational psychology] and rational physics as related to *natura formaliter spectata* [nature regarded formally]. "Rational" sciences are distinguished from empirical sciences. While the latter observe, classify, and seek to grasp the laws governing matters of fact, the former explore the essential determination of the region of being underlying these matters of fact. The principle stating that spatial being is extended, does not, for example, issue from an inductive generalization based upon matters of empirical fact. Extension is a determination of the *essence* of spatial being. Subordinate to rational physics are material ontologies of lower stages of generality, which are related to bare moments of physical being (cf. Kant's "phoronomy," "dynamics," and "mechanics"). With respect to its logical form, every material ontology is a materially determinate particularization of certain universal categories of formal logic.[37]

The *mathematical character* of formal ontology is visible even in the bare definitions of its disciplines. The "theory of multitudes" or "theory of numbers" and the "theory of multiplicities" or (set theory) are recognized mathematical sciences (cf. *FTL*, § 24). The discussions in the *Philosophy of Arithmetic* concerning the concept of sets or numbers and its relation to the formal "something-as-such" were steps in the direction of the "formal arithmetic" planned for part two, steps, therefore, in the direction of the development of a formal ontology (cf. § 27a). According to the *Formal and Transcendental Logic*, formal apophantics can also be formulated as a mathematical science.[38] Is pure logic, therefore, finally nothing but mathematics? However evasive and unconvincing the answer given by Husserl to this question in the *Prolegomena* (*PPL*, § 71), the *Formal and Transcendental Logic* provides a clear criterion for distinguishing between the "mathematics of the mathematician" and the mathematics of the logician, namely, the characteristic interest of the latter in the theory of cognition and science (*FTL*, §§ 51f.). We shall be able to understand how this interest manifests itself only when we have progressed further in our elucidation of the distinction between formal apophantics and formal ontology.

The distinction between the apophantical doctrine of signification and the formal-ontological theory of objects corresponds with that between "judgements about judgements and judgements about objects." This distinction rests upon that between the various attitudes or orientations and is grounded in a distinct theoretical interest. The orientation toward objects is the more natural. Formal ontology grows from a formalization of the objects of straightforward natural experience and scientific research. The orientation toward significations is secondary. Formal apophantics turns its gaze from the straightforward objects and directs it reflectively upon the semantic medium of their givenness. This reflection, characteristic of apophantics, is the expression of an interest in the critique of cognition (§§ 44, 48). In addition to this difference of subjective interest, the two-sidedness of formal logic is also to be characterized in respect of the objects of formal logic. As objects of apophantics, significations are "objectivities" in a secondary and derivative sense. They are not " 'true' or 'real' objectivities" but "*intended objectivities as intended*, [. . . regarded] purely as the *posited as such* in the syntactical process of positing" (§ 44bβ). Objects and significations do not come to consciousness within the same orientation. In the original judging consciousness, significations are not known "objectively" at all. Nevertheless, as objects of apophantical logic, significations become a derivative form of the straightforward objects of natural experience (§§ 44f.). In this sense, therefore, formal apophantics is dependent upon formal ontology. This priority of formal ontology does not, however, preclude the transformation, on their side, of formal-ontological assertions into formal-apophantical assertions or the comprehension of formal-ontological objects as objects considered in respect of the manner in which they are intended [*Gegenstände-im-Wie*], that is, as "object-senses" [*Gegenstands-Sinne*] (§ 53).

The essential reason for transforming objects of judgement into "object-senses" or objects *qua* judged, lies in the critical interest characteristic of apophantics, in accordance with which objects are no longer treated as straightforward objects. This interest in the theory of cognition on the part of the logician first attains its full expression, however, only when the logician has posed the question regarding the agreement of the significations or the contents of judgement with the actual matters of concern. We have already seen how this "attitude of cognition" of the logician reaches a first point of satisfaction in the formal logic of truth, that is, in the investigation of the forms of judgement and "their adequation to the things themselves." However, the "evidence of clarity" attained in the *formal* logic of truth is still not "evidence as the having of the meant itself, the final goal" (*FTL*, § 16c, see also § 89). Formal, that is, analytic conditions of truth appear as a mere "anticipation" of ultimate, material-synthetic conditions of truth. In other words, the interest of cognition, which guided the development of pure-formal logic, pushes beyond the borders of this logic. A *material* logic of truth, which concerns the adequation of judgements determined in their content to reality, can be developed only through a "transcendental logic" of subjective acts of knowledge.

Just as the distinction between *formal* logic of truth and formal logic of consequence is based upon a "subjective-phenomenological" consideration of their corresponding types of evidence (i.e., of "clarity" and of "distinctness") (§ 70a), so too is a *material* logic of truth grounded *a fortiori* in "evidential criticism of experience" (title of chap. 4 in part II of *Formal and Transcendental Logic*). The description of ways of givenness of things and affairs, or rather the subjectively oriented description of modes of experiencing, asserting, and verifying is thereby a fundamental task of this material logic of truth.

The phenomenological theory of cognition, and more particularly, the phenomenological doctrine of evidence and intuitive fulfillment, is the authentic instrument of this material logic of truth that takes the form of a transcendental logic. For Husserl, this *material* logic of truth is, however, more than a mere supplement or deepening of the *formal* logic of truth, rather, it functions as its "critic" and "fundament." The material logic of truth "criticizes" the "idealizing presuppositions of logic" (*FTL*, part II, chap. 3), namely it refers to the circumstances of possible experience without accounting for it. Formal logic presupposes the unity of possible experience; it refers to the order of things in the world, without giving the slightest attention to the experience of the world. Formal logic cannot help but presuppose ultimate cores of syntactical formation, without being able to determine them as individual objects of sensuous perception. In the *grounding* of formal logic by transcendental logic, the analysis of pre-predicative experience and the therein grounded conditions of possible truth must thus play a preeminent role.

The insight into the necessity of a foundation of the objectively oriented formal logic in a subjectively oriented theory of cognition can be found in a nascent form already in the *Prolegomena*. There, Husserl advances a "Noetics" as a necessary complement of pure-logical theory of science (*PPL*, §§ 63, 32). While pure logic explores the objective "content" of ideally possible cognition (§§ 65f.), this noetics investigates the "subjective" ideal conditions which enable thinking beings "to perform all the sorts of acts in which theoretical knowledge is made real" (§ 65, 238 / F, 233). What Husserl calls there "noetics" is nothing other than "phenomenology." It is that which constitutes the most intrinsic interest and the overriding aim of his entire work.

§ 3.   The Phenomenological Theory
of Cognition

> Logic, as the science of the logical as such, and, in its highest
> form, encompassing all other forms of the logical, as the
> science of science as such, is oriented in *two directions*. It
> is everywhere a matter of the performances of reason
> [*Vernunftleistungen*], and this in the double sense of the *perform-
> ing activities and habitualities*, [on the one hand,] and the per-
> formed and henceforth persistent *results*, on the other hand.
> [*FTL*, § 8]

This Husserlian conception of a "two-sided," subjectively and objectively oriented, logical inquiry already governed the systematic structure
of the *Logical Investigations*. Before we enter into a closer discussion of
the method and the results of such a subjective logic or phenomenological theory of science in the following chapters, we would like in this preliminary consideration to reflect upon the motivation for such a logic. In
so doing, we shall see that it is an *epistemological* interest which sets in
motion the phenomenological exploration of the "performing activities." Husserl defines this phenomenological theory of cognition as a
fundamental science, that is, as a science which systematically explores
the ultimate basis of justification not only for objectively oriented logic
but for every science pure and simple. What initially presented itself as
the task of a subjective supplementation of objective logic, expands into
an exploration of the universal *a priori* in the correlation "of cognition,
sense of cognition, and object of cognition" (*IP*, 22), and finally flows
into the conception of an absolute science that Husserl characterized
already in 1908 as

> an exploration of the ultimate sense of the validity of cognition
> by way of a return to the . . . transcendental-phenomenological
> origins, that is to say, a transcendental-phenomenological ex-
> ploration of the constitution of the . . . objective element [*das
> Objektive*]: the origins of objectivity [*Objektivität*] in transcen-
> dental subjectivity, the origins of the relative being of objects
> [*Objekte*] in the absolute being of consciousness. [*EP* I, 382]

According to its program, phenomenology in the *Logical Investigations* remains oriented entirely toward the epistemological clarification
of pure logic.

[P]henomenology discloses the "sources" from which the basic
concepts and ideal laws of pure logic "spring," and back to
which they must again be pursued in order to provide them
with the "clarity and distinctness" requisite for an epistemological understanding and critique of pure logic. [*LI* II/1 (I), 3 /
F, 249f.]

These "sources" [*Quellen*] are nothing other than the immanent experiences [*Erlebnisse*] in which the logical concepts and objects are intuitionally realized (4 / F, 250), that is, in which they come to *intuitional
givenness* (5 / F, 251). Such intuitional givenness of pure-logical objects
is, however, a higher form of immanent experience, one which already
presupposes the givenness of objects pure and simple. Thus, the phenomenological clarification of the connection between ideal-logical objects and their (categorial-) intuitional givenness implies at once the
clarification of the (sensuous-) intuitional givenness of objects pure and
simple. The epistemological clarification of pure logic is necessarily confronted with the "*most general questions of basic concern to the theory of cognition,*" questions such as the following: "In what sense might it be that the
'in itself' of objectivity could be 'experienced' and in the end become
subjective again"; how is it possible that "all thinking and knowing is
related to objects [*Gegenstände*] or states of affairs which it ostensibly
meets . . ." (8 / F, 253f.)? The traditionally basic epistemological question that Husserl here raises, sees itself placed before the paradoxical
task of explaining "that human thinking, when it proceeds according to
logical method, encounters something like a thing [*Dinglichkeit*] existing
in itself, [a] nature [existing in itself], or a mathematical entity existing in
itself" (*LE*, 401). At the same time, of course, one must ask the following:
"What concern have the matters themselves for the courses of our thinking and the logical laws regulating them?" (*IP*, 3)

Such basic epistemological questions are stirred by various motives. The *Logical Investigations* name the oscillating and equivocal significations of words as the primary hindrance to the progress of pure-
logical science (*LI* II/1 [I], 5 / F, 251). Some years later, the chief motive
for phenomenology is said to be skepticism as called forth by the confu-
sions and ultimate countersense of a theory of cognition founded in the
naturalistic presuppositions of biology, psychology, or history (*IP*, 18ff.).
Husserl appeals throughout, however, to the *evident givenness* in which
"the logical ideas, the concepts and laws, are able to be brought into
epistemological clarity and distinctness" (*LI* II/1 [I], 5 / F, 251), and
which is able to set thinking free from the countersensical presupposi-

tions of natural theories of cognition and the resulting "skeptical despair" (*IP*, 30). The requisite instances of evident givenness are thus located primarily in the acts of categorial intuition in which the logical concepts and laws come to adequate givenness. Particularly during the concrete elaboration of the first, fifth, and sixth *Logical Investigations*, as well as in the ensuing years, Husserl gained an increasingly more distinct awareness of the fact that, while those acts of cognition which are directed toward the objects of pure logic are, to be sure, epistemologically the most important acts of cognition, nevertheless their exploration represents only one special domain of the general inquiry into the theory of cognition.

This expanded awareness of the problem is documented in a letter to Brentano written in 1905. In reference to the suggestion made in the *Prolegomena* (§ 65) for the incorporation of the epistemological problematic into the program of pure logic, Husserl writes the following: "It now seems to me more practical to separate pure logic and the critique of cognition" (cf. *Hu* XVIII: p. xxxvi). The "enigma" of cognition (*IP*, 36 and passim) concerns not only the relation of logically ideal being and subjectively real being; rather, more generally, it concerns the relation of *transcendence and immanence.* In this context immanence designates the sphere of evident givenness and possible, adequate intuition. Transcendence is determined negatively as the sphere of the non-immanent. The *Logical Investigations* already designate the sphere of immanence as a domain of presuppositionless givenness (*LI* II/1 [I], 15 / F, 259), and in *The Idea of Phenomenology* of 1907 this sphere of immanent evident givenness is determined, in an emphatic appeal to the systematic doubt of Descartes, as the sphere of indubitable givenness (*IP*, 30 and passim). The enigma of cognition thus has essentially to do with the sphere of transcendent being insofar as this is exposed to epistemological doubt; or, more precisely, it has to do with the givenness of transcendence within immanence and the epistemological relation of immanence to transcendence. As traditional theory of cognition shows, however, this enigma cannot be solved as long as immanence and transcendence are regarded in the form of an ontologically grounded opposition which could only be overcome by constructing a connecting "bridge." The appeal to the sphere of evident givenness as the proper domain of epistemological inquiry is, to be sure, a necessary condition for a presuppositionless epistemology. Nevertheless, such an appeal contributes to the solution of the basic epistemological question only if the *relation* between immanence and transcendence is itself able to be explored within the compass of evident, immanent givenness.

> The relation to transcendence . . . is unclear; . . . the [phe-
> nomenon of] "meeting the transcendent," which . . . is
> ascribed . . . to cognition, . . . is unclear. Where and how
> might we find clarity? There and then, when . . . the relation it-
> self was able to be given as something to be beheld, something
> intuitable. [37]

As a purely *intuitive* exploration of the *intentional* acts of consciousness, only the *phenomenological theory of cognition* is in a position to explore
in such manner the relation between immanence and transcendence. It
thus seeks to explore "the unity binding cognition and the object of cognition, a unity indicated by the word 'soundness' [*Triftigkeit*]" (37), and seeks
to do so without overstepping the domain of evident givenness. Phenomenology satisfies the demand for presuppositionless and evident exploration precisely in confining itself to a consideration of the cognitive
processes and freeing these from all transcending apperceptions. We shall
return later to a detailed discussion of this *phenomenological reduction* of
consciousness (see below, chap. 2, § 1). The exclusion of every form of
transcendence from the domain of phenomenological consideration does
not mean, however, that transcendence utterly disappears for phenomenological inquiry. Rather, the relation of consciousness to transcendence
is given evidentially in phenomenological-reflective consideration. It is for
this reason that in *Ideas I* Husserl writes as follows regarding the phenomenological reduction of transcendence: "We have actually lost nothing,
rather we have gained absolute being in its entirety. Understood correctly,
absolute being is seen to shelter within itself all worldly transcendencies"
(*Id* I, § 50). This assertion rests essentially upon the determination of the
epistemologically presuppositionless, that is, phenomenologically reduced sphere of immanence as *intentional consciousness*. We shall also return later to this fundamental phenomenological doctrine (see below,
chap. 3, § 1). In the present context, we are interested merely to observe
that, by virtue of the intentional relation of the processes of consciousness
to an object, every kind of intentional relation—whether fully knowing or
emptily asserting, whether oriented toward immanent or transcendent objects—can be brought to phenomenologically evident givenness.

At least in their express self-understanding, the *Logical Investigations* still conceive the phenomenologically evident givenness of
transcendence rather narrowly. Only intentional *acts*, given in phenomenological reflection, count as presuppositionless epistemological
data. The acts of cognition relevant for the basic epistemological question about truth are intuitionally fulfilled acts in which the intended

object comes to intuitional self-givenness. Strictly speaking, nothing can be said about the object of cognition except that it is intended in an act that must be more closely determined. When, from the end of 1906 onward, Husserl proceeded to designate as a phenomenological evident datum not only the act but also the intentional correlate of this act, that is, the intentional object just as it is intended in this act, there followed very decisive consequences for carrying through the phenomenological theory of cognition. Within the framework of phenomenologically reduced data it thenceforth became possible to study not only the intentional referral in the act of cognition but also "the pure *correlation* between objectivity and cognition . . . [and to do so] purely immanently and essentially" (*EP* I, 387f. [1908]). This consideration of correlation first unfolds its full consequence, however, only when it comes to include the correlation between the synthetic connection of multiple acts of cognition and the unitary intentional object that is intuitionally given in these acts. If in such manner one oversteps the boundaries of the merely point-for-point correlation of the present act of cognition with its respective intentional correlate; if one considers how, for example, a uniform thing is self-given, that is, how it appears in a continuous synthesis of manifold intuitive acts; then one acquires a phenomenologically evident understanding of the continuous process of cognition implicit in the perception of a thing.

Husserl calls this phenomenological investigation of the correlation between a regulated multiplicity of cognitive acts and the unitary intentional object of consciousness that shows itself in these acts, a *constitutive analysis*. Such a constitutive analysis, which, viewed more precisely, is seen to rest both upon the concept of the intuitional representation [*Repräsentation*] of an intentional object in the act and upon the concept of the fulfilling synthesis of manifold acts, is the proper phenomenological answer to the enigma of cognition.

> The task is now to pursue all forms of givenness and all correlations within the compass of pure evidence or self-givenness. . . . Naturally it is not only the individual acts which come into consideration here but also their complexes, their interconnections of agreement and disagreement, and the teleologies that emerge within them. These complexes are . . . unities of cognition which, as cognitive unities, also have their unitary objective correlates. . . . In this way we come at last to understand how the transcendent, real object . . . can be encountered in the act of cognition as what it is initially intended to be and how the sense of this intention, this opinion, is . . . progres-

sively fulfilled in the continuous complexes of cognition. We then understand how the object of experience is continuously constituted. [*IP,* 13, cf. also 75]

From about 1908 onward, Husserl calls the constitutive exploration of this complex correlation of the manifold acts and the object of cognition a *transcendental-phenomenological* task. "It is the task of *transcendental phenomenology* to make clear the connections between true being and knowing and thus in general to explore the correlations between act, signification, and object" (*LE,* 427). As constitutive analysis, transcendental phenomenology explores the way an object, in respect of its sense and validity, is built up, evinced, constituted in the fulfilling interconnections of the intuitive acts of cognition. As constituted, every object of cognition is necessarily relative to its determination and its justification within the context of intuitionally constituting consciousness. Correctly understood, this epistemological conception of the origin "of objectivity [*Objektivität*] in transcendental subjectivity, of the relative being of objects in the absolute" being of consciousness (*EP* I, 382), will be seen to determine as well the sense of Husserl's *epistemological* idealism.

> [The transcendental-constitutive consciousness] is the root, . . . the source of all else that is called being. . . . It is . . . not a unity of multiplicity: it does not refer to something further, from which it could or must have been derived. All other being is precisely unitary and points mediately or immediately back to the absolute flow of consciousness. If the flow of consciousness *is* in accordance with *its* mode of being, then everything else— whatever it might be—*is* also. Nothing further is required. . . . This state of affairs justifies our designating the . . . root-giving consciousness as absolute consciousness in opposition to consciousness and to the laws that belong essentially to consciousness. . . . On the other hand, there is a certain disadvantage involved in saying, "there is only absolute consciousness," as if one wished to say: all other being is only seeming. . . . This would, of course, be *fundamentally false*. The objects of nature are evidently true objects. Their being is true being. . . . It is fundamentally false to apply to such being a standard other [than] the one it itself requires in accordance with its category and to discredit something because it is "constituted" or rooted in consciousness. [*Ms. B IV 6,* 91b f. (1908)]

2

The Methodical Founding
of Phenomenology as
the Science of Pure,
Transcendental Consciousness

§ 1. The Phenomenological or
Transcendental Epoché and Reduction

Part two of the lectures of 1923/24 concerning "First Philosophy" is
devoted to the "Theory of the Phenomenological Reduction" (*EP* II,
title page). In the course of these lectures, at the close of a series of
discussions concerning the "Cartesian method of transcendental reduction," Husserl says the following:

> [It has] become clear not only that we in fact have the de-
> scribed method to thank for our *access to transcendental subjectiv-
> ity*, but that *this or a related method* is altogether indispensable in
> order to discover such subjectivity. I emphasize: *to discover*. . . .
> Understandably, transcendental subjectivity had first of all to
> be discovered historically as well. In an initial, immature . . .
> form, this discovery comes to the fore in the Cartesian *ego co-
> gito*. . . . A pure, actual demonstration of transcendental sub-
> jectivity is first accomplished in the *method of phenomenological
> reduction* familiar to every phenomenologist. [78–80]

In Husserl's view, and speaking very generally, what he calls the phenomenological or transcendental reduction forms the indispensable method that the philosopher must follow in order to attain to pure or transcendental subjectivity, that is, in order to attain to the domain of research proper to phenomenology as the "basic science of philosophy" (*Id* I, 1 / G, 42). Even in his contemplations of the history of philosophy, carried out primarily in his later years, Husserl endeavored to provide a critical disclosure of the steps taken by past thinkers in preparing the way to a basic transcendental science. He did so by attempting to track down in their own works instances in which they had caught sight of but missed the proper sense of the phenomenological reduction (cf. *EP* I, part I; *CES*).

In order to gain some clarity in the face of the manifold problematical aspects of this method in Husserl's extensive work, we shall try first, in abstraction from its philosophical motivation, to outline the simple sense of the *fundamental achievement* of the phenomenological reduction as a method of access to the sphere of phenomenological research. Only then will we concern ourselves with the problem discussed by Husserl regarding the *motivation* for the performance of the reduction. We shall subsequently come to grips with the question of the various *ways* of executing the reduction and close with an allusion to Husserl's *idea of philosophy*, intimately bound up as it is with the performance of the reduction.

The Fundamental Achievement of the Phenomenological Reduction

In a text from the 1920s, Husserl writes the following: "Subjectivity, and this universally and exclusively, is my theme. It is a purely self-enclosed and independent theme. To show that this is possible and how it is possible is the task of the description of the method of phenomenological reduction" (*Hu* XIII, 200). Only after the appearance of the *Logical Investigations* in 1900/01 did this "pure theme of subjectivity" (203) gradually clarify itself to Husserl in methodical reflection. It can be said summarily, however, that the achievement proper to the phenomenological reduction, as conceived by Husserl about 1905, consists in *methodically and distinctly delimiting* in its *characteristic ownness* the domain of research of phenomenological analysis already treated in the *Logical Investigations*, that is, in methodically securing for this domain its *pure*, unmixed *givenness*. In this work, Husserl circumscribed the concrete complex of immanent experiences belonging to a psychical individual, the stream of consciousness, as he would later say, as the domain of research of descriptive psychology or phenomenological analysis. This domain attains thematic givenness exclusively by way of the "counternatural direction of intuition and thought" characteristic of *reflection*. "Instead of being absorbed in the performance of the acts built manifoldly one upon the other, and hence, [instead of] being turned exclusively toward the objects of these acts, we are supposed rather to 'reflect,' that is, to *make these acts themselves into objects*" (*LI* II/1 [Intro.], § 3; V, § 14).

The decisive thought for the phenomenological reduction now rests on this, that beyond the achievement of the *Logical Investigations* in reflectively turning our gaze toward the acts of consciousness as such, there is still required a methodically *pure* apprehension of consciousness itself, now made an object of research in reflection. In the *Logical Investigations*, Husserl had not yet worked out a consistently *pure mode of apperception* for consciousness itself. Rather, in the fifth *Investigation*, dealing with the theory of consciousness, he conceived consciousness thoroughly and expressly in natural-empirical apperception, that is, in the manner of psychology. Consciousness is taken to be quite simply a *component* of the empirical, corporeal-spiritual, thus and so determined human "I" of this or that personal individual, psychophysically characterized, localized in objective space, and ordered in respect of objective time. In the *Logical Investigations* Husserl thematized consciousness with a kind of philosophical unconcern[1] by employing an order of reflection that rested *upon the basis* of natural-empirical apperception. In his later manner of speaking, reflection remained bound to the "mundane experience" in which prephilosophical, natural life runs its course. As Husserl clearly recognized as early as 1905/06, the attitude of natural life, "the entire natural bent of thinking," is oriented toward empirical apperception. Immanent experiences undergo an "habitual relation to the empirical 'I,' " "whereas proper schooling is required in order to stay within the bounds of pure givenness" (*Ms. F I 26*, 3a, 5a).

Again and again, Husserl associates the difficulty in performing the phenomenological reduction with its *unnaturalness*. Even more sharply than in the bare *habitus* of reflection [*Reflexion*] and reflective research, the unnaturalness proper to phenomenological self-meditation [*Selbstbesinnung*] can be seen in the demand for "purification" by way of the reduction, a demand which comes to the fore in respect of the *data given by reflection itself*. For, as it was characterized by the phenomenological analysis of the *Logical Investigations*, "bare reflection—however carefully it may observe and analyze, however truly it may be directed toward my pure psychical life, toward the pure inwardness of my soul—remains *natural, psychological reflection* as long as it is without such a method" (*Hu* VIII, 79), as long, that is, as it is without the phenomenological reduction.⟩ By contrast, it is the proper achievement of the phenomenological reduction, by way of consistently disconnecting the *natural empirical apperception* of consciousness, to keep methodically to the pure givenness of consciousness. Husserl metaphorically describes the reduction as a "method of doffing the empirical-objective robe . . . with which I again and again drape myself in an habitual apperception that remains unnoticed in the course of naive experience" (78; cf. also 12ff., 427). By way of this methodical suspension of empirical apperception within the reduction, consciousness ceases "to be human, or otherwise empirical consciousness," the word "consciousness" "loses all psychological sense, and one is finally led back to an absolute that is neither physical nor psychical being in the natural-scientific sense. Yet throughout the domain of phenomenological contemplation this absolute is the field of givenness. One must simply break with that supposedly so evident thought stemming from natural thinking, that all that is given is either physical or psychical" (*LE*, 242). Thus writes Husserl as early as 1906.

In conformity with this methodically reflected "purification" of consciousness itself, Husserl henceforth modifies his concept of reflection. With a backward glance at the *Logical Investigations*, and over against the natural, empirical perception which he subdivides into outer and psychological (inner, adequate) perception (reflection, in the *Logical Investigations*), he sets forth what he calls "*phenomenological perception (reflection)*," an expression which I should now like to prefer to the expression, 'adequate perception,' I employed earlier. To begin with, the essential concern is not adequacy but the phenomenological reduction and phenomenological position-taking [*Stellungnahme*]. Phenomenological perception relates to the *pure phenomenon of this reduction*. Within such perception, the perceived has *no position in objective space* but likewise none in objective time. Nothing of transcendence is posited along with it: The pure phenomenon is a pure, simple 'this,' an absolute givenness and unquestionableness." By contrast, inner, psychological perception bears an "apperceptive relation to the body of the 'I' [*Ichkörper*] and to [all] other 'external nature.'" It remains within the "sphere of naturalness" (*LE*, 371f. [1906 or possibly 1909]).

The phenomenological reduction has to engage the "*pure* mode of apperception" of consciousness, to elevate us from the level of what is prior with respect to us, namely, natural consciousness, to the level of philosophical consciousness (*LE*, 212 [1906]). In a manuscript dating from 1910, Husserl writes the following:

> Consciousness, and this is the fundamental error constituting the ultimate error of psychologism (an error to which not only all empiricists succumb but all rationalists as well), is not a psychical experience, not a network of psychical experiences, not a thing, not an appendage (state, action) to a natural object. Who will save us from the reification of consciousness? He would be the saviour of philosophy, indeed, the creator of philosophy. [*Ms. A I 36*, 193b]

As is set forth so clearly in the "Considerations Fundamental to Phenomenology" from the "General Introduction to Pure Phenomenology," *Ideas I,* published in 1913, Husserl at bottom wanted nothing else with the method of phenomenological reduction than consistently to desist from making consciousness a theme of research within such a "reification" or naturalization. He sought rather to clarify consciousness in its *own essentiality* [*Eigenwesentlichkeit*] (*Id* I, cf. esp. §§ 33, 39, 46, 49–51, 53). Stating the matter concisely, for the transcendental consciousness or "I" it is a question of "becoming aware of itself, experiencing itself thematically in its purity and making of itself the thematic field of cognition." In order to do so, Husserl adds, the "I" must first "come upon motivations . . . and end up by practicing [the] phenomenological reduction" (*EP* II, 417).

Motivation for the Performance of the Phenomenological Reduction

We may gather from the foregoing discussions that, in view of the fundamental significance which Husserl ascribes to the phenomenological reduction, the motivation for the performance of this reduction might well hang together very closely with his motives for philosophizing, that is, with his idea of philosophy. Indeed, Husserl's gradually attained clarity regarding the basic form of the method of reduction as a return to pure consciousness or, as he will come to say more and more, a return to transcendental subjectivity, can be understood as an expression of the insight finally gained into what philosophy ought to be about and into the basis upon which, and the manner in which what is thus aimed at can actually be attained.

As carried forward in a radicalized manner after the appearance
of the *Logical Investigations*, Husserl's attempt to come to terms with the
problems of a critique of cognition and reason, that is, with the problems
of a logic of experience, became decisive for the taking up of a genuinely
philosophical thematics. He extended the horizon for his posing of the
problem beyond specifically logical-mathematical cognition so as to en-
compass cognitive, theoretical reason, and objectivity cognized as such
by reason (*FTL*, § 100). The requirement for a *universally* conceived clarification of the possibilities for cognition grew from a deepened meditation on the skeptical arguments that crop up again and again in the
history of philosophy and concern the relation between cognition and
object. Putting the matter quite generally, Husserl was not interested in
the naturally and objectively oriented thematic of cognition characteristic of the various scientific disciplines, whose evident factual achievements he always recognized (cf. *LE*, 425; *EP* I, 246f.). His interest lay
rather in a "clarification of cognition in accordance with the *essential
possibilities* for its achievement [*Leistung*]," a clarification which is not to
be found "upon the paths of objective science" (*IP*, 6) and which in general is thoroughly alien to the natural attitude (cf. *IP*, lecture 1). The
possibility of cognition which is self-evident to natural thinking, namely,
the possibility of cognitively reaching [*treffen*] an objectivity that is in itself what it is, this "reaching the object" [*Triftigkeit*], as an achievement
of cognition, becomes radically questionable in philosophical skepticism.
The possibility of *objective* cognition and objective science comes to be
denied and a radical subjectivism is maintained for all cognizing.

The skeptical argumentations (especially those of Hume and the
ancient sophists Protagoras and Gorgias) made a deep impression upon
Husserl. At the same time, however, they seem directly to have given rise
in him to the "transcendental turn" so decisive for his idea of philosophy. He discovered in skepticism itself the hidden *transcendental motivation* for this turn and proceeded to work this motivation out in a
consistent fashion.[2] If the naive *pregivenness* of the world as the natural
basis of all objectively oriented cognition became *problematical* in the
skeptical argument, and if the world itself was thereby drawn into question both in respect of the essential possibility of its being known and in
respect of the fundamental sense of its being-in-itself [*Ansichsein*], then
the task, according to Husserl, was to elucidate the enigma of the possibility of cognition as such, doing so on an *ultimate* or *in itself primary*
basis, beyond which one can go no further and which is presupposed as
valid in all other cognition. According to him, such a clarification will
succeed thanks precisely to the phenomenological reduction. This re-

duction no longer sets free the psychologically apperceived consciousness, the consciousness conceived as a constituent of the now enigmatic world. Rather, it discloses the *pure* consciousness as an ultimate, "absolute" basis for research. In this transcendental attitude everything depends upon holding with *radical consistency* to just such a pure and absolute point of view, for, as Husserl wrote as early as 1906, "he who in even a single point . . . relies upon factors pregiven in natural apperception, has to pay for it with countersense and absurdity" (*LE*, 187f.) In other words, over against natural-objective cognition and science, everything depends upon making "the following a theme and a pure theme in principle":

> How the cognizing subjectivity, in its pure, conscious life,
> brings about this achievement of sense [*Sinnesleistung*], this
> achievement of judgement and insight [which constitutes] "objectivity"; not how it theoretically and progressively determines
> an objectivity which it *has* in advance within experience and experiential belief, but how in itself it comes thus to *have* such an
> objectivity in the first place. For it *has* only what it achieves
> within itself; the simplest having-a-thing-over-against-oneself in
> perception is itself already consciousness and accomplishes a
> bestowing of sense and a positing of reality in super-abundant
> structures: except that reflection and reflective study are required in order to gather something from this accomplishment,
> and they are required all the more in order to gather something which would be of use scientifically. [*EP* I, 67f.]

Thus, "*transcendental science*" has "a totally different theme from all the objective sciences; [it] is separated from them and yet related to all of them as a correlate" (68). In lectures delivered as early as 1907, Husserl emphasized quite distinctly that "philosophy is situated in a new dimension over against all natural cognition" and that there would correspond with this dimension "a new, radically new method contraposed to the method of the 'natural' dimension." It becomes clear in these lectures that Husserl's idea of philosophy went forth originally from the problematic of skepticism and the critique of cognition, found its proper footing with the discovery of the transcendental reduction, and began to unfold itself in the universally situated problem of transcendental constitution. Husserl argues here that whoever would deny this utterly new dimension and method will have failed to understand not only the whole stratum of problems peculiar to the critique of cognition, but also "what it is that *philosophy actually wants to be and should be* and what, over against all natural cognition and science, lends to philosophy its own distinctive character and warrant" (*IP*, esp. 24ff.). Not long afterwards, in the *Ideas I* of 1913, it becomes fully clear that the theory of transcendental constitution has the task of building the "new 'theory of cognition' " (*Id* I, § 55).

As the one who is philosophizing seeks to reach an understanding of just "what it is he is actually aiming at under the title 'philosophy' and just how far he must desire something fundamentally other than [what] 'positive' science [desires]," there finally arises, according to Husserl, "a necessary motivation," "which drives one out beyond the natural positivity of life and science and makes necessary the transcendental change of attitude, the phenomenological reduction." In his work, Husserl "struck out on various, *equally possible* paths, in order perspicuously and forcibly to set forth a motivation such as this one," that is, in order to lead from the natural to the philosophical attitude, to show that the *transcendental* basis laid open by the phenomenological reduction is the basis of the specifically *philosophical* mode of experience (cf. *Id* III, "Nachwort zu meinen Ideen," 147f.).

The Several Paths of the Phenomenological Epoché and Reduction

It is possible to identify three principal types of path taken in the work of Husserl. In the present context, we wish not so much to follow these paths in their basic forms and in their mutual connections and intersections throughout the individual works and creative phases,[3] as rather to attempt to characterize them in broad strokes within the horizon of Husserl's attempt to come to terms with the history of modern philosophy.[4] Albeit his early cry "to the things themselves" may have resounded with an antihistorical tone,[5] Husserl himself not only stood more or less unconsciously under the influence of contemporary philosophical doctrines but, in reflection upon the intellectual content of the philosophical works he studied, found an aid for the clarification of the "demands issuing from the problems themselves" as well as a stimulus for deepening these problems and asking new questions (cf. *PSS*, 340). In his mature, critical history of ideas (1923/24) stands the following famous sentence: "The deepest sense of modern philosophy lies in there having inwardly accrued to philosophy in the modern era a task whose motive power, even if unexplained, sets philosophy perpetually in motion. This is the task of redeeming in a higher sense the truth of the radical subjectivism of the skeptical tradition," and doing so "by way of *transcendental subjectivism*" on the basis of the phenomenological reduction (cf. *EP* I, 61).

In his own eyes, three moments in the tradition were of exceeding importance for the path to transcendental subjectivism as travelled by Husserl in transcendental phenomenology, "the secret longing of all modern philosophy" (*Id* I, § 62). These were: (1) Descartes's "fundamental reflection" in the *Meditations Concerning First Philosophy*; (2) Kant's "Copernican turn," in the *Critique of Pure Reason*, from the ancient ontological thematic to the transcendental interpretation of the sense of the world as a world of possible experience; and (3) the psychology of "inner experience" associated with British empiricism (from Locke to Hume) and transmitted to Husserl by way of Brentano. We may thus speak of a "Cartesian path," an "ontological path," which we may perhaps also designate as a "Kantian path," and a "path through descriptive, intentional psychology."

The "Cartesian" Path

In 1923/24, Husserl wrote the following: "Historically, we find the seed of transcendental philosophy in Descartes" (*EP* II, 4). It was nearly twenty years earlier that Husserl had first introduced the method of phenomenological reduction into his phenomenology. Then, under the spell of arguments directed skeptically against the possibility of cognition as such, Husserl had noted the following:

> If it has become unclear and uncertain how cognition could reach its object, and if we become inclined to doubt whether such a thing would be possible, we must first of all have in mind indubitable cases of cognition or possible cognition in which the objects of cognition are actually reached or would be reached. . . . Here the *Cartesian method of doubt* offers us a beginning: . . . the *cogitationes* are the first absolute data [*Gegebenheiten*]. [*IP*, 4]

It is especially in connection with these skeptical arguments and their usually attendant appeal to Descartes's procedure of a return to the *ego cogito* that Husserl names his own method the phenomenological or transcendental epoché. The prevalent thought in this regard is the methodical disengagement, bracketing, or suspension of the entire world of transcendent experience as it is known in straightforward or "positive" cognition and science. The aim hereby is to bring into view the pure, immanent, constitutive subjectivity which would be "left over" (the idea of "residue") even if the world did not exist (the idea of "world-annihilation") and from the viewpoint of which one might therefore commence with the novel, transcendental science (cf. *IP* [1907]; *Id* I [1913]; *EP* II [1923/24]; *CM* [1929]).

According to Husserl, Descartes had set forth scientifically "the very realm of 'that merely subjective element' to which skeptical relativism—albeit skeptically—reduced all cognizable being" (*EP* I, 66). Thus, Husserl never wearies of underscoring the "unprecedented importance of the Cartesian beginning, its importance," concealed from Descartes himself no less than from subsequent theories of cognition, "as a laying open of the realm of pure consciousness by the pure ego." Again and again, Husserl seeks to emphasize "the necessary and exclusive backward reference of the theory of cognition to this realm." In the first two *Meditations* of Descartes he finds "the sole onset for a true beginning of such discussions as could lead to *pure* formulations of the distinctive problematic of reason" (*EP* II, 328).

However, what is decisive for Husserl's own path is the *phenomenological reduction*, which already is to be applied to the Cartesian *cogitatio* (cf. *LE*, 216 [1906/07]; *IP* [1907], 7). As early as 1906, Husserl had written that "the first and basic methodological component in the theory of cognition" is the "skeptical position-taking [*Stellungnahme*], the *absolute epoché* which recognizes no pregivenness and sets its *non liquet* ['it is not clear'] as an abstention from judgement over against all natural cognition" (*LE*, 187). Notwithstanding his estimation of Descartes's revolutionary return to the *ego cogito* as methodologically exemplary, it was Husserl's persistent criticism that Descartes himself had continued to understand the *ego cogito* as a "part of the world" and that pure transcendental subjectivity had hence escaped him. In the phenomenological reduction, that is, in the *pure* apperceptive mode of consciousness, lies the "*necessary correction* of the Cartesian contemplation of evidence," and this in the sense that henceforth one may speak only "of the evidence of what is demonstrated directly in the strictest phenomenological reduction and is purely and immanently cognizable on this basis." One may no longer speak of the "evidence of the *sum* which establishes my existence in the natural, psychological sense" (*LE*, 216).

The question is no longer this, "How, in my immanent experiences, can I, this human being, possibly reach a being in itself [*Sein an sich*] outside, beyond me, and the like?" Rather, on the basis of the phenomenological reduction, we now pose "the *pure basic question*: How can

the pure phenomenon of cognition reach something that is not immanent to it?" (*IP*, 7). Howsoever he may have touched upon it, in Husserl's
eyes Descartes failed to arrive at the *pure* formulation of the problem
because he "had not learned the right lessons from skepticism" (*EP* I,
64). "In the attempt to *demonstrate* the right of evidence and of its
transsubjective bearing," he lost himself "in circles of reasoning which
were seen early on and were much deplored" (65). For Husserl, by contrast , the matter does not at all depend upon a "demonstration," upon a
"guarantee" of transcendence or objectivity (cf. *EP* I, 65; *CES*, 193 / C,
189). As mentioned above, his sole concern lay with a *clarification* of the
essential possibilities of cognition, a clarification which would be based
on the pure thematization of the intentionally performing life of consciousness as constitutive of objectivity in manifold ways.

This consequently reflective onset, which radically transforms the
sense of any talk about objectivity "straight away" and makes consciousness visible as the function of constituting actuality within itself (cf. *Ms.
M I 1*, 89), also comes to bear on the discussion of the possibility of the
non-being of the objective world (the "*world-annihilation*"), a discussion
which has often given offense and was probably expounded even by Husserl himself in a partially misleading manner. For Husserl, the discussion
constitutes a particularly effective mental experiment on the "Cartesian" path, an experiment which effects a radically executed annulment
of the natural attitude of life and the theoretical attitude of science in
which the world is there for me (*EP* I, 340). In this experiment, too, it is a
question of attaining to the intentionally performing life of consciousness in its *transcendental* purity as the absolute phenomenological datum,
that is, as an "*own* field of being, given in its own experience *independent*
of the experience of the world, a field of being which can now become *eo
ipso* a field of possible judging, even of insightful and scientific judging"
(*Id* I, 635). In Husserl, the thinking-over of the possible non-being of the
objective world, this "fictive hypothesis" (*EP* I, 340), in fact maintains
itself solely on the basis of the purely reflective thematic of consciousness. It does not regard world and consciousness somehow speculatively
"from the outside" in order then, for example on the basis of a methodical doubt, to establish that, in spite of the annihilation of the world, consciousness remains as a "residue"—a thought which surely could not be
carried to fulfillment. Rather, "world-annihilation" is the title for an insight gained solely from reflecting on the life of consciousness and its
possible course, an insight into the "style of correlation [*Korrelatstil*]
characteristic of the discordance in the universe of my possible *cogitationes*," and hence an insight into the "essential possibility of modifying"

the style of concordance (*EP* I, 337f.; *Id* I, 634). Conversely, applied "positively," as it were, the reflective thematics of consciousness is concerned in the phenomenological reduction to understand how belief comes about with "world" as its content (cf. *Id* I, 634).

Guided by the skeptical problematics Husserl initially restricted the field of his research to reflection on the actually present stream of consciousness. He did not yet have at his disposal the means for making our acceptance of the existence [*Daseinsgeltung*] of the intentional object, much less our acceptance of the existence of the whole "world" (*qua cogitatum*), transcendentally intelligible on the basis of merely momentary immanent experiences. Within such a restriction, he was also denied access to a subjective clarification of the objectifying achievement [*Leistung*] "world as *intersubjective* unity." A "transcendental solipsism" seemed to be the lot of the radicalized return to the *ego cogito*. Such a consequence seems also to cling to Husserl's later introductions to transcendental subjectivity by way of the Cartesian path. As Husserl will later say in the *Crisis,* the great disadvantage for the reader who is led on this path to the phenomenological point of view lies in the fact that this path "does indeed lead, as if by a leap, to the transcendental ego but, inasmuch as every preliminary explanation must fall short, brings this ego into view in a seeming emptiness of content in which one is initially at a loss to know what is thereby supposed to have been gained and even how, from such a beginning, a fully novel and philosophically decisive basic science should ever have been acquired" (*CES*, 158 / C, 155).

The "Ontological" Path

⟨On another possible path to the transcendental attitude Husserl maintains "order in a direction opposite that suggested by the Cartesian onset" (175 / C, 171f.): Here he does not begin "directly" with the *ego cogito* but rather from the objective, ontological side. He wishes to awaken us to the need for a correlative transcendental-subjective consideration that will make the sense of objectivity intelligible. This procedure also corresponds to Husserl's own course of development beginning from the formal sciences (cf. above, chap. 1, § 2; *PP*, § 3; *FTL*, § 100).⟩ From about 1907/08 onward, the procedure under discussion was also strongly marked by Husserl's attempt to come to grips with Kant's idea of transcendental philosophy.[6] It is worthy of note, therefore, that even Kant himself had been led to establish his transcendental interpretation of the world under the influence of the skeptic Hume. In the course of the development of his transcendental phenomenology, Husserl sees himself, "in the essential results" of his work, to be "at one with Kant as regards the broad lines" of their respective approaches (*EP* I, 235).

Generally speaking, Husserl's ontological path to transcendental subjectivity consists in making us attentive to what is in principle an ultimate *"unintelligibility"* as the basic character of all natural, prescientific or scientific cognition of objects (beings, *onta*). Such a lack of intelligibility continues to hold sway as long as this "straightforward" cognition fails to be considered as such and universally in the full concrete context of intentionally performing subjectivity, as long as it fails to be clarified in this concrete *correlation*.

> Every positive science possesses . . . an abstract *onesidedness* by virtue of the fact that the transcendental life and performance of the experiencing, thinking, researching, and founding consciousness remains anonymous within it, remains unseen, untheoretized, uncomprehended. [*EP* II, 27]

Like Kant, Husserl poses the "transcendental questions." He seeks "in subjectivity or, more precisely, in the correlation between subjectivity and the objective, the final determination of the sense of objectivity as apprehended in cognition" (*EP* I, 386). As with Kant, so it is with Husserl a question of the *"transcendental subjectivizing* which is not only compatible with genuine objectivity but constitutes its *a priori* reverse side" (*FTL*, 226). The "*a priori* of subjectivity" or the "phenomenological *a priori* of constitution" counts for Husserl as "the ultimate in intelligibility and that which first makes everything else intelligible."[7]

This attitude, leading consistently from the world of experience, accepted as given, to the very *experience* of the world, thus has its prototype in Kant's "Copernican turn" as a reversal of the entire natural manner of thinking. With respect to the search for a more concrete understanding of the transcendental interpretation of the sense of the world, the advantage of this path over against the Cartesian path lies above all in the fact that here it is not necessary to perform a skeptical epoché in the sense of a disengagement of our acceptance of the existence of the world and a retreat to an absolutely given foundation. Rather, the things of experience and finally the whole world come to be grasped in their basic structures or in their ontological structures as an "*index*" or "*guide*" to the subjective *a priori* of constitution. This orientation toward natural experience precedes the transcendental turn, and it is through this orientation that the transcendental thematic itself receives from the very beginning a fullness of content and a stable guidance. The task then consists in making the ontological or objective structuring of the naturally experienced world intelligible as complexes of phenomena, and doing so purely from the subjective sources of the intentional achievement of consciousness.[8]

On the ontological path, it is the things themselves which demand that we break through the confinement of the phenomenological field to the actually present stream of consciousness. The objective *a priori* of the things themselves *indicates* the phenomenological interconnections of consciousness, that is, the actual and possible regulations of consciousness as pure consciousness of the objective [*das Objektive*] (cf. *PI* I, 180, 182). In phenomenological experience we arrive at the reflective thematics of a whole system, stylistically determined as an horizon and composed of temporally sequential, actual and possible immanent experiences, *intentionally implied* in one another. Above all, we find here an expansion of the phenomenological reduction so as to include *intersubjectivity*. It is alone in respect of intersubjectivity that the full sense of objectivities as "intersubjective unities" can be constitutively clarified in accordance with their objective *a priori* (cf. §§ 36ff.; *EP* II, Appendix XX). In thus leading up to transcendental subjectivity by way of the ontological path, Husserl is able to characterize the phenomenological reduction in a manner somewhat reminiscent of Kant's "Copernican turn." He says the following:

> Phenomenological reduction is nothing other than a *change of attitude* in which the world of experience comes to be contemplated consistently and universally as a world of *possible experience*, that is, the experiencing life comes to be regarded, that life in which what is experienced is in every case—and universally—a sense of experience with a determinate intentional horizon. [436]

However, Husserl reproaches Kant, on the one hand, for lacking in radicality or for "operating at an elevated level [*Hochstufigkeit*]" in the onset of the transcendental problematic. Right up to and including the *Crisis* he plays Descartes's return to the *ego cogito* off against Kant (*CES*, 102f., 437 / C, 99f.). On the other hand, and above all, from the very earliest and again up to and including the *Crisis*, Husserl criticizes Kant's "mythical formation of concepts" and his talk of "transcendental-subjective 'faculties,' 'functions,' 'formations,'" of the "I of transcendental apperception" and of the "thing in itself," as "*constructive concepts*" (§§ 30f., 57). He holds it up to Kant that, "coming from the Wolffian ontology" as he did, Kant remained "always *essentially ontologically oriented*, even in matters of transcendental philosophy," and considered "the systematic execution of a correlative, *concretely intuitive* study of performing subjectivity and its functions of consciousness . . . to be dispensable for the completion of his problematic." In spite of an "initially penetrating look into the *a priori* of the sense-bestowing life of consciousness"—especially in the "subjective deduction" of the first edition of the *Critique of Pure Reason*—Kant, in Husserl's mind, had "constructed a transcendental subjectivity" (cf. *EP* I, 227, 281f.; *CES*, § 31; p. 120 / C, 117f.).

Husserl detected the reason for this mythically constructive procedure in Kant's fear of "any *recourse to psychology* as an absurd perversion of the genuine problematic of the understanding." This fear arose because Kant, "in his conception of the soul and of the range of tasks of a psychology," remained dependent upon the very same empiricism which he had combatted in other domains. It arose because for Kant what "counts as the soul is the naturalized soul, the soul conceived as a component of the psychophysical human being within the time of nature, that is, within spatio-temporality. There the realm of transcendental subjectivity could never be the realm of the soul. But in "distinguishing [Kant's] transcendental subjectivity from the soul, we fall into an unintelligibly mythical domain" (117f. / C, 115f.).

The Path through Descriptive, Intentional Psychology

This last mentioned reproach of Kant by Husserl helps us toward an understanding of Husserl's peculiar *clarification of the transcendental problem* with express regard for the "related function of psychology" (cf. the title of part III of the *Crisis*). Above all during the 1920s and again in the *Crisis*, Husserl methodically thought through the relation between phenomenology and psychology which was constantly present in his own development, and projected a "path from psychology to phenomenological transcendental philosophy" as a further possibility for leading up to the transcendental-phenomenological reduction.

The psychology in which Husserl was interested, however, is not to be confused with the then contemporary positive-scientific experimental psychology, which studied the psychical as a natural event, a real-causal annex of animal bodies. Husserl called his psychology a pure, descriptive, phenomenological or intentional psychology. In all of his considerations regarding the idea of such a psychology, the central thought lay in his conceiving it as the thematization of the *essentiality proper to the psychical* [*Eigenwesentlichkeit des Psychischen*]. This means above all that he viewed psychology as a study of the essence proper to the psychical over against the physical and as an eidetic science over against a factual science.[9] In Husserl's conception of what is properly essential to the psychical we find the deep influence, always stressed by Husserl, of *Brentano's* characterization of the essence of the "psychical phenomena" as such, namely, the "relation to a content" or "direction toward an object." In his phenomenology, Husserl developed the full consequences of Brentano's doctrine of the various "modes of relation of consciousness to a content" (cf. *LI* II/1 (V), § 10), that is, in Husserl's terminology, the various modes of *intentionality*[10] as the basic trait of the essence of all psychical life. His radical dissociation from the then current conception of the life of the soul as an "analogue of the physical events of nature" was decisive for his own idea of "descriptive psychology." Even for Brentano, as Husserl critically remarked, the soul had remained just such an ever freshly self-transforming complex of elements with corresponding causal laws. Husserl, by contrast, laid down the firm principle "that it belongs to the essence of conscious life to shelter within itself neither the spatial outside-of-one-another, inside-of-one-another, or throughout-one-another, nor the spatial totality, but rather an intentional implication and motivation, an intentionally mutual self-enclosure of intentional objects, such that according to form and principle no analogue whatsoever obtains in the physical domain" (*PP*, 36f.; *EP* II, 123f.).

It is of particular significance that the most general essential-characteristic of the intentionality of psychical life permits itself to be drawn directly from the *evidence of inner experience* (reflection) and set forth descriptively as "a performance accomplished in multifariously demonstrable forms and appurtenant syntheses" (*PP*, 36, cf. 31). Following Brentano, Husserl takes up the tradition of British "empiricism" from Locke to Hume and never ceases to esteem this tradition highly or to underscore its importance for his phenomenology. Nevertheless, by means of the phenomenological reduction or the pure apperception of consciousness, he radically transforms the sense of this empiricism which finally ended in the skepticism of Hume. The reflective "inner experience" of psychological consciousness becomes a thematization of the anonymous "transcendental experience" of pure consciousness, and the descriptive psychology of "psychical phenomena" becomes an analysis of the intentionality of consciousness, leading Husserl ever further into the depths of the essential structure of an individual's pure consciousness and a group's intersubjective consciousness. On the basis of the subtly analyzed "intentional implications" of consciousness (cf. below, chap. 5) and the inseparably appurtenant, universal, intentional corre-late, Husserl endeavored to render visible that proper essentiality of souls which appears in the natural-mundane attitude as an outside-of-one-another localized in bodies. He attempted to show this to be "a pure intentional inside-of-one-another" or an "all-inclusive unity of an infi-nite continuity of life," and he tried to make the simply existent [*schlicht seiende*] world intelligible as "the communal phenomenon 'world,' 'world for all actual and possible subjects,' of which none can withdraw itself from its intentional implication" (*CES*, 259 / C, 255f.; cf. *EP* II, 153).

According to Husserl, if we remain radically and universally within the boundaries of the pure thematics, we shall discover the sud-den shift into the transcendental-philosophical contemplation of the world to be latent and necessarily contained in the "pure development" (*CES*, 259 / C, 256) of descriptive psychology understood as pure, re-flective analysis of the manifold intentionalities of consciousness with their implications and correlates. This shift is the radical change of atti-tude in which the world and objectivities of every kind come to be con-ceived *exclusively* as *intentional correlates* of the multiplicities of consciousness, rather than being naturally and straightforwardly presup-posed as pregiven (259 / C, 256, passim). The "psychical," which ap-pears in the natural attitude, and in positively oriented psychology, as a dependent stratum of being in humans and animals, thereby loses even the sense of a mundanely phenomenal event. It *is* the "purely apper-ceived," the transcendentally subjective (cf., e.g., *EP*, 427).

Against the background of the *Aufhebung* of pure-descriptive psy-chology that takes place in transcendental phenomenology and mirrors Husserl's own development, the idea of a *path* through pure psychology to transcendental phenomenology acquires its full significance as an ex-cellent "*propadeutic.*"[11] Since the 1920s at the latest, Husserl speaks of the phenomenological-*psychological* reduction in which "*pure psychologi-cal* subjectivity" comes to be thematized in phenomenological or pure psychology. This occurs without in any way drawing into question, sus-pending, or bracketing that belief in the being of the world of experi-ence which is self-evident for the natural attitude to which even pure psychology remains subjected. In a thoroughgoing parallel with pure psychology, it is precisely this reflective cognition of the essentiality proper to the life of consciousness, that is also acquired by the one who has entered the transcendental-phenomenological attitude (cf., e.g., *PP*, 343; *Id* III, 144ff.). Husserl writes finally in the *Crisis* that *pure psychology,* which except in his own pure phenomenology is supposed to have no historical precedent whatsoever,[12] is "and can be nothing other than that which was sought *from the very beginning in the philosophical intention [of our investigation]* as an absolutely founded philosophy, and which can be fulfilled only as phenomenological-transcendental philosophy" (*CES*, 263 / C, 259). Modern psychology, as it developed in historical consequence of British empiricism, had failed, in Husserl's eyes, because it neglected "to inquire about what in essence was the only genuine sense of its task as a *universal science* of psychical being." The "consistent and pure execution of this task" would have had "to lead [psychology], of itself and with necessity, to a science of transcendental subjectivity and thus to its transformation into a universal transcendental science" (207 / C, 203). The particular interest of the path from pure psychology to transcendental phenomenology lies, perhaps, in the rather impressive success that Husserl had on this path in making intelligible, not merely "constructively" but rather concretely and intuitively, the clarification and execution of the transcendental problematic inaugurated by Kant.

The Phenomenological Reduction and the Idea of Philosophy

Husserl's philosophical intention to redeem the truth of skeptical subjectivism in a higher sense in the form of "transcendental subjectivism" would seem to become more concretely intelligible by way of a meditation on his method of reduction. Objectivity, our world in its entirety, has in the transcendental-phenomenological contemplation of consciousness only the sense of an intentional correlate of subjects reciprocally and intentionally implied in one another. Another world, unrelated to our subjectivity and intersubjectivity, has no sense for us whatsoever (cf. *CES*, 257f. / C, 253f.). *Objectivity* is itself a correlative achievement [*Korrelatleistung*] of the communalized transcendental consciousness. Again and again Husserl sets forth as an achievement of the reduction the *emancipation* from the absolutization of the world, *an absolutization* which ultimately, though covertly, underlies even skeptical argument.

In summarizing, we may maintain with Husserl the following: "My calling" as a phenomenologist "is the study of pure subjectivity" (*EP* II, 431); the phenomenological reduction provides the way of access to this thematic.

> The characteristic feature of phenomenology consists in its being *radical and universal* in *reflection* and accepting *no* natural datum in a simple and straightforward manner. Rather, it leads

(handwritten margin note: i.e. to realize the 'inner truth' of Descartes' attempt to the cogito & British Empiricism?)

every datum back to consciousness, to the universe of actual
and possible consciousness in which natural being is given in
consciousness, intended, possibly "demonstrated as true," etc.
[It thus reduces every datum,] not in hazardous isolation, but
every one together with every other actual and possible [da-
tum]—in the unity of a radical resolve to assume no natural
existence [*Dasein*] as given, but rather *to make a theme of the universe of consciousness and of this alone* and thus to wish to have
and regard natural existence solely *as* that which is experienced
or otherwise intended, thought, etc. [430]

The essential feature in Husserl's problematic of the phenomenological reduction seems to us to lie in the "philosophical will to ultimate
and absolute knowledge, the will to philosophy" which, in fact, first
arose as a rejoinder to skeptical argument (cf. 500). It would seem to us
mistaken, however, to characterize this will without further ado as "Car-
tesianism" or even as exuberant soaring off beyond and in disregard of
human factuality. It is rather the case that Husserl, much like Kant, appears within modern European philosophy as a renovator of the Socratic-Platonic " 'Know thyself!' from which, as becomes ever more
clear, the whole of philosophy issues" (121, cf. 166f.). Husserl constantly, and no less so during his years in Freiburg, stood as an alien over
against the speculative philosophers of German Idealism.

With a radicality and consistency not foreseeable from the outset,
Husserl attained or renewed the "idea of *philosophy as absolute knowledge*," as *episteme* over against mere *doxa*, which in his understanding had
originally been established by Socrates-Plato. This *episteme*, as the true
idea of the rationality of the original Greek establishment of European
philosophy so often conjured up by Husserl, was in his thinking connected essentially with self-knowledge.

Perhaps . . . it is true in the strictest sense that *self-knowledge*,
but only radically pure or *transcendental* self-knowledge, is the
sole source of all the knowledge that in the ultimate and highest sense is genuinely and satisfyingly scientific, namely, the
philosophical knowledge which makes possible a "philosophical" life. In that case *philosophy itself* would simply be the systematic self-unfolding of transcendental subjectivity in the
form of systematic transcendental self-theorizing on the basis
of transcendental self-experience and its derivatives. [167, cf.
also 5]

What was expounded "rhetorically" in the context from which this citation stems was thoroughly the opinion of Husserl. "But the goal is distant, the path is difficult and must first be cleared. Without guiding thoughts one cannot search. But the paths, and the theories which prepare them, must be gained by hard labor, step by step" (169).

Thus understood, <u>philosophy forms</u> in Husserl's eyes "<u>an</u> *idea*." It is "able <u>to be realized only</u> in a style of relative, temporary validity, and <u>in an infinite historical process</u>—but in this way it is indeed able to be realized" (*Id* III, 139). In the same sense, Husserl stressed again and again that the accomplishment of a genuine and pure transcendentalism would not be the task of *one* man and *one* "system," but rather the scientific task of generations (cf., e.g., *CES*, 459 / C, 379f.). Not least of all, "philosophy as a strict science" means precisely this working together of those who philosophize, as over against a "philosophy of world-views [*Weltanschauungsphilosophie*]" bound to the style and capacities, the creative genius of a single personality.[13] In the inquiry back into " 'transcendental subjectivity' as the original site of every bestowal of sense and confirmation of being," an inquiry set in motion by the performance of the phenomenological reduction, Husserl puts into practice philosophy as "a strict science in the radical sense," born "of ultimate self-responsibility" (139).[14]

§ 2. The "Eidetic" Reduction:
Phenomenology as the Eidetic Science
of Consciousness—The Method of
Eidetic Inquiry

When around 1905 Husserl set his phenomenology in motion on the basis of the phenomenological reduction, he recognized immediately and quite clearly the problem of whether *pure phenomenology* were really *possible as a science* and, if so, how.[15] For the chief difficulty regarding scientific, and therefore not solipsistic but intersubjectively verifiable, objectively valid research into the phenomenologically reduced consciousness,[16] stems from the fact that in pure reflection, that is, upon performing the phenomenological reduction, we find ourselves "in a *ceaseless flux of never-returning phenomena*," in an eternal Heracleitean flux.[17] It is a "characteristic of consciousness as such to consist in a fluctuation that takes its course in various dimensions" (*Id* I, § 75). The phenomena may even "be given indubitably in reflective experience. Mere experience is not a science."[18]

> A descriptive knowledge that ascertains and determines a phenomenological "world," such as in the case of our knowledge of the natural world, is utterly excluded. *After the phenomenological reduction, scientific ascertainments* regarding the phenomena are not possible, *nota bene*, if we wish to fix and conceptually to determine these phenomena as absolute, one-time particulars. [*LE*, 224]

> [For] even the single philosopher, by himself and within the epoché, can seize hold of nothing from this incomprehensibly streaming life, retrieve and repeat it, always with the same content, and become certain of its being-this and its being-thus, so as to be able to describe and, as it were, document it in stable assertions (even if only for his own person). [*CES*, 181 / C, 178]

In view of this difficulty, Husserl maintained again and again that it was the aim of the exploration of consciousness to be not an empirical science but a science of essences and that it could in general arrive at *scientific* results only as an exploration of *essences*, as an eidetic inquiry. But what is *eidetic* science according to Husserl? He constantly stressed that empirical science is not the only kind of science,[19] that over against the "sciences based on experience and induction" there are *pure, a priori* sciences. The *purity* from which phenomenology takes its name is "not merely that of pure reflection," that is, not merely that which is made possible by the phenomenological reduction, but also purity in the sense of the *a priori*.[20] Husserl's doctrine of phenomenology as an eidetic science, his doctrine of the "eidetic reduction," as he says from time to time, is now connected extremely closely with his conception of just such a pure, *a priori* cognition. In turn, this conception is imprinted with the mathematical style of thinking as understood by Husserl. If we pursue these connections to some extent, we shall arrive at a closer determination of the kind of science that Husserl strived for with his pure phenomenology.

The following passages may serve to point out the relations in question. In his *Formal and Transcendental Logic* (1929), Husserl wrote the following: "Of the concepts belonging to the ambiguous expression '*a priori*,' [the concept of the *eidos*] defines the only one to which we grant philosophical recognition. It is exclusively the *eidos* which is meant wherever I speak in my writings about the '*a priori*' " (*FTL*, 219 fn.). In a manuscript stemming probably from the first half of the 1920s and bearing the title "The Method of Eidetic Inquiry," we may read the following: "Everyone has a practical knowledge of the *a priori* from the study of pure mathematics. One knows and approves of the mathematical style of thinking. . . . It is toward this style that we orient our concept of the *a priori*" (*AV*, 13). Finally, in the *Ideas* of 1913, Husserl addresses the mathematical disciplines, especially geometry and arithmetic, as "the ancient highly developed eidetic disciplines." Parallel and in contrast with them he conceives the "new eidetics" of transcendentally pure consciousness (*FTL*, § 71).

Husserl considers the fundamental characteristic of his, as it were, mathematically modelled *a priori thinking* to consist precisely in this, that there is accomplished in such thinking a *liberation from the fact*, or a shaping of the fact into the form of an *arbitrary example*. Expressed differently, "the mathematician abstains in principle from every judgement concerning real actuality [*reale Wirkichkeit*]" and, instead of actualities, concerns himself with *ideal possibilities* and their related laws.[21] The pure geometer, Husserl's favorite example, thematizes spatial figures. In doing so, however, he is *not* interested in figures experienced in individual perception or *quasi*-experienced in imagination, figures lying on the table or produced through representation. Rather, he thematizes "pure" spatial figures. These exhibit in themselves a *structure of universality* which is able to be determined by the "multiform mental activity" of ideation or eidetic vision (*PP*, 76). Husserl describes this method for the viewing of ideas or essences more closely as a *variation* performed in *pure phantasy*, in which only pure, ideal possibilities can be constituted, a *variation* in which the universal is able to be viewed actively as the *pervasively identical* (invariant, inseparable) trait found throughout the figures and objectivities that are constituted as *possible* actualities.[22] In order mentally to run through the particular variables and get a view of the ἐν ἐπὶ πολλῶν (cf. *PP*, 78; *EJ*, 414 / C&A, 343), it is crucial that one attain to the level of pure phantasy and remain within its boundaries, for it is only on this ground that one can grasp the *pure* eidetic universality that is independent of every positing of correspondingly real being and is bound to no presupposed actuality (*EJ*, 426f. / C&A, 352f.). The insight into this pure eidetic universality permits every imaginable particularization to be known in advance (*a priori*) as a particularization of its essence, that is, in the consciousness of mere *exemplification* (as a member of the range of singular, pure possibilities). On the basis of the *eidos* it is possible to set forth "laws of necessity which determine what must necessarily belong to an object if it is to be able to be an object of this kind" (ibid.). There obtains here the correlation between eidetic universality and eidetic necessity as this correlation was expressed by Husserl in the *Ideas*: "Every eidetic particularization and singularization of an eidetically universal state of affairs is, as such, an eidetic necessity" (*Id* I, § 6); or, there obtains here the "necessity which is understood as the not-able-to-be-otherwise of a matter of universal insight in its application to any particular case whatsoever as such."[23]

According to Husserl, the basic attitude exercised by mathematicians can, "in view of the universal and essential relationship between actuality and possibility, between experience and pure phantasy," be universally extended.

> The way stands open from every concrete actuality and from every actually or potentially experienced trait of such an actuality into the *realm of ideal or pure possibilities* and thereby into the realm of *a priori* thinking. [*AV*, 1; *EJ*, 428 / C&A, 353f.]

Within this attitude, actuality is itself treated "as one possibility among other possibilities, in fact, as an arbitrary possibility in the realm of phantasy" (*PP*, 74). The "basic accomplishment [*Leistung*] upon which all else depends" consists in the "transformation of one or another experienced or phantasized objectivity into a variation," a transformation which Husserl finds performed in exemplary fashion in the domain of pure mathematics. According to Husserl, however, there are various kinds of eidetic science corresponding with the various domains of actuality (*AV*, 17f.; *MS. F IV 1*, 62a; *Id* III, passim).

It is important to notice that in the orientation toward the pure *eidos* "the *factual* actuality of the particular case produced in variation" gets treated "as wholly irrelevant" (*PP*, 74). This is so not because the factually experienced actuality must be *skeptically* denied or abandoned (71); rather it is a consequence of the proper sense that characterizes the orientation toward the essence. Such an actuality is first drawn into consideration in the transference of eidetic universality that takes place in the "application." Stated differently, "the essence of purely eidetic science consists in its *exclusively eidetic* procedure" (*Id* I, § 7);

> [I]ntuitive experience of an essence does not in the least imply the positing of an individual existence; pure eidetic truths do not contain the slightest assertion regarding matters of fact; and thus from eidetic truths *alone* not even the most trivial matter-of-factual truth can be inferred. [13 / G, 57]

Within the factual sciences, we find, for example, the activity of a natural
scientist who observes and experiments and establishes empirically given
existence; for whom, therefore, *"experiencing* is a *founding act* which could
never be replaced by mere imagining." On the other hand, within the
orientation of the eidetic sciences, "factual experience" provides "only
an *exemplary point of departure,* a point of departure for the style of free
phantasy which I shape in accordance with factual experience *without* for
the rest *employing it as something posited and accepted [als Geltung zu
benutzen]"* (§ 7; PP, 71).

Sciences of Fact and Sciences of Essence; Fact and Essence. The "Application" of *A Priori* Cognition to Factual Existence

The distinction between sciences of fact and sciences of essence, which
constantly reappears in Husserl's general deliberations on the theory of
science, is rooted in his doubtlessly "Platonically inspired" conception
of the relationship between facts and essences. Concisely formulated,
the guiding thoughts as expressed by Husserl in section 1 of the *Ideas* of
1913 are the following: matters of fact, matters of individual, spatiotemporal existence, are *"accidental."* "It is thus; but in accordance with its
essence it could be otherwise" (*Id* I, § 2). Possible, valid laws of nature
here express "only factual regulations which could after all read quite
differently" (§ 2). The following statements are now decisive for Husserl's conception:

> When we said: "in accordance with its own essence" every mat-
> ter of fact could be otherwise, we already expressed thereby
> the thought that an *essence,* and thus a purely apprehensible *ei-
> dos,* belongs to the sense of every accidental matter and that
> this essence is now subordinated to eidetic truths of various
> levels of generality. An individual object is not merely as such
> an individual, a "this, here!", a unique instance. As constituted
> thus and so *"in itself [in sich selbst],"* it has its own distinctive
> character, its stock of essential predicables which must accrue
> to it (as that "being, as it is in itself"), in order that other, sec-
> ondary and relative determinations might accrue to it. [§ 2][24]

This relationship "founds a corresponding relation among sciences of
fact and sciences of essence" (§ 7) and their "relationships of interdependence"(§ 8).

Husserl divides the eidetic (*a priori*) disciplines very generally into so-called "*formal* ontology," as an eidetic science of the formal region "objectivity as such," and into *material* or *regional* ontologies (cf., e.g., *Id* I, § 8; *Id* III, § 7; *AV*, 18f.; above chap. 1). For their part, the sciences of fact (empirical sciences) refer essentially both to the formal-eidetic disciplines and to the corresponding material-eidetic disciplines, that is, they have their "essential, theoretical foundations in the eidetic ontologies" (*Id* I, § 9).

Of particular importance is the relationship of the *application* of *a priori* cognition to factual existence. This relationship can be made intelligible from the standpoint of the relationships of interdependence between fact and essence or between the sciences of fact and the sciences of essence (cf. below, chap. 10). According to Husserl, it is possible to form "the idea of a completely rationalized science of experience" (*Id* I, § 9) resting upon the following considerations: Eidetic universality can be placed in relation with occurent actualities because every *actually* occurent objectivity is at once, in the pure sense, a *possible* objectivity that can be regarded as an example, as an instance of pure possibility, and transformed into a variant (*EJ*, 426 / C&A, 352). The relationship discussed above with regard to an *eidetic necessity* in the case of eidetic particularization and singularization "*holds as well for all factual existence.*" We can see, in other words, that everything belonging inseparably to the pure *eidos* must also belong to every corresponding factual occurrence (*EJ*, § 90; *Id* I, § 6; *Id* III, 40f.).

Rationalization of factual existence thus takes place by way of judging factual actualities in accordance with the laws of their pure possibilities, that is, in accordance with the *a priori* conditions of *possible* experience (*AV*, 16f.; *EJ*, § 90). It is clear that such a rationalization, according to its own sense, is itself neither competent nor able to perform, nor finally, as it were, to make superfluous the corresponding empirical-scientific cognition. The *real* conditions of possibility will always have to be determined in accordance with the methods of the empirical sciences (cf. *Id* III, 39f.; *Ms. F I 17*, 22). Husserl believed, however, that an empirical science whose regional domain is rationalized, even if only partially, is "raised to a new level" as a science and that the constitution of the eidetic discipline "has to mean a decisive step forward for the corresponding empirical science" (*Id* III, 43).

Husserl discerned such an event in seventeenth-century physics when the "*mathesis of nature*" came into force through the application of a "geometry that had been highly developed as pure eidetics" (cf. *Id* I, § 9; *Id* III, 43; *CES*, § 9). In this way "an infinity of truths valid with unconditional necessity for everything experienceable within this re-

gion," came to be established "for one of the great regions of experience" (*Id* III, 43). Mathematics articulates *a priori* conditions for nature
"without ever treating of nature 'itself' as a fact" (*EJ*, 427 / C&A, 353).
The *a priori* and always possible *application* of eidetic, mathematical cognition broke onto the scene when material nature was recognized as being *essentially res extensa* and geometry was seen as a corresponding
"ontological [eidetic] discipline related to an essential moment [in the
make-up] of such [a] thing [*Dinglichkeit*], that is, to the spatial form" (*Id*
I, 20 / G, 65). The actuality "material nature" thus became capable of
being judged in accordance with the laws of its pure possibility, just as is
the practice of mathematical physics.

Such an application of an appurtenant eidetic science is regarded
by Husserl as a "universal and thoroughly necessary task, to be related to
every sort of actuality"; for only in this way can the "scientific cognition
of *empirical actuality* be 'exact,' only in this way can it partake of genuine
rationality, namely, insofar as it refers this actuality to its eidetic possibility" (*AV*, 16f.; *EJ*, 427f. / C&A, 353f.). In the *Cartesian Meditations*
(1930), Husserl still writes that " 'in itself' [*an sich*] the science of pure
possibilities precedes the science of actualities and first makes the latter
possible as science" (*CM*, 106; cf. *Id* I, § 79).[25]

Pure Phenomenology as Eidetics of Consciousness

For Husserl, all the foregoing considerations concerning the theory of
science come to a peak in the transcendental-philosophical thesis of the
"*essential relation*" between all ideas of Being and consciousness (cf. *Ms.
F IV 1*, 62a). Husserl is of the view "that all possible *a priori* disciplines
form a coherent '*universitas*,' an innermost unity within multiplicity, that
they cohere in an *a priori* science of the primordial sources of all possible
consciousness and Being—in a 'transcendental phenomenology' of
which they must be treated as the essential and necessary ramifications"
(*AV*, 18f.). *All* eidetic sciences "cohere with one another by way of the
eidetics of consciousness" (*Ms. F IV 1*, 62a).

> That which is *specifically phenomenological* consists in the eidetic
> deliberation [*Wesenserwägung*] which transports us into the in-
> tentionally all-encompassing consciousness and thus sets every-
> thing yielded by eidetic contemplation [*eidetische Betrachtung*]
> into a relation with the eidetic essence of consciousness in
> which . . . all being is "constituted." [*Id* III, 133]

With this reference of all actual and possible objectivities to the corresponding experiencing acts of consciousness, to the subjective, *constitutive a priori* of consciousness as such, the central theme in Husserlian pure phenomenology as an eidetics of consciousness has been reached.

Ever since the *Logical Investigations* Husserl had referred the specifically phenomenological thematic to the intentional experiences immanent in consciousness. Now, the liberation from the *fact* of the empirical contingencies pertaining to the course of consciousness of our organization, even of the universal-human organization, is *equally fundamental* for the study of those experiences. The laws which can be exhibited through such an orientation belong "to all possible organizations as such insofar as these are able to be built up from acts which have taken on the form of the pure species" (*LI* II/2 [VI], § 64). What is at stake here, even as early as the *Logical Investigations*, is Husserl's understanding of the *pure a priori*, in critical contrast with that of Kant, as the insight into an *eidetic* interconnection which holds good as such not only "on the basis of our factual subjectivity."[26]

The immanent experiences of consciousness given reflectively in actual, psychological experience, do *not*, as such actual experiences, *bind* the phenomenologist.

> In precisely the same way . . . as pure geometry desists from binding itself to the shapes observed in actual experience and rather pursues possible shapes and transformations of shape in free, constructive, geometrical phantasy and determines the eidetic laws of these shapes: *precisely in this way* pure phenomenology wishes to explore the realm of pure consciousness and its phenomena, in accordance not with factual existence but *with pure possibilities and laws.*[27]

The empirical science of consciousness is psychology. Phenomenology, by contrast, establishes itself as the pure, *a priori*, eidetic science, "pure" in the sense of the " 'purity' of geometry and mathematical analysis." It investigates the ideal, *a priori* laws under which the pure *possibilities of* consciousness stand,[28] and rules out all questions concerning real existence. "Thus, when the phenomenologist says, *there are [es gibt]* immanent experiences, there are psychical states such as perceptions, memories, and the like, his 'there is' means precisely what is meant by the mathematical 'there is,' e.g., 'there is' a series of numbers. . . . In both cases, the 'there is' is founded not by experience but rather by eidetic vision," which comprehends "not particulars of existence but rather essences of the lowest order of universality or [essences] as species and genera of a higher order of universality" (*Id* III, 47).[29]

In consequence of the "Heracleitean flux," pure phenomenology can concern itself only with a conceptual and terminological determination of the essences of a higher degree of specificity (perception as such, remembering as such, empathy as such, volition as such, etc.) and the universalities of the highest order, "immanent experience as such, the *cogitatio* as such" (*Id* I, § 75; *Id* III, 41). On the other hand, this or that flowing *concretum* or, as Husserl also says, the "singular idea" or "eidetic singularity," as the "lowest universality," belongs "to the sphere of the 'unlimited,' the ἄπειρον, the scientifically indeterminable, no less than do the individual *cogitationes* themselves" (cf. *Ms. F I 17*, 46a [1909]). As Husserl still maintains as late as the *Crisis*, the following holds true with respect to the particular case of this or that immanent experience which must serve as a basis for the phenomenological eidetic analysis:

> The fact is here *as* the fact of its essence and is determinable only *through* its essence; there is no analogous way of empirically documenting it through inductive experience such as in the case of objectivity. [*CES*, 182 / C, 178]

The question of the eidetic attitude or ideation runs as follows:

> *What is* "perception" as such, what is "judgement," what is "remembering"? We could also ask: What do we mean by . . . ? Or: What do "perception," etc., mean? [*Ms. F I 17*, 45a (1909)]

As Husserl says elsewhere, the question is aimed at determining "what lies in such perceptions [etc.] so that *without this* they cannot be thought?" (*Ms. F I 4*, 9b [1912]); or, we strive for the insight that these moments and those are constitutive for this or that form of consciousness (perception, remembering, etc.), the insight that one may *omit none* of these moments and need add no further moment to the determination. In a word, eidetic determination of immanent experiences concerns that which "belongs to 'perception as such,' [that which] belongs, as it were, to the *eternally same sense of possible perception as such*" (*Id* III, 40) and, *mutatis mutandis*, to every possible kind of consciousness as such.

Directed in such manner toward the *pure possibilities of consciousness*, the eidetic phenomenologist, in respect of his positing the being of the universal, the *eidos*, in no way depends upon positing the being of the exemplary, "arbitrary," and particular case. The particular case, for example this or that passing perception or phantasy, merely forms the "basis of abstraction" (*Ms. F I 17*, 426) for determining the universal essence of perception as such, phantasy as such, possible consciousness of this or that kind as such, for which the mode of being of the particular case is a matter of "indifference" (*Ms. F I 4*, 10b).[30]

If "only the universal essence itself, the idea, as it were," is set forth by way of ideation, then we have "a unity which is not in flux, which merely particularizes itself in what does flow, but in so doing is not itself drawn into the flow. Ideas or essences are '*transtemporal*' objectivities. Essences of phenomenological data are free from individuation [*Individuation*] by way of phenomenological temporality, free from the individualization [*Individualisierung*] in the transformation of the now and of what has been, which belongs to the phenomenologically individual as such" (*Ms. F I 17*, 45a). Thus, even for the domain of the fleeting, temporally bound, pure, immanent experiences, eidetic analysis permits "the task involved in a comprehensive scientific description to be meaningfully posed" (*Id* I, 140 / G, 210).

As the eidetic science of consciousness, pure phenomenology also forms in Husserl's eyes the *rational* discipline corresponding with *empirical* psychology as a factual science of consciousness; for it makes possible a clarification of the fact studied in psychology, the fact of psychical life itself, whether individual or communal. It makes this clarification possible on the basis of the eidetic grounds of possible consciousness as such and therein makes possible an *application* of the rationality of the necessary, *a priori* laws of consciousness to factual events.

In closing, it must be emphasized that, in spite of the exemplary character of *pure mathematics* for the eidetic attitude, Husserl always contrasted the *descriptive* eidetics of phenomenologically reduced consciousness with the type of *exactness* possible in mathematics owing to "ideal concepts" (*Id* I, §§ 71–75; *Id* III, 44, and esp. § 11). The possibility of the "exactness of conceptual formation" lies neither in our free will nor in logical technique. Rather, it presupposes "exactness in the comprehended essences themselves" (*Id* I, § 73), or, as Husserl also says, in the "regional *a priori*." If the idea "space" belongs to this *a priori*, then a mathematical eidetics is appropriate (cf. *Id* III, 44); for in Husserl's view *space* must be understood as a "definite multiplicity," that is, as "definable in a mathematically exhaustive manner" (cf. *Id* I, § 72). Over against this, in accordance with its own essence the *flow of consciousness* possesses *neither* a *spatial structure* nor an ordinal system of coexistence analogous to space. Therefore it does not form a mathematical field (*Id* III, 44). Even a mathematization in the sense of a purely formal, axiomatic, deductive theory, which would itself not necessarily have to be bound to the idea "space," would, applied to the multiple intentionalities of consciousness and to the intentional implications of consciousness within consciousness (cf. below, chap. 5), yield no genuine insight into that which distinguishes consciousness in and of itself [*an ihm selbst*], that is, in its proper essentiality, as intentional. "As a descriptive, eidetic science, transcendental phenomenology belongs . . . to a totally different basic class of eidetic sciences than do the mathematical sciences" (*Id* I, § 75), which are distinguished by a constructive character that also makes possible purely *deductive* derivations of conclusions (cf., e.g., *AV*, 15f.; *Id* I, § 72; *Id* III, 44, 132).

In looking back on the two methodological sections, we may recall in closing what Husserl says in the *Cartesian Meditations*.

> Thus we raise ourselves to the methodological insight that, in addition to the phenomenological reduction, eidetic intuition is the basic form of all special transcendental methods and that both [of these methods] thoroughly determine the legitimate sense of a transcendental phenomenology. [*CM*, 106]

3

The Universal Structures
of Consciousness in
the Phenomenological Sense

We have seen that the true object of phenomenological science is the activity of consciousness explored in pure phenomenological reflection with an eye to the essential structure of that activity. Our further considerations will show both how this universal class, the activity of consciousness, is differentiated into various kinds of conscious acts (perception, phantasy, memory, apperception of the other) and how various modes (actuality and potentiality, spontaneity and receptivity) can be distinguished in the performance of these acts of consciousness. All of these various kinds of consciousness, as well as their constitutive performances, nevertheless agree in this respect, that on the one hand they are *intentional*, while on the other hand they occur in the *stream of immanent temporality*.

§ 1. Intentionality

It seems a trivial fact to many thinkers that conscious, immanent experiences possess the property of being related intentionally to corresponding objects. For such thinkers, Husserl's careful analysis of the intentionality of consciousness and the continual modifications that this doctrine undergoes in the course of the development of his work would thus amount to a proof that the entire Husserlian phenomenology is a thoroughly trivial philosophy. Other thinkers, those with a greater affinity to Husserl's work, are of the contrary opinion that intentional analysis is in fact the most essential merit of the Husserlian phenomenology, although the latter's description of intentional consciousness urgently requires further development and radicalization. It would be necessary, for example, to overcome the separation of subject and object that still sets the direction for the Husserlian concept of intentionality. At the same time, a deepened understanding of the intentional phenomenon would be the most appropriate means for slipping under the guard of Husserl's rationalistic attachment of phenomenology to the tasks of epistemology. In any case, this debate, which we cannot here enter into more fully, is a clear proof that not only for Husserl but for the entire phenomenological movement "intentionality . . . [is] not a password but the title for a central *problem*" (Heidegger, *PITC*, xxv / C, 15).

In the following account, however, we must neglect not only the further development of Husserl's concept of intentionality but also its prehistory, as it were (concerning which, see Hedwig), and its contemporary development. It is well known, of course, that Brentano and his scholastic training exercised an important influence on the development of Husserl's concept of intentionality. Furthermore, the reader of the fifth of the *Logical Investigations* knows that Husserl developed his concept of the intentional or "objectifying act" in the course of attempting to come to terms and take issue with Brentano's concept of "psychical phenomena." Nevertheless, in seeking to determine Brentano's own position, one can by no means rely exclusively on Husserl's presentation of that position. A serious exposition of the relationship between Brentano's and Husserl's doctrines of intentionality would rather have to enter into the issue of the extent to which Husserl's critique correctly rendered Brentano's standpoint, particularly in the case of the "mental inexistence" of the intentional object, as well as the extent to which this critique then moved Brentano to an elucidation or alteration of his doctrine. Thereafter, a central task would still remain, that of pointing to the diverse philosophical background of Husserl's and Brentano's occupation with intentionality. Brentano's interest lies clearly in the theory of science. His interest is classificatory and is articulated within the framework of a realistic metaphysics. Husserl, by contrast, is concerned with a metaphysically neutral, functional determination of every activity of consciousness, be it an act of true cognition or a mere presumption, be it directed toward conscious being or toward spatially transcendent being, whether it posits the being of the intentional object or neutralizes this positing, and so on. Finally, yet a third participant, namely Meinong, must be admitted to this fundamental debate. Here, too, we must remain content merely to point to the fact that the relation among Brentano's, Meinong's, and Husserl's occupations with intentionality remains "even today . . . the title for a central problem" and that familiarity with Husserl's concept of intentionality does not permit one to dispense with a study of the writings of his presumed predecessors (cf. Mohanty).

The most important condition for the possibility of a presuppositionless, phenomenological science of consciousness, is the restriction of this science to evident data. For the early Husserl, only *adequate* data count as *evident*, self-given data. In the *Logical Investigations* he defines this realm of adequate data as the field of the really immanent contents of consciousness given in phenomenologically pure reflection. The really [*reel*] immanent contents of consciousness, in opposition to the real [*real*] and ideal objects, are the moments of consciousness lying in the temporal stream of phenomenological consciousness itself and constantly appearing anew and flowing away there. It is these fluent moments that phenomenological science in its eidetic attitude describes in terms of their eidetic structures. Really immanent contents of consciousness do not necessarily have the form of intentional acts, yet even the nonintentional, really immanent data of sensation stand in possible connection with intentional acts or apperceptive apprehensions. In *Ideas I* the domain of phenomenologically evident data is expanded beyond the sphere of real immanence. Not only intentional acts but also their intentional correlates, that is, the objects as they are intended in these acts, are adequately self-given to phenomenologically pure reflection. If we call all pure data of phenomenological reflection "immanent," then we have accordingly to distinguish between "really immanent" contents, such as the intentional acts, and "intentionally immanent" contents, such as the intentional correlates. (By contrast, if, as Husserl occasionally does, we confine the application of the concept of immanence to really immanent data, then the intentional correlates must be called "transcendent" and at once distinguished from the transcendence of natural reality.) Employing the terminology of *Ideas I* (§ 88), we have to differentiate between noetic and noematic phenomenological data. Naturally, the inclusion of noematic data within the field of phenomenology has its consequences for the doctrine of intentionality. Husserl even speaks on occasion of "noematic intentionality" (§§ 101, 104). Nevertheless, it is sensible first to present the expressly noetic formulation of the inten-

[handwritten marginal note: this occurs even earlier, i.e. in Idea of Phen.]

tional function of consciousness, for even after the introduction of the noema this formulation retains its full validity. It owes this enduring validity to the fact not only that noesis and noema are parallel structures but also that in *Ideas I* the mode of givenness and the essential determination of the noematic correlate are clearly derived from the determination of the noesis, that is, from the determination of the intentional experience (§ 98).

The Intentional Act (Noesis)

Intentional acts are distinguished not only in being related to or aiming at objects (*LI* II/1 [V], §§ 10, 13) but also insofar as this intentional direction undergoes differentiations (§ 14). Brentano had already distinguished between various kinds of intentional relation or various "psychical phenomena." Husserl distinguishes himself from Brentano (as well as from Natorp) by grounding this differentiation of the intentional relation exclusively in the eidetic structure of the intentional act rather than in the various kinds of intentional object. As such, everything that a noetic phenomenology can say about the intentional object derives immediately from the description of the intentional act.

> The object is an intentional object, that is, there is an act with a determinately characterized intention, an intention that in this determinateness makes up precisely what we call the intention toward this object. [§ 20]

> There are . . . not two things present in immanent experience; the object is not immanently experienced and then next to it the intentional, immanent experience itself; . . . rather, only one thing is present, the intentional, immanent experience, of which the essential descriptive characteristic is precisely the relevant intention. [§ 11a]

This characteristic, that of "presenting . . . an objectivity," is common to all intentional experiences regardless of their diversity in other respects. The various kinds of intentional experience all belong to the same class of "objectifying acts" (§ 41).

This moment, common to all objectifying acts and having the function of presenting an intentional objectivity, Husserl calls the "material" [*Materie*] of the act.

> The material counted for us as the moment of the objectifying
> act that brings it about that the act will present just *this* object
> and in just *this way*, that is, in just these articulations and
> forms, with particular reference to these determinations or re-
> lations. [*LI* II/2 [VI], § 25]

Every word of this definition is important and pregnantly comprises a
whole series of considerations from the fifth of the *Logical Investigations*.
The most important determination of the material is doubtlessly that it
refers the act to "just this object" and in a way that implies *at the same
time* the "determinations" of this object. Thus, the material determines
which object the act will refer to (*denoting*) and, within this "objective
relation," it determines *at the same time* the characteristics of this object
(*connoting*): "The material firmly determines not only the object as such
which is meant by the act, but also the way in which it is determined" (*LI*
II/1 [V], § 20). According to the above quotation from the sixth of the
Logical Investigations, this "way" comprises not only the characteristics
attributed to the object but also the "articulations and forms" in which
these characteristics are thus attributed. The simplest, because most immediate way of relating to a determinate object is by means of names
(§§ 33f.). In naming, the intentional act is related directly to the object,
pointing to it "as if with the finger," meaning or intending the object in
one ray of "meaning or intention [*Meinung*]." The material of such a
"single-membered (simple) act" (§ 33) is a "single-membered material"
(§ 42). Such "single-rayed" acts of naming are to be distinguished from
the multi-rayed acts, that is, the "propositional" or "synthetic" acts
(§§ 33, 36, 38). Here Husserl names only predicative judging as an example of a propositional act. He might have referred as well to other
intentional acts such as collecting, relating, and so on, that is, to all those
acts that he designates in the sixth of the *Logical Investigations* as categorial acts. Without wishing to anticipate our later discussions, we must
nevertheless emphasize that these categorial acts are founded acts and,
indeed, are ultimately founded in single-rayed acts. The articulated material of a "synthetic, multi-rayed, uniform act" (§ 42) presupposes acts
of single-rayed intention or "single-membered materials" in which the
members of the synthetic intention are simply intended. Thus, according
to Husserl's conception, the predicative proposition, for example, "The
pencil is red," is founded in the simple presentation of the pencil.

   Our leading text from the sixth of the *Logical Investigations* also
designated the material as a moment of the objectifying act. According
to the terminology introduced in the third of the *Logical Investigations*,

"moment" means a "dependent part." We must therefore also ask to what independent whole the material contributes and in conjunction with what other dependent moments. The answer runs as follows: "In the descriptive content of every act we have *quality* and material as two moments mutually requiring one another." We designate "the unity" of these two "thoroughly essential and thus indispensable components of an act . . . as the *intentional essence* of the act" (§ 21). Quality and material, just like their unity, the intentional essence, are really inherent moments of the intentional act which, though they do "not make up the complete, concrete act," nevertheless constitute the essential conditions for its intentional function. In describing the act, Husserl's interest lies not in its full psychological concretion but merely in those structural moments of every intentional act which are the bearers of the intentional relation of the subject to an object.

The *quality* designates the mode in which a certain, thus and so determined intentional object, is intended (§§ 20, 26, 30). Diverse intentional acts with the same material are distinguished insofar as "the same content . . . can be the content of a question, a doubt, a wish, and the like" (§ 20). The quality is thus related to a variety of diverse, subjective attitudes in the performance of the intentional or objectifying acts. However, the structural unity that binds together these various modes of questioning, doubting, and so on, is not yet brought into clear relief in the *Logical Investigations*. It is *Ideas I* (§§ 103ff.) that first provides a clear answer to this question and defines doubting, wishing, questioning, and so on, as modalizations of the manner in which an intentional object can be intended by being *posited*. The primordial form of positing is the positing of being or the belief in being ("primordial belief [*Urdoxa*]"). Questioning, doubting, and so on, are modalizations of this doxic belief in which the determinate intentional object is consciously intended as being-questionable, being-doubtful, and so on. Nevertheless, positional-intentional consciousness need not take the form of an actually performed positing. The positing can also be a merely potential one (§ 113). The quality thus designates the positional character that belongs to all intentional acts whereby this positing, which can be actually or only potentially performed, can assume the form not only of primordial belief but also of questioning and the like. The characterization of the quality of the act as a cognitive positing (which needs to be rationally justified), and the characterization of the noematic correlate of this quality as a characteristic of being, set the direction for the terminological designation of the intentional act as noesis (§§ 85f.). However, the modalization of the positional quality of the intentional act is not the only way that acts of like material can nevertheless be contrasted with one another. A perception and a memory may be related in the same doxic attitude to the same intentional object, with an identical determination and an identical articulation. What distinguishes these acts from one another is the way they intuitively "present" their intentional object. Although the intuitive fullness of an act stands in very close connection with doxic positing or cognitive pretension, it is better not to designate it as a modification of the quality of the act. The *Logical Investigations* define the quality of the act as a moment that is essentially common to all intentional acts (and not to intuitional acts alone). *Ideas I*, too, distinguishes between noematic "characteristics of being" (*Id* I, § 103) and (possibly intuitive) "manners of givenness" (§ 99).

Just as Husserl distinguished between single-membered and founded materials of the act, so he now differentiates as well between intentional, immanent experiences, accordingly as they exhibit either a simple or a founded quality of act. Acts of simple quality include all objectifying acts (*LI* II/I [V], §§ 37f., 41), not only those performed in the primordial mode of belief in actual being but also the acts that posit an intentional object in the mode of doubting, questioning, and so on. An intentional act of founded quality is not, in the strictest sense, an objectifying act. Rather, it has "an objectifying act . . . in its 'foundation,' that is, it has . . . within itself an objectifying act as a necessary component, the entire material of which is at the same time and, indeed, individually identical with the entirety of its own material" (§ 41). These qualitatively complex acts are of concern within the spheres of emotion, volition, and valuation. An experience of joy, for example, is not a straightforward objectifying act, but a (merely) subjective attitude which, however, presupposes the intentional relation to the object that has been experienced as joyous (cf. also *Id* I, § 116). Naturally enough, this founding, objectifying act can be an act with a single-membered material (joy at an object presented in a single ray) as well as an act with an articulated material (joy at an object presented synthetically and formed categorially, for example, the clattering mill by the brook . . .).

Husserl called quality and material "mutually requisite moments" of the intentional act. It is easy to see in what respect quality needs to be supplemented by material.

> The quality determines only whether what has already been "presented" [*das vorstellig Gemachte*] . . . in a determinate way is intentionally present [*gegenwärtig*] . . . as desirable, questionable, . . . and the like. [*LI* II/I (V), § 20]

Husserl establishes the necessity for the correlative supplementation of the material by the quality in the form of taking lengthy issue with Brentano's concept of mere presentations [*Vorstellungen*] (chaps. 3, 4, 5). Brentano had ascribed the dependent functions of the material presenting an object, on the one hand, and of the quality, that is, the doxic attitude, on the other hand, to two diverse and independent forms of consciousness, namely, the mere presentations and the acts of doxic positing. The core of Husserl's critique consists in demonstrating that all those phenomena adduced by Brentano for the support of his concept of the mere, nonpositional presentation (for example, understanding while not concurring with a judgement), could be taken in a phenomenally more plausible and logically more consistent fashion as modifications of the class of doxic, or positing, objectifying acts. There is no doxically unqualified relation to an intentional object, no isolated occurrence of the material: "One would regard as unthinkable a material that were neither the material of a presenting [*Vorstellen*] nor that of a judging and the like" (§ 20). In virtue of the necessary, mutual supplementation of material and quality, and in view of the series of modifications characterizing both of them, we also have the following classification: (1) objectifying acts with single-membered material (nominal presentations) or (2) with articulated material (multi-rayed, synthetic acts, for example, predicative judging); if we pass over to intentional experiences with a founded quality we obtain the following: (3) emotional acts with single-membered material and (4) with articulated material. Every intentional act can be aligned with one of these four classes, yet consideration for the intuitive fullness of the acts in question allows further differentiations within each of these classes (acts of perception and phantasy, for example, both belong in class [1]).

The Intentional Correlate (Noema)

Ideas I takes over from the *Logical Investigations* the basic content of their determination of the essence of the intentional act. In addition to the new doctrine of the doxic character of emotional and volitional acts and the more precise analysis of the phenomenon of intentional implication, one essentially new contribution of *Ideas I* to the noetic analysis of intention consists in its transferring the function of intentional belief to inactual [*inaktuell*] or potential consciousness (cf. *Id* I, §§ 35, 113). Not every intentional, immanent experience is the experience of a " 'wakeful' ego," a " 'cogito' " in the "pregnant sense," one that is "actually" directed toward an intentional object which is meant "explicitly." Just as a thing is arranged with respect to the order of certain objective surroundings, so, too, every actual immanent experience is "surrounded by a 'fringe' of inactual [immanent experiences]." Each of these inactual immanent experiences is "also . . . a 'conscious experience' or, more briefly, a 'consciousness' . . . 'of.' " Furthermore, every "implicit" intentional consciousness is able to be explicated; every "potential" immanent experience is potentially *actual*, a motivated possibility of an intentional act performed in the mode of the cogito (§ 35). We shall see later what a decisive role these potential immanent experiences play within the structure of both the consciousness of temporal objects and the perception of the thing.

However, the most important contribution made by *Ideas I* to the further development of the phenomenological analysis of intentionality doubtlessly concerns the determination of the intentional correlate, the forms of noematic givenness and function. The relevant discussions from *Ideas I* rest upon the voluminous investigations from 1906 to 1912 preserved in the literary remains in the form of lectures and research manuscripts. As is to be expected from a text "written down as if in a trance, in six weeks, with no drafts as a basis" (cf. *Id* I, xxxix), and, moreover, intended as a "general introduction to pure phenomenology," the discussions of *Ideas I* frequently remain quite far behind the point of advance reached by the manuscripts in the development of the pertinent problem. Most of the numerous controversies occasioned by the interpretation of *Ideas I*, in particular the interpretation of the concept of the noema, can be properly decided only on the basis of a study of these extremely carefully elaborated texts from the literary remains. If in the following account we nevertheless orient ourselves primarily with respect to the wording of *Ideas I*, our reason for doing so lies not merely in the restricted scope of our presentation but rather because the bulk of the pertinent texts from the literary remains is still unpublished.

The noema owes its earliest consideration within the compass of phenomenological data to the reflection that, on the one hand, the givenness of the intention relating to the object and, on the other hand, the givenness of the object, just as it "lies" there in this intention, are not merely correlative but also equally evident.

> [The phenomenologist] looks both to the phenomena and to
> the objectivities that appear in the phenomena or are intended
> in them by thought. . . . On the basis of phenomenological evi-
> dence we can . . . describe an object and the way it is deter-

mined when it is presented in the mode of . . . [phantasy, as an example of an intentional act]; we can describe . . . what belongs to the essence of consciousness insofar as consciousness is consciousness of a certain objectivity [*Objektivität*]; . . . and [we can describe what belongs] to the correlative objectivity to the extent that and in the manner that it is intended in this thus constituted consciousness. . . . We are thus continuously occupied with the objective [*das Gegenständliche*] and yet we do not accord it the status of an existent. [*LE*, 230f.]

The most important motive for considering the intentional correlates as belonging to the realm of phenomenological data is clearly to be found in an epistemological interest. The concern here is to make possible the study of the cognitive relation within the compass of purely phenomenological data.

Thus, this wondrous correlation between the phenomenon of cognition and the object of cognition shows itself everywhere. . . . The task now, however, is . . . to pursue all correlations . . . within the bounds of pure evidence or self-givenness. . . . The phenomenology of cognition is a science of the phenomena of cognition in a double sense; [it is a science] of cognitions as . . . acts of consciousness in which this or that objectivity [*Gegenständlichkeit*] presents itself . . . and, on the other hand, [it is a science] of these objectivities themselves as thus presenting themselves. [*IP*, 12ff. (1907)]

The intentional correlate or noema is thus introduced as a structure of being objectively-intended or as an object of cognition "to the extent that and in the manner that" it may be laid claim to within the phenomenological reduction.

If we now perform the phenomenological reduction, every transcendent positing, especially the positing that lies within perception itself, receives its own suspending parenthesis. . . . Hence we ask in general, maintaining these suspensions in their clear sense, what is it that "lies" evidentially in the whole "reduced" phenomenon. Now then, this, too, lies within perception, that it . . . has its "percept as such," "this blossoming tree there in space—with the quotation marks understood— precisely the correlate that belongs to the essence of the phenomenologically reduced perception. [*Id* I, § 90]

And this " 'percept as such' " is nothing other than the "perceptual noema" (§ 88).

No less than the noesis, this noematic correlate is given adequately (§§ 88, 90, 98, 144, 149). However, the noema is distinguished from the naturally real object not only in virtue of the absolute evidence of its givenness but also in virtue of the reflective character of that givenness. "The primary orientation is toward what is objective; the noematic reflection leads to the noematic and the noetic [reflection leads] to the noetic components" (§ 148). It remains unclear, however, by exactly what means this "peculiar" noematic reflection (§ 89) is distinguished from the noetic reflection. This unclarity concerns at once the whole relation between noesis and noema. On the one hand, the "correlate of consciousness [is] inseparable from consciousness" (§ 128), a "dependent object" (§ 98), while on the other hand, the following holds true: "In spite of this dependence, the noema is able to be regarded for itself" (§ 98). This unclear determination of both the peculiarity of the noematic reflection and the independence of the noematic givenness finally leads us to the insight that, as regards the noema as such, its status in regard to consciousness remains unclear. In this respect, the only thing that is clear from *Ideas I* is the consistent ascertainment that the noema cannot be a datum really immanent in consciousness (§§ 88, 90, 97f., 128). However, when Husserl later became more explicitly interested in the temporal individuation of the momentary correlate of a particular phase of the act, this point, too, began to waver.

> Every memory intends something and what it intends has, as such, the same position in time as the memory. . . . Thus, it again becomes clear that there are no grounds for removing the "noema" from the immanent experience and denying it the character of a really immanent moment. [*APS*, 335]

To be sure, however, in saying this one is not simply and generally placing in question the distinction between noema and noesis. The question of the really immanent inclusion of the noema within the performance of consciousness concerns only a rather particular and narrow concept of the noema, namely, the noema regarded as the individual, point-by-point correlate of a momentary act-phase of consciousness. Moreover, Husserl is working in the above quotation with the somewhat problematical presupposition of a "simultaneity" (in the sense of the same position in the same stream of time) of act-phase and individual, noematic correlate. In any case, there are no grounds for designating noematic unities, such as the ideal-

identical noematic sense or an "objectivity" (in quotation marks) constituted in consciousness, as really immanent data and inserting them into the
stream of consciousness as moments of that stream. A critical reflection
upon the status of the noema with regard to consciousness would thus have
to concern itself primarily with differentiating the various forms of possible
noematic givenness more clearly than did Husserl in *Ideas I*.

In any case, it is clear that the noema, as phenomenologically
pure and reflective givenness, stands in very close connection with the
noetic performance of intentional acts. As an "object" given, just as it is
intended, the noematic correlate exhibits a structure that is parallel with
that of the corresponding intentional act. Just as diverse acts of questioning, doubting, and so forth, can possess an identical intentional material, so also it is possible to isolate in the manifold, noetic correlates of
these acts, a "noematic nucleus" provided with diverse characteristics of
being [*Seinscharaktere*] (§§ 99 102, 129, 133). With the primordial, doxic
mode of belief that uniformly structures the quality of the act, there corresponds the characterization of the noematic nucleus as being actual
(§ 104). As the correlate of an intentional act of questioning, the intended object accordingly is given precisely as being questionable. This
parallel structuring concerns not only the material of the act and the
noematic nucleus, as well as the quality of the act and the noematic characteristics of being; it also concerns the respective stages of founding to
which these components belong. With the formation of stages on the
side of the act there corresponds a noematic formation of stages. Husserl speaks of "noematic intentionality" in respect to the manner in
which noemata of various stages refer to one another (§ 101). In the end,
the material of the act and the noematic nucleus correspond with one
another not merely in respect to their stages of founding but also in respect to their intentional function. Even as the material of the act
designates a certain object and determines this object by means of character traits, so, too, the intentional object is, *qua* intended, a certain object with various characteristic traits. And just as diverse acts can be
related to the same object, albeit under diverse determinations, so it is
possible for diverse noemata or, more precisely, diverse noematic nuclei
(="whats") to have a common object (="X") in spite of their diversity.

> Here several act-noemata have everywhere diverse nuclei, in
> such a way, however, that in spite of this they merge into a
> unity of identity, a unity in which the "something," the deter-
> minable component that lies in every nucleus, comes to con-
> sciousness as identical. [§ 131].

If, in a sense reaching beyond the sphere of the judgement, one calls the determinations of the determinable "something" "predicates" (§ 130), then this identical "something" is a "central noematic moment . . . : the 'object' [*Gegenstand*], the 'object' [*Objekt*], the 'identical,' the 'determinable subject of its possible predicates'—the pure X in abstraction from all predicates" (§ 131). If one calls the noematic nucleus "sense" (§§ 99, 129, 132), and calls the X qualified as the "subject of the sense" (§ 145) an "object," then the description of the connection between the noematic nucleus and the X also affords an answer to "the phenomenological problem concerning the relation of consciousness to its object" (§ 128). Examined more closely, this answer proves to have a twofold meaning. On the one hand, the following holds generally true: "Every noema has its 'content,' namely, its 'sense' and is related by way of this to 'its' object" (§ 129; cf. also §§ 128, 135). On the other hand, we understand not only that "every" noema is related to an object but also how it must be related to this object in order that the actuality of the "object" be epistemologically demonstrated. The investigation of the "actual object" is the "title for certain eidetically regarded rational connections in which the X that they have in common in virtue of their sense receives its positing in accordance with reason" (§ 145; cf. also §135). This positing in accordance with reason is justified in the uniform coherence of intuitively fulfilled senses or noemata (cf. §§ 142, 144f.).

In the context of both the analysis of the judgement and the perceptual constitution of the thing, we shall enter still more closely into this theory concerning the relation of the noematic correlate to "its" object. What strikes one above all else in the discussions of *Ideas I* is the equivocal use of the term "noematic sense." The following are designated as "sense": (1) the phenomenologically reduced object (the object within quotation marks) or the intended as such (§§ 80, 90)—where one would have to distinguish still more precisely between the multiple noematic correlate of an individual, momentary act, and the (unitary) noematic correlate of a continuously uniform synthesis of manifold, constitutive acts of consciousness; (2) a merely abstract moment of the full noema (=1), namely, the noematic nucleus (§§ 99, 129, 132); and (3) "the identical noematic 'what,' " that is, the noematic signification of the judgement (§ 94). This equivocation in the noematic concept of sense is also the reason that *one* interpreter of *Ideas I* designates the noema as an ideal-identical content of intention [*Vermeintheit*] and *another* designates it as an individual, phenomenal datum; that for *one* interpreter all talk of an objective relation of the noema "through" or "by means of" the sense is taken as metaphorical or simply inappropriate, while *another* takes it as a valuable supplement to a Fregean semantics. In spite of the uncertainty about what may constitute the proper meaning of Husserl's concept of the noema, this concept has become for contemporary philosophy a privileged starting point in the attempt to come to terms with Husserlian phenomenology.

§ 2.   Time-Consciousness

According to Husserl, the most fundamental consciousness, presupposed in all other forms and structures of consciousness, is the consciousness of time.

> In the *ABC*'s of the constitution of all such objectivity as enters
> consciousness, and of subjectivity for itself as being, the *A* is to
> be found here. It consists, as we are able to say, in a formal,
> universal framework, in a synthetically constituted form in
> which all other possible syntheses must participate. [*APS*, 125]

To be sure, Husserl did not always begin with this *A* in his portrayal of the structures of consciousness. Rather, in the first volume of his *Ideas*, he suspended consideration of this "sphere of problems of exceeding difficulty" (*Id* I, 162f. / G, 236; *Id* II, 102f.; *FTL*, 252f.)

Husserl's problematic of time-consciousness follows two main directions. On the one hand, it follows an *objective* direction, objective in the sense that it begins from the question regarding the possibility of comprehending a temporal object [*Zeitobjekt*] (that is, a duration, such as the duration of a tone or of a temporal lapse, for example, a melody); on the other hand, it follows a subjective direction whose theme is consciousness both as a temporalizing [*zeitigend*] "absolute subjectivity" constituting all temporal appearance and, in its self-appearance or self-temporalization, as a constituted flow of consciousness. The order of problems indicated by this twofold problematic will guide us in the following exposition.

In his first line of questioning, with the question as to how a temporal object can be constituted within consciousness, Husserl starts from Franz Brentano's theory of time. Brentano had established his theory of time upon the ascertainment that, in the comprehension of a temporal process, what has once been perceived will for a while immediately thereafter remain present to us in consciousness. At the same time, however, it will appear as something more or less past, as something that has been pushed back in time, as it were. When we hear a melody, it is not the case that with the sounding of a fresh tone the preceding, now faded tone has fully disappeared. Otherwise the comprehension of a melody would not be possible. Still, the faded tone does not simply linger as a tone-sensation but rather is modified by its temporal determinateness. Otherwise we would have no melody, that is, no sequence of tones, but only a chord or even a mere muddle of tones. Brentano explains this phenomenon in the following manner: There is a psychological law according to which a continuous series of presentations [*Vorstellungen*] is adjoined to a single presentation, each member of the series *reproducing* the content of its predecessor and attaching to it a *temporal moment of the past*. This is a primordial association, an achievement [*Leistung*] productive in creating a new moment, namely, the modifying and constantly different temporal moment. According to Brentano, time, succession and alteration, is not *perceived*. It is comprehended only by means of reproductive and productive phantasy. Supported upon the presentation of the past, phantasy, according to Brentano, also forms the presentation of the future as a kind of transference or transposition of the past (cf. Husserl's exposition of Brentano's theory, in *PITC*, 10 ff. / C, 29ff.).

Over against this theory of Brentano's, Husserl raises two main critical questions. (1) Does that which has just passed [*das unmittelbar Vergangene*], let us say in hearing a melody, really appear in the manner of an object of *phantasy*; is there not an essential distinction between the *phantasizing* of a temporal object and the consciousness of what has just passed in the course of our perceiving a present [*gegenwärtig*] temporal object? (2) Is the mere attachment of a new moment, namely, the "temporal moment of the past," to something that is reproduced and present [*ein reproduziertes Gegenwärtiges*], able to explain the "transcending consciousness" of the past? Husserl's own thoughts on time-constitution seek to take account of these critical questions.

Husserl begins with an analysis of the comprehension of a present flow [*Ablauf*] of time. His basic example is the hearing of a sequence of tones, for instance, the hearing of a melody. Here he distinguishes three moments which of necessity belong together. (1) First of all, there is the *"primordial impression [Urimpression]"* (67, 100 / C, 92, 130f.) or "primordial sensation" (77ff., 325f., 372 / C, 102ff.). To this corresponds the now-moment of the temporal object, let us say the immediately sounding tone. In a "momentary simultaneity [*Momentanzugleich*]" it is possible for several primordial sensations to be found together with one another (376). (2) "At the same time" as the primordial impression, there exists a "continuity" of "fresh" or "primary memories" (a "trail of memory, a comet's tail of 'memory' " [377f.]). It is this, a "further-consciousness that holds back [*zurückhaltendes Noch-Bewusstsein*]" (81 / C, 106f.), to which there corresponds in the temporal object the "a while ago," the "just past," or the "no longer"; in the example of the melody, the tones or tone-phases which have just sounded and faded away. From 1909 on, Husserl increasingly preferred the expression "retention" to the expression "fresh or primary memory" (335ff.)[1] Each retention in this continuity of retentions has a definite mode in which a definite, earlier point of time, a "just now" lying more or less in the past, is adumbrated.[2] The farther into the past the points of time belong, the more dimly they are retained. "The whole disappears into darkness, into an empty retentional consciousness" (26, 621 / C, 46f., 85f.). Husserl also speaks of a kind of "temporal perspective" in which the object increasingly "contracts" and becomes dim in proportion with its ever greater remove in time (26 / C, 47). (3) The third moment is expectation or *protention*. It intends the immediately approaching, the not-yet. According to Husserl, it is a prefigurement or anticipation of what is to come on the basis of retentional consciousness (*APS*, 186); a "projected shadow" or a projection of the past, as an expectation, into the future (287, 186).

These three moments—primordial impression, retention, and protention—constitute for Husserl the concrete living present, that is, the "originary temporal field [*originäres Zeitfeld*]" (*PITC*, 31 / C, 52). This field consists in a now with a "temporal fringe," that is, with a living horizon of the no-longer (the just past) and the not-yet (the now approaching) in various gradations.

Yet according to Husserl these three moments, themselves forming a continuity, serve to describe only a momentary phase in the perception of a temporal object. In every phase this perception has its originary temporal field in all three moments, in the primordial impression, the retention, and the protention. But this phase is constantly passing over into a new phase. The perception is under constant change; it is in constant flux (75 / C, 100). A new now is continuously pushing the earlier now back into the past (43, 63 / C, 65f., 86f.). The primordial impression is being continuously transformed into retention, this into modified retention, and so on (*Id* I, 164 / G, 237; *PITC*, 40 / C, 62). The primordial impression is constantly new, a living source-point of being (*PITC*, 67, 69, 100 / C, 91f., 93f., 130f.). This ever new now is the essential element, the "motor," as it were, of time-constitution.

> For it would, indeed, be inherently thinkable that the clarity of immediate memory [=retention] not dwindle, while, apart from the addition of a new now, time-consciousness would be wholly unthinkable. [425]

Husserl conceives this entire change, proceeding as it does from the constantly new now, as a continuity of iterated modification. The primordial impression is modified into a retention of the primordial impression; the retention is modified into a retention of the retention; this retention of second degree is modified into a retention of third degree, and so on. The retentions of higher degree are a "continuous implication [*Ineinander*] of retentions of retentions" (*Id* I, 164 / G, 237). In this manner of modification and modification of modification, the retention bears "within itself the heritage of the entire preceding development in the form, as it were, of a series of adumbrations" (*PITC*, 327). In this view of time-consciousness, Husserl distances himself from the so-called content-apprehension-schema [*Inhalt-Auffassungs-Schema*] originally attempted by him in this same realm and according to which particular characteristics of the act would give to "nontemporal contents of apprehension" a relation to a determinate temporal position (cf. 36, 40, 62 / C, 58, 62f., 85f.). He states that the temporal gradation already affects all contents (47ff. / C, 71ff.) and that "not every constitution has the schema 'content-of-apprehension and apprehension' " (7 anm. / C, 25 fn.). Furthermore, within this change of the originary temporal field, Husserl also describes the fulfillment or disappointment of protentions by way of primordial impressions (cf. 52ff. / C, 76ff.).

In its change, the originary temporal field is "originarily self-given" (38 / C, 60f.). In this sense it is *perceived* and is not, as Brentano taught, an object of reproductive and productive phantasy. The reproduction or phantasy—for example, recollection ("secondary memory" over against "primary memory," retention)—is to a certain extent a *reiteration* of this *whole* "temporal fringe." It is a reproduction of this whole perceptual flow (36, 52 / C, 58, 76). "The whole phenomenon of memory has, *mutatis mutandis*, precisely the same constitution as does perception." For example, in the recollection of a melody it is " 'as if' we hear first of all the first and then the second tone, etc." A tone resounds, as it were, and sinks into the just-past. The reproduction is therefore a reiteration of primordial impression, retention, and protention (35, 46, 51 / C, 57f., 69f., 74f.). However, this reproduced melody is not presence [*Gegenwart*]; rather, it is "presentiated [*vergegenwärtigt*] presence" (36 / C, 58). It is not itself given "in immediate intuition [*leibhaft*]," not perceived, but "only presented [*vorgestellt*]" (41f. / C, 63f.). This presentiated time "points back necessarily to an originally given, not phantasized but presented [*präsentiert*]" time (45 / C, 68f.). That is to say, reproduced time points back to perceived time such that a perception of time must be assumed as the origin of the presentation of time [*Zeitvorstellung*].

In this context, and in opposition to Brentano, Husserl points to a radical distinction between retention ("primary memory") and recollection ("secondary memory").

> The modification of consciousness which transforms an originary now into a reproduced now is something quite different from the modification which transforms a now, whether originary or reproduced, into a past. [46f. / C, 69f.]

There exists between primordial impression and retention a "continuous mediation," a "continuous transition," a "constant adumbration"; "by contrast, there is no talk of a steady transition from perception into phantasy, from impression into reproduction; the latter distinction is a discrete one." (41, 47 / C, 63f., 70). The distinction between retention and recollection (reproduction) does not consist in the fact that recollection would simply reach further back in time. For recollection can also "recapitulate" something which is retentionally still more or less clearly beheld by consciousness, as when, let us say in hearing a melody, I recall the beginning of this melody in "reiterating" it (62, cf. 50, 153f. / C, 86, cf. 73). The distinction is much rather structural. While primordial impression passes continuously into retention and this into retention of retention, and so on, recollection turns back temporally and reiterates a *whole* perception.

The principal distinction between retention and recollection also becomes clear in the novel temporal form which recollection brings forth over against the perception of time, retention being a dependent moment of this perception. Perceived, present time is perpetually in flux (108 / C, 143f.). A new now is continuously springing up and every temporal moment sinks retentionally down into an ever more distant, ever darker past. Over against this fluid time oriented within the now, we have the idea of an *objective* time as a stable order of the earlier and the later with respect to identifiable points of time (64 / C, 88f.). While in our perception of time the temporal events, beginning from the now, sink steadily back into the past, in *objective* time they never change their position. According to Husserl, this objective time is the achievement of reproduction, primarily of recollection (69 / C, 93f.).

> To be sure, in recollection time is also given as oriented within each moment of memory, but every point presents an objective point of time which can be identified again and again, and the stretch of time is formed from purely objective points and is itself identifiable again and again.

> Identity of temporal objects is thus a constituted unity produced by certain possible coincidings in the identification of recollections. [108 / C, 143f.]

An objective temporal order, existing in itself [*an sich*] and to whose positions and positional relations I *can come back again and again by way of identification*, is brought to consciousness only by way of reproduction. Such a temporal order is the product of an idealization in reproduction. It is the correlate of the consciousness that "I can identify this and come back to it *again and again*."[3] Over against this objective time, Husserl calls the fluid, oriented time the "time of givenness."

Time, time of givenness and objective time, is constituted within consciousness. Is this constitution itself a temporal process? Is the time-constituting consciousness itself within time? With this question we enter into the subjective orientation of Husserl's problematic concerning time-consciousness. Husserl writes as follows:

> In the *natural attitude* one will say quite as a matter of course and one will deem it a matter of course to say: I now comprehend a tone which maintains itself throughout its duration. . . . In attending to the *constitutive appearances* of inner consciousness, I comprehend them as being now, I now comprehend the consciousness of the now and the entire continuity of the before-consciousness [*Vorher-Bewußtsein*] [the consciousness of the before, of the just past], and this entire continuity is *contemporaneous*, it belongs to the now, takes place now, stands there as that. And if I pursue the *flow* of these continuities, I find them taking place one after the other, and the whole fills a duration. This duration is, of course, the same as that of what appears inwardly. The duration of the immanent tone is the same as that of the consciousness in which this tone is steadily constituted in accordance with its duration. [369]

Husserl himself, however, in texts from the lecture course of 1904/05 which form the foundation of *The Phenomenology of Internal Time Consciousness* (*Hu* X), placed the time-constituting consciousness *in* time. According to his later judgement, he would therefore at this earlier date still have been caught "within the natural attitude." In these early texts he explains as follows:

> It is indeed evident that the perception of a temporal object possesses a temporality of its own, that the perception of a duration presupposes in its own right a duration of the perception, that the perception of a random temporal figure has a temporal figure of its own.[4]

At that time, he identified the time of sensation and the time of the sensed, the time of perception and the time of the perceived. They are "contemporaneous."[5]

During the years 1908/09, however, Husserl underwent a change in his position and the moment of this change of position seems still to be within reach of exact determination. We discern it in a manuscript published for the first time in *Husserliana* X as text number 50. Rudolf Boehm, the editor of this volume, dates the text in question between October 1908 and the summer semester of 1909. At the beginning of the text, Husserl still places the time-constituting consciousness in time.

> [W]hen consciousness of the tone-now [*Ton-Jetzt*], the primordial impression, passes into retentional memory, then this memory is itself another now, that is, it belongs to a new tone-now. [326]

After discussing retentional modification and the problem of comprehending the time-constituting flow, Husserl closes with the following lines:

> Is there something absurd in the temporal flow's being regarded as an *objective movement*? Yes! On the other hand, memory is nonetheless something that has *its own now* and [it has] the same now as, let us say, a tone. *No.* There lies the basic mistake. *The flow of the modes of consciousness is not a process, the now-consciousness [Jetzt-Bewußtsein]* [that is, the consciousness of the now,] *is not itself now.* The "co"-existence of retention with the now-consciousness is not "now," not contemporaneous with the now, which, on the contrary, would make no sense. . . . *Sensation*, therefore, if by this we understand *consciousness* (not the immanent, enduring red, [the immanent enduring] tone, etc.; thus, not what is sensed), *exists non-temporally*, that is, it is

> *nothing found within immanent time,* just as is the case with *reten-*
> *tion, recollection, perception,* etc. (The extent to which it is able to
> be objectified in nature, in "objective time," is a question in its
> own right.) These are highly important matters, perhaps the
> most important in the whole of phenomenology. [333f.]

The reason put forward by Husserl in this text for maintaining the
nontemporality of the time-constituting consciousness seems to be
found in his consideration of the infinite regress which would otherwise
result. Were this consciousness within time, then another consciousness
would be necessary which would constitute this consciousness as temporal, etc. (cf. 332f.). The basic thought here is that everything given (appearing) as temporal, even the immanent experiences given as temporal
(*cogitationes*), is *constituted* within consciousness. Hence, the "consciousness presupposed in all constitution" (73 / C, 98), the ultimately *constituting* consciousness, which is not a whole of temporally constituted
immanent experiences but "a consciousness with a different sense" (*Id*
II, 102), cannot itself be temporal.

In another text from *Husserliana* X (text no. 54), probably not
written before 1911[6] and already introduced into the lectures on the
"Phenomenology of Internal Time Consciousness" collated by Edith
Stein in 1917 and edited by Heidegger in 1928, Husserl explores more
closely the nontemporality of the time-constituting consciousness. Here
he cites other reasons for this nontemporality than those just mentioned
and, in fact, such reasons as serve to remind us of Kant's "Paralogisms
of Pure Reason." Husserl tells us that a temporal alteration or non-
alteration is a process in an identical object such that the object has its
duration in this process. By contrast, the time-constituting flow is not an
object, not a substrate which is altered or not altered in the course of its
duration. Husserl further remarks that the alteration of a temporal object has a velocity and can be thought of as accelerated or retarded and
as converted into rest (non-alteration). By contrast, he says that the
change, the "alteration" of the time-constituting flow, is marked by "the
absurdity that it passes just as it does pass and can run neither 'more
swiftly' nor 'more slowly' " (*PITC*, 369f., cf. 73f. / C, 98f.).

> It is thus evident that the time-constituting appearances are
> fundamentally different objectivities from the appearances con-
> stituted in time, that they are neither individual objects nor in-
> dividual processes and that the predicates of such objects or
> processes cannot be sensically ascribed to them. Thus, it like-

wise makes no sense to say of them (and to say this in the same
sense) that they are in the now and were before, that they followed after one another temporally or that they are contemporaneous with one another, etc. [370, cf. 74f. / C, 99f.]

Whereas in the previously cited text (no. 50) Husserl is thinking primarily of
perceived time, he is concerned above all in the text presently before us (no.
54) to oppose the time-constituting consciousness to *objective* time.

The nontemporal, time-constituting consciousness, which Husserl designates as the "absolute, primordially constituting consciousness" (*Ms. B IV 6*, 215f. [ca. 1908]), as the "true and ultimate absolute"
(*Id* I, 163 / C, 236), is, as will have become clear from the above discussion, not able to be regarded as a bare, timeless form, through which the
temporal would, so to speak, drift along. The consciousness of primordial sensation and the primordial time-consciousness as such are understood by Husserl as

being in constant change. . . . The change consists in the fact
that the immediately intuited [*leibhaft*] tone-now is steadily
modified (sc.: *in consciousness, in respect to consciousness*) into the
mode of having-been and that the tone-now which has passed
into the modification is steadily superseded by an ever new
tone-now. [*PITC*, 326; our emphasis, I.K.]

This is to say that consciousness changes insofar as that of which it is
conscious changes temporally. A temporal change can appear within
consciousness only by way of a change of consciousness. Yet the change
of the time-constituting consciousness is not a temporal sequence (376).
Husserl also speaks of an "at once" or a "together" of the primordial
impressions of what is presently contemporaneous (let us say, of a tone
and a color), impressions which are themselves as little contemporaneous, however, as are the retentions which preserve the phases of time
just past and which belong to this "at once."

This entire "at once," comprising a primordial presentation
[*Präsentierung*] and the continuity of preterite phases, makes
up the mobile moment in the actuality of consciousness, an actuality which constitutes the immanent object in incessant alteration. [378]

Husserl thus attempts to grasp the truly absolute consciousness in which
the whole of time makes its appearance, as an actuality which is mobile

within itself [*in sich*]. In his later manuscripts he calls it the "primally standing-streaming pre-presence [*urtümlich stehende-strömende Vorgegenwart*]" (*Ms. C 3*, 3a ff. [1930]), thus designating it at once as mobile-streaming and immobile-standing, as a source-point which at once constantly flows and yet abides at the same site. Or, he calls it a "primordial presence which is not a modality of time" (*PI* II, 667f. [1934]), that is, which does not have next to it a past and a future, since, as pure actuality, the time-constituting consciousness cannot be moved into the past.

How is it ever possible, according to Husserl, to comprehend this "true and ultimate absolute"? Husserl writes the following:

> One can and must say: A certain phenomenal continuity, that
> is, such a one as is a phase of the time-constituting flow, *belongs*
> to a now, that is, [it belongs] to the now which this continuity
> *constitutes*, and it belongs to a "before," that is to say, that con-
> tinuity which is (we may not say: "was") constitutive for the
> "before."[7] But is the flow not a one-after-the-other? Does it
> not indeed have a now, an actual phase, and a continuity of
> pasts now consciously preserved in retentions? We cannot help
> this but can say only: This flow is something that we name such
> *in accordance with that which is constituted*, but it is not some-
> thing that is temporally "objective." It is the *absolute subjectivity*
> and has the absolute properties of something to be designated
> *in an image* as a "flow," the absolute properties of a point of
> actuality, a primordial source-point "now," etc. Within the ex-
> perience of actuality we have the primordial source-point and a
> continuity of moments of resonance. We have no names for
> any of this. [*PITC*, 371]

According to this passage the time-constituting consciousness seems to be not an object of direct apprehension (intuition) but something that has been constructed, that is, constructed as the condition for the possi-bility of what is experienced temporally.

However, in the subsequent course of this text Husserl says the following: "Yet I know of this flow as flow, I can look towards it" (378). This flow thus seems to be no mere construction. It is not something merely supposed as a condition of possibility. Husserl attempts the fol-lowing solution:

> It is the one, unique flow of consciousness (possibly inside of an
> "ultimate" consciousness) within which the immanent-temporal
> unity of the tone and the unity of the flow of consciousness it-

self are constituted at one and the same time. However shocking
(if not at first downright contrary to good sense) it may appear
to be that the flow of consciousness should constitute its own
unity, it is nevertheless so and it can be made intelligible on the
basis of the essential constitution of this flow. [378]

In fact, Husserl attempts to make the self-appearance [*Selbsterscheinung*]
of the flow intelligible in the following manner: Every retention has a
"double intentionality": the retention of a past phase of the tone (for
example, the point at which the tone "c" is struck) is also the retention of
the retention, now having flowed away, of this same phase of the tone;
and in this retention itself the preceding retention of this phase of the
tone is again implied, and so the regress continues until we reach the
primordial impression of this phase of the tone (379ff., 326ff.). Thus,
the retention which I am having of the past phase of the tone is necessarily also a retention of the preceding continuity of retentions right up to
the primordial impression of this phase of the tone. Husserl calls the
intention toward the tone (toward the "object" [*Objekt*]) the "transverse
intentionality" of the retention. He calls the intention toward the retentions (toward the flow of consciousness) the "longitudinal intentionality" of the retention (379ff., 82ff./ C, 108ff.). Within this longitudinal
intentionality of the retention, the time-constituting flow itself appears
to itself. This longitudinal intentionality is not a *supplementary* retention,
in addition to the retention of the tone (that is, the retention of the constituted temporal object). Were this the case, it would, indeed, lead to an
infinite replication of the flows, since this supplementary retention
would itself in turn have to be held fast by means of a supplementary
retention, and so on. Rather, the longitudinal intentionality is in actuality none other than the characteristic that structures the *modification* of
the retention. The modification refers as such to that of which it is a
modification, in the present case to the preceding retention and ultimately to the primordial impression as the primordial mode.

> This does not lead to an infinite regress, in virtue of the fact
> that within itself every memory [=retention] is a continuous
> modification which, as it were, bears within itself the heritage
> of the entire preceding development in the form of a series of
> adumbrations. [327]

The flow appearing in the longitudinal intentionality is not temporal in
the way that the tones (the "temporal objects") are temporal. Husserl

does speak, however, of a "quasi-temporal arrangement of the phases of the flow" (381, 83 / C, 109f.), and we must understand this in the sense of a quasi-temporal coordination of the constituting subjectivity with the objectivity which is constituted in it. Husserl speaks further of a "pre-phenomenal, pre-empirical temporality" of the (appearing) flow (381).

> It thus seems that all of this, however difficult it may be, actually permits of understanding. There are, accordingly, two inseparable intentionalities, mutually requiring one another like two sides of the same thing; these are woven together within the one, unique flow of consciousness; in virtue of the one intentionality, immanent time is constituted, an objective time, a genuine time in which there is duration and alteration of that which endures; in the other intentionality, the quasi-temporal arrangement of the phases of the flow [is constituted]. . . . The flow of the consciousness constitutive of immanent time *not only is*, rather, its nature is so remarkable and yet so intelligible that a self-appearance of the flow must necessarily subsist within it and hence the flow itself must necessarily be comprehensible in its flowing. The self-appearance of the flow does not require a second flow; rather, as a phenomenon, it constitutes itself within itself [*in (sich) selbst*]. The constituting and the constituted coincide. . . . [381]

But do they really coincide? Husserl explains the self-appearance of the flow by way of the longitudinal intentionality of the *retention*. Yet within the retention it is only the preceding moment which is known, just as within the longitudinal intentionality of the retention it is only the preceding phases of consciousness which are known. Thus, the time-constituting consciousness, as pure actuality and hence precisely as the "true and ultimate absolute," cannot appear within the retention. Husserl continues the above quotation in the following manner:

> The constituting and the constituted coincide and yet they cannot, of course, coincide in every respect. The phases of the flow of consciousness, in which phases of the same flow of consciousness are phenomenally constituted, can not be identical with these constituted phases, and, of course, they are not thus identical. What gets brought to the level of appearance within the momentary actuality of the flow of consciousness is, in the sequence of the reproductive moments of this flow, past phases of the flow of consciousness. [381f.]

Husserl ponders the question whether the currently actual phase of consciousness can still be known within an "ultimate consciousness" and concludes with the following remark:

> It should be seriously considered whether one must assume
> such an ultimate consciousness, a consciousness which would
> be a necessarily "unconscious" consciousness; that is to say, as
> the ultimate intentionality it cannot (if attention always already
> presupposes a pregiven intentionality) be something attended
> to; thus, it can never, in this particular sense, come to con-
> sciousness. [382]

In other texts, Husserl calls this "ultimate consciousness" that he here puts into question "internal consciousness" (*PITC*, app. XII) or "primordial consciousness" [*Urbewusstsein*] (app. IX). It is a (self-)consciousness of the actual flow of consciousness which, however, can never be attentive, intending, positing:

> Consciousness necessarily is *consciousness* in each of its phases.
> Just as the retentional phase is consciousness of the preceding
> [phase] without objectifying it, so too is the primordial datum
> [the actuality of consciousness] already consciousness . . . ,
> without being an object. It is just this primordial consciousness
> that passes into retentional modification. . . . If it [i.e., the pri-
> mordial consciousness] does not exist, no retention would be
> conceivable either. [*Hu* X, 119]

According to these considerations, however, the absolute time-constituting consciousness cannot in itself be grasped attentively, but can be grasped so only in the distance of an appearance that is quasi-inserted in time.

By way of clarification and summarization, we can say that in his phenomenology of time Husserl distinguished among the following three basic kinds of time, that is, between their variously structured constitutions: (1) the time of the present [*Gegenwartszeit*] (the *perceived*, originary temporal field, or the time of givenness), constituted in the continuous flow of impression-retention (transverse intentionality) -protention; (2) *objective* time, constituted in reproduction and in the *identification* made possible within reproduction; in respect to objective time, Husserl further distinguishes between objective, transcendent time (time of space or of nature), and objective, immanent time (an "infinite continuum of duration," as discussed in § 81 of *Ideas I*); (3) the pre-phenomenal, pre-empirical time of the flow appearing to itself, constituted in the longitudinal intentionality of the retention (a quasi-temporal arrangement). Over against all three of these times stands the absolute, time-constituting consciousness, the primordial present, which is not a modality of time. To this "ultimate" consciousness belong impression-retention-protention; retention in respect of its transverse and longitudinal intentionality, also, the reproductions belong to it; and, in fact, all consciousness as such insofar as it is understood purely as constituting actuality as the primordial present [*Urgegenwart*]. On the other hand, insofar as it appears itself within the longitudinal intentionality of a retention (and is thus far constituted), it belongs to pre-phenomenal time; and, insofar as it comes to be objectively identified in reproduction as immanent experience, it belongs to objective, immanent time (and under certain conditions to the objective time of nature as well).

4

Perception, Thing, and Space

T
he phenomenological analysis of perception occupies a fundamental position in Husserl's theory of cognition. Perceptions belong to
the epistemologically distinguished class of intuitional acts referring intentionally to an object that is self-given. As sensuous acts
they are at once the paradigm and the foundation for the determination
of every other kind of intuitional act. The phenomenological analysis of
the acts of intuitional presentation [*Vergegenwärtigung*] as well as of intuitional thinking and judging, reserved for the next chapters, rests essentially upon the concept of a sensuous act in which the intentional
object is itself given in immediate intuition. Inasmuch as the determination of the essence of so-called "inner" perception has been treated in
our earlier discussions of phenomenological reflection as well as in our
analysis of the constitution of temporal objects, we shall confine ourselves in what follows to an analysis of the perception of spatial objects.
On the other hand, we shall not analyze this mode of perception merely
as a standard example of the epistemological privilege ascribed to intuitive acts. Rather, we wish to show how physical things, as well as the
space encompassing them, are constituted by perceptual experience.

   Again, we may properly maintain that the constitution of the
thing functions as the paradigm for all Husserlian constitutional analyses
as such. This explains why it is elaborated by Husserl in such a careful
and thorough fashion. Unfortunately, the limited scope of the present

exposition does not permit us to follow Husserl's analyses in every detail or to bring into consideration the full compass of the pertinent sources, published or unpublished. Above all, we would like to look into Husserl's analysis of visual perception and the kinaesthetic motivation of such perception. In doing so, we shall confine ourselves in particular to his earlier discussions of the matter, such as are to be found in *Husserliana* XVI ("Thing and Space. Lectures from 1907") and in the *Logical Investigations*. It will become clear that this delimitation of our textual sources makes it impossible that certain pertinent and important themes be given all the attention they deserve, themes such as the *passive* constitution of the perceptual appearance, the transition in constitutional analysis from the visual phantom of the thing to the physical-material or causal-substantial thing-in-itself, the insertion of the single, detached thing into the encompassing horizon of mundane experience, the interlacing and experiential integration of the various sensory fields (for example, the visual and the tactile), and also the dual constitution of the subject of perception as a body and a soul.

§ 1. Appearance as Mixed Representation [*Repräsentation*] and as Partial Self-Givenness of the Thing

As one might expect, the phenomenological analysis of the perception of spatial objects begins with the way in which these objects are given in and for consciousness. Its first and most important observation concerns the circumstance that spatial objects are never fully given in intuition with respect to all their sides and characteristics. Reflection upon the modes of givenness teaches us that only certain "sides" or "aspects" actually come to be seen in the visual perception of a thing, whereas other sides of the same object fall entirely outside of the field of vision (for example, the rear side, the underside, a hidden side, and so on). And yet, in the simple, prereflective performance of a perception of a thing, we do intend to see the thing and not merely its front side; and likewise in reflection, the side which has actually been seen necessarily refers to the as yet unseen sides and to the entirety of the uniform thing. It is the first and most fundamental task of a phenomenological analysis of the perception of a thing to make intelligible this necessary connection between partial or perspectival givenness and the whole or uniform thing. The specifically phenomenological character of this analysis of the perspectival mode of givenness of the thing consists in one's thereby moving exclusively within the compass of phenomenologically reduced data. *Partial* intuitive givenness may not, then, be understood as if but a piece were given of a thing existing in itself and fully differentiated within itself in respect of its content. By the same token, partial intuitive *givenness* may not be understood as if there were to be found in consciousness a representative of the noumenal thing such that this representative would then be conceived, by means of a causal inference, as the phenomenal givenness of the noumenal thing (cf. *DR*, § 40). Perceptual experience alone can be laid claim to as the phenomenological givenness of a thing. The totality of the thing and the partiality of its givenness can be differentiated only in reflection upon the phenomenological givenness of the intentional act of perception (and its noematic correlate). Husserl did not succeed right away in discharging this task. He had particular difficulty determining the nature of the "surplus" of the perceptual intention in respect of the fact that this surplus stretches beyond the partial self-givenness of the object; in other words he had difficulty determining the nature of the reference of the partial perceptual givenness to the full thing. For one may say neither that the thing is intuitively given in this surplus that reaches beyond the actual seeing of the thing, nor that the thing does not attain to givenness at all in this surplus. But how, then, is the absence of that which I cannot actually see nevertheless present in my seeing?

Let us consider that moment of the act of perception which can be designated as "seeing" in the strict sense, that moment in which a "side" of the thing is given in full intuition. Husserl calls this eminent givenness "authentic [*eigentlich*] appearance" and distinguishes it from the empty co-intention or from the apperceptive surplus that he calls "inauthentic [*uneigentlich*] appearance" (§ 16 and passim). In this authentic appearance an aspect of the thing is *itself given* in intuition, that is, it is given "in its physical presence [*leibhaft*]" or "originarily." This (partial) intuitive *self-givenness* characteristic of the act of perception (in its entirety) is to be distinguished on the one hand from other modes of *intuitive* givenness in which the object is not given itself but rather is given by means of an image. On the other hand, it is also to be distinguished from modes of givenness in which the object as such is given not in intuition but merely by means of a (conventional) sign representing the object. Thus, talk of the perceptual self-givenness of the object also has a polemical connotation related to an epistemological theory which reduces perception to representation by images and signs.

Husserl criticizes this theory in particular in his attempt to come to terms with K. Twardowski's essay *Zur Lehre vom Inhalt und Gegenstand der Vorstellungen* (1894) (cf. esp. *LI* II/I [I], § 13; [V], § 45; *Id* I, § 129; for a more comprehensive portrayal of the problematics, see B. Rang). Twardowski adopts the view that every intentional relation to an actual object is mediated by a mental "content" or "secondary" object that, as an image seated in consciousness, serves as a substitute for the "primary," that is, the extramental object. Accordingly, perception is a complex act, a "double activity of presentation," which is related to the actual object (*id quod*) by way of the "content" of consciousness (*id quo*). It is quite wrong, however, in Husserl's view, to understand perception by analogy with imaginal consciousness [*Bildbewußtsein*] inasmuch as consciousness of the image, on the contrary, presupposes the possible perceptual self-givenness of the original. Moreover, Husserl points out that the doubling of the structure of intentional objectivity into "content of consciousness" and "real object" leads to an infinite regress (cf. *LI* II/I, 421ff. / F, 593ff.; *Id* I, §§ 52, 90).

Husserl describes immediate, perceptual self-givenness, a givenness mediated by neither image nor sign, as an intentional act of a perceptive "animation" of the representational contents (*DR*, §§ 14f., 40, and passim). This act owes its *intuitiveness* to the complex of sensational data interwoven with the apperceptive act into "a most intimate unity" (§ 40). Nevertheless, these data function as intuitional representatives of an intentional *object* merely in virtue of their being animated by the intentional act. The authentic appearance of an object of perception is the intentional act inasmuch as and to the extent that this act is interwoven with corresponding sensational data. The inauthentic appearance is the apperceptive surplus, that is, that moment in the intending of an object which is wanting in corresponding sensational data. Husserl understands the authentic appearance or partial self-givenness of the thing as the "pure perceptual tenor [*Gehalt*]" of the perceptual intention (*LI* II/2 [VI], § 14b) or, again in the language of the *Logical Investigations*, as the intuitive moment within the total complex making up the perceptual representation of an intentional object. In this context, "representation" means nothing other than the (noetic) complex of apperception, hence, the nexus of sensational data and the intention (or, more specifically, its intentional matter) which pervades these data and relates them to the object (§ 26).

In the *Logical Investigations*, the model for this apperceptive representation is the semantic intention [*Bedeutungsintention*], that is, the intentional act which both bears and instantiates the signification of the linguistic expression and which in doing so relates the signs composing this expression to the signified object of reference. Such an "interpretation" does not regard the signs of a linguistic expression for their own sake but understands them as the signitive representatives of this object. Intuitive representation of the intentional object is distinguished from this model of signitive representation by the fact that in intuition the representational data, in contrast with the linguistic signs, are neither physical objects (signs) nor even (signitive) representatives of the object but are rather understood as being the object itself, inasmuch as and to the extent that it is intuitively given. In a purely phenomenological consideration of the (noetic) complex of representation, the distinction between signitive and intuitive representation is the fact that, in signitive representation, the apprehension and the representational content form a merely "accidental, outward" connection, while in intuitive representation, they form an "essential, inward" connection. In intuitive representation there "obtains an inner, necessary connection between the matter [of the intentional apprehension] and the representative [content]" (§ 26). From the objective standpoint, this means that "only a content which is . . . like it [i.e., the object] can serve as [the perceptual-] intuitive representative of the object" (§ 26). Thus, for example, the color of a thing can be intuitively represented only by means of a datum of color.

The perceptual givenness or appearance of the thing is accordingly an intuitive representation in which, however, the intentional object is itself only partially given. It is, in other words, a partially intuitive representation. It may be misleading to designate even the immediate, perceptual givenness of the thing as *representation*, for in common parlance "representation" means substitution or at least mathematically stable coordination, but scarcely concrete, intuitive self-givenness of an object. This terminology was first introduced in the *Logical Investigations*—part two of the "Psychological Studies Concerning Elementary Logic" (1893) still made a sharp distinction between "intuitions" and "representations"—and was dropped shortly thereafter. Yet it is more than a mere terminological awkwardness which is of concern in the *Logical Investigations*. In respect of the perceptual givenness of a thing, Husserl speaks there of intuitive *representation* because the intuitive self-givenness of the thing is merely partial, that is, it is fitted into a total, (noetic) nexus of representations in which it is supplemented by a signitive representation, a givenness of the perceptual object which is mediated by the apprehension of a sign. Thus, that which, with regard to the "Lectures on the Thing" of 1907, we have called an inauthentic perceptual appearance, that is, the apperceptive "surplus" (*LI* II/I [V], § 14) over and above the "pure perceptual tenor," is to be understood as a signitive representation which brings to givenness the sides of the thing which are not intuitively given in perception (*LI* II/2 [VI], §§ 14, 15, 23). Accordingly, "the same content," that is, the same sensational complex, should be apperceived by one part of the intentional act as an intuitive representation of the intentional object, and by another part of the act as a merely signitive representation (§ 26). It is Husserl's view that the connection of these two forms of representation within the act of perception is one in which attention is aimed primarily at the performance of the intuitive apperception, whereas the surplus of apperception represents the merely co-intended aspects of the object in the manner of signitive representation (by means of "adjacency" to [§ 10] or "contiguity" with [§§ 15, 23, 26] this intuitive representation). A full act of perception or the full appearance of a thing, that is, the unity of authentic and inauthentic appearance, is thus a sum (cf. § 23) of diverse forms of representations or it is a "mixed" form of representation, at once intuitive and signitive (§§ 14b, 23, 25, 26).

In order to initiate our line of criticism, it is not necessary that we develop further this doctrine of the total appearance of the thing as a mixed form of representation. Since in carrying it out we can rely on Husserl's own insights, this critique is exceptionally well suited to serve as a guide for portraying the development of the problematics subsequent to the *Logical Investigations*. First of all, it seems exceedingly questionable whether one may define the inauthentic appearance of the merely co-intended aspects of the thing as signitive representation. Sensations are not signs in the sense of physical objects and, unlike linguistic signs, do not function as the merely conventional representatives of the sensuous object of perception. Looked at more exactly, the merely co-intended aspects of the thing are represented neither signitively nor imaginatively, that is, in the intuitiveness proper to acts of phantasy. Rather, they are not represented at all.

> [I]nauthentically appearing objective moments are represented
> in no way whatsoever. The perception is . . . a complex of full
> and empty intentions (rays of apperception); the fulfilled intentions or fulfilled apperceptions are those which represent authentically; the empty ones are simply empty of any
> representational material whatsoever, they really represent
> nothing. [*DR*, § 18; cf. also *Ms. M III 2 II 2*, 7a ff. (1913)]

If the apperceptive surplus in the perception of the thing is defined in this manner as the horizon of empty co-intention or of motivated perceptual possibility, then it follows immediately, as the second point of the critique, that authentic and inauthentic appearance are not merely connected with one another in the manner of associative contiguity but form an essential unity.

> Authentic and inauthentic appearance are not separated but united within the appearance in the broader sense. Consciousness is consciousness of the bodily [*leibhaft*] presence of the house: it means, and quite in the sense of the whole perception: The house appears. . . . The authentic appearance is not something separable. [*DR*, § 16]

A third point in the critique concerns not only the *Logical Investigations* but even large portions of the lectures on the thing, held in 1907 (*DR*). Of concern there is the fact that the partition of the perceptual act into diverse forms of representation, but also the distinction between authentic and inauthentic appearance, is derived from the determination of the real object; that the natural actuality of this object may not, however, be laid claim to within the bounds of a phenomenologically pure consideration. (Compare, for example, the following passage omitted in the above citation from § 16 of *Thing and Space* [*DR*]):

> The house appears. It does so, however, with the limitation that but a mere side of the house is actually represented. . . . A side, however, is a side of the full object. It is nothing for itself; as a being-for-itself it is unthinkable. This evidence means: The authentic appearance is not something separable.

Indeed, this derivation of the phenomenological structuring of the appearance from the physical reality of thing and space is questionable. It can even be said to be countersensical, and it is so, just insofar as the phenomenological description of phenomenal givenness is supposed to be of service to a constitutional analysis of the sense of being that characterizes the actuality of thing and space (and not the reverse). We shall return shortly to the real reason for this circular, countersensical definition of the reality of the thing.

If we first consider the consequences of this definition, what leaps to our attention above all is the spatialization of consciousness in analogy with the "*partes extra partes*"–structure that characterizes physical nature alone. Not only ought parts of the thing and moments of the perceptual act correspond exactly, according to this questionable doctrine; not only ought the act of perception break down into diverse forms of representation conjoined with one another by mere contiguity; but even within one selfsame form of representation—for example, in the intuitive moment of the perceptual act—the "intentional matter of the apprehension" and the "content of the apprehension" ought to be connected with one another "piece for piece" (*LI* II/2 [VI], § 26; cf. also *DR*, §§ 55, 60). This breakdown of the activity of consciousness (noesis) into (independent ?) "pieces" is not, however, merely the upshot of an intellectualistic construction or a naturalistic reification of consciousness. Rather, it also bears witness to the fundamental difficulty of the constitution of space by the nonspatial, transcendental consciousness. As we shall see, Husserl finds himself forced to ascribe to the thing-constituting consciousness, and especially to the sensational data interwoven with this consciousness in really [*reell*] immanent fashion, a "pre-phenomenal" or "pre-empirical" spatiality or extension (cf. *DR*, §§ 20–22, 25, 46; app. III). We shall have then to entertain the more general question of whether Husserl does not find himself compelled, in his analysis of the constitution of thing and space, either to expand the concept of the constituting consciousness or, at least, to designate supposedly really immanent contents of consciousness as noematic contents of the intentional act of perception.

The at all events surprising splitting-up of the simple act of sensuous perception into a bundle of rays of "partial intentions" (cf. *LI* II/2 [VI], § 47; *DR*, § 18, and passim), as well as the countersensical presupposition of thingly reality by a phenomenological, constitutional analysis, finally leads us back again to the basic problem of a phenomenological analysis of perception, namely, how to determine appearance as *partial self-givenness*. The paradoxical difficulty consists in the fact that the appearance, as *self-givenness*, is the appearing object, while at the same time, as *partial* self-givenness, it is not this object, that is, it is never identical with the thing which appears in it. Once again, both the portrayal of the attempted solution to this problem in the *Logical Investigations* and the critique of this attempt are excellently suited to serve as approximations to a satisfying answer. The *Logical Investigations* determine the partiality of the phenomenal self-givenness of the thing against the background of full self-givenness, as full self-givenness is able to be realized only in the realm of inner perception (*LI* II/I [V], §§ 5f.). Adequate self-givenness is characterized by the fact that "here [the] representing and [the] represented content are *identically* one" (*LI* II/2 [VI], § 37). By contrast, in partial self-givenness the intuitive representative is not simply identical with the "object itself, just as it is in itself." Rather, partial self-representation or "self-adumbration" is "representation by *similarity*" (§ 37; cf. also § 29).

It may, indeed, be feasible in phenomenological contemplation to establish a relationship of similarity among diverse appearances of one and the same thing (*DR*, § 55). Such a relationship may not, however, be alleged between the appearance and the appearing thing. Apart from the circumstance that the appearance and the thing "just as it is in itself" cannot be compared with one another within phenomenologically pure contemplation, it is furthermore countersensical to define the partiality of the thing-constituting appearance by looking to the dogmatically presupposed being of a thing that is intrinsically fully determined in itself. Looked at more exactly, however, the countersense does not consist only in a circular, constitutional analysis which, in critically determining the being of the thing, already dogmatically presupposes the natural concept of the thing. The deepest contradiction consists rather in defining the partial self-givenness or perspectival character of the appearance of the thing by looking to the adequate givenness of a nonspatial, psychical entity within inner perception; and, moreover, in designating this nonperspectival givenness as a teleological ideal of adequation regulating the progressive experience of a spatial object (cf. *LI* II/2 [VI], § 14b).

It is easier, however, to criticize the *Logical Investigations*'s attempt at a solution than to produce an alternative solution. It does not suffice to point to the fact that every appearance of a thing is necessarily a merely partial self-givenness of the thing, that the progressive cognizance of the thing in a continuous perception is necessarily an inconclusive, infinite process, and that, accordingly, the conception of an adequate "*intuitus originarius*" of spatial being is countersensical (cf. *DR*, §§ 30, 33–35, 39). Over and above that, it must be shown, firstly, how the partiality of the appearance can be determined without the dogmatic presupposition of a thing-in-itself; secondly, it must be shown to what extent the phenomenological description of the continuous experience of a thing is nevertheless legitimately guided by a preconception of the very object which is yet to be constituted; and thirdly, it must be shown how the epistemological ideal implied in the progress of perceptual cognizance is to be determined, if the idea of an adequate givenness of the thing is countersensical.

Husserl takes up the first task as early as the lectures on the thing of 1907 (*DR*). He does so by understanding the partiality of the self-givenness of the thing as a need for a supplementary self-givenness. Accordingly, he determines it with respect to the horizon that necessarily surrounds the authentic appearance and points to further, diverse, possible appearances of the same object. We shall examine still more closely this dynamization of the distinction between authentic and inauthentic appearance when we pass on to the phenomenological description of the *continuous* process of perception.

The second task also has to do with the structure of the continuous perceptual process, namely, insofar as the phenomenological analysis of this process departs from a regional-ontological preconception of the thing. In the language of *Ideas I*, this means that "the region 'thing' " serves "as [a] transcendental clue [*Leitfaden*]" for the phenomenological-constitutional analysis (*Id* I, § 150, also § 149). This concept of the thing, pregiven in a "straightforward alignment of vision," assigns what it has to investigate to the phenomenological-reflective experience of the thing; at the same time, it prescribes the "rules" governing the "course" of this constitutive experience of the thing. Thus, for example, the phenomenologically investigated perspectival character of the appearance of the thing, and the "limitlessness in the progress of harmonious intuitions" of the thing, are "necessities" conditioned by the eidetic concept "thing-as-such." Does Husserl not thereby fall back again into the countersensical presupposition which we censured in our interpretation of the *Logical Investigations* and the lectures on the thing, namely, the presupposition that derives the determination of phenomenologically constitutive experience (for example, the perceptual appearance) from the pre-phenomenological determination of actuality which is, however, yet to be constituted by this phenomenological experience? The answer is no, for in the first place it is no longer an empirically actual object, but rather a material-ontologically explored essence that guides the transcendental-constitutional exploration of the actuality of thing and space; and in the second place the results of this phenomenological exploration cannot be derived from the material-ontological conception of the thing; rather, these results had necessarily to remain hidden from the "straightforwardly" oriented, regional-ontological science. With the essence of spatial objects that is acquired in geometrical eidetic intuition, "however, we know nothing of the very processes of intuition and the essences and eidetic infinities which belong *to it* [i.e., intuition]" (§ 150). The geometer is not a phenomenologist. The phenomenological doctrine concerning orientation, depth, and distance within the field of appearance is not an analytical consequence but rather a subjective supplement or a transcendental foundation of the geometrical doctrine of three-dimensional space. The eidetic preconception of the thing does, to be sure, necessarily imply the impossibility of an adequate appearance of the thing. It says nothing, however, concerning the structuring of this appearance and its reference to an ordered multiplicity of further and supplementary appearances of the same thing. Yet this is not all. In carrying out the phenomenological investigation, we do not merely substitute a phenomenological description for a pregiven eidetic preconception; rather, in the course of this investigation, the meaning of the eidetic preconception and its guiding role for the incipient phenomenological investigation come to be understood for the first time. The transcendental-phenomenological analysis of the process of experience not only determines what it means for a thing actually to be, rather, it likewise concerns the process of acquiring material-ontological essences and hence determines the sense of being and the epistemological function proper to these essences.

The third task similarly concerns the continuous process of perception, no longer, however, in its relation to the material-ontological preconception of the essence of the thing, but in its characterization as a continuous process of fulfillment or as a process of sensuous cognition aligned teleologically with the idea of maximum fullness or ultimate givenness of the thing. The dispatch of this task proves to be as difficult as it does, because, on the one hand, the experience of the thing is necessarily an infinite process and hence excludes an adequate self-givenness of the thing; and because, on the other hand, progress in perceptual cognition would remain unintelligible apart from a teleological anticipation of the adequate givenness of the thing-in-itself. Again, only in *Ideas I* did Husserl succeed in solving this *aporia*, and he did so by designating the adequate givenness of the thing as an "idea (in the Kantian sense)" and by defining the latter more precisely as a "system of *infinite* processes of continuous appearing" (§ 143). Thus, the thing-in-itself is now understood as an idea, in particular, as a regulative idea resulting from the idea "of limitlessness in the progress of harmonious intuitions" (§ 149). In contrast with the real thing-in-itself of the *Logical Investigations*, the idea of the unity of the thing in an infinite process of experience is a purely phenomenological idea, an idea adequately given and free of the countersensical presupposition of a spatial object given in a nonperspectival appearance. In spite of this, however, one may ask whether the teleologically regulative idea of an *infinite* progress in cognition is actually capable of motivating the cognitive interest which lives in the process of perception, or whether it does not rather permit this interest to founder in despair (cf. Bernet, 1978a and 1978b).

§ 2. The Continuum of Appearance and its Constitutive Achievement

Up until now, our treatment of perceptual experience has remained abstract. To be sure, it cannot be denied that a consistent determination of the concept of appearance represents a necessary and fundamental precondition for any philosophical and quite especially for any phenomenological theory of perception. On the other hand, however, the genuine accomplishment of phenomenology consists precisely in having introduced into the compass of a philosophical analysis of perceptions concrete phenomena such as the determination of diverse types of alteration in the continuum of appearances and the kinaesthetic motivation of this alteration, phenomena such as the arrangement of sensations within the encompassing organization of different "fields" and the relation of these sensuous fields to corresponding, diverse systems of kinaesthetic capability, and so on. In this section, we shall confine ourselves to a schematic description of the continuous flow [*Ablauf*] of perception and its constitutive function. Only when we have completed this task will we move on to treat the kinaesthetic motivation not only of the continuum of appearances but also of every single appearance.

A concrete act of perception is, in fact, always a temporally extended act. In our preceding analysis of the concept of appearance we removed by abstraction a single, momentary phase. If we now reinsert this phase into the nexus of the continuous course of appearances, the question arises in the first place as to how the transition from phase to phase is to be understood. The next question, a question fraught with consequences, is how, in this continuum of appearances, a "harmoniousness [*Einstimmigkeit*]" can arise that does not merely coordinate manifold appearances with a selfsame object but is at the same time experienced as the progressive satisfaction of a cognitive interest bearing on this object.

Husserl understands the continuity of appearances that characterizes the course of the perceptual act as a synthetically unified multiplicity of intuitive phenomena belonging to the perceptual object. The form of unity which binds together the multiplicity of appearances is, above all, the temporal form of the stream of consciousness. The appearances lie in the actually present flow of pre-empirical temporality, and the continuity of the process of appearance or, respectively, the duration of the object appearing in this process (*DR*, §§ 19f., 48, 56; pp. 223f. and 335) is in this flow. (Here we may disregard the fact that these manifold appearances are for their part already temporal unities and, to be sure, unities constituted in the absolute, nontemporal consciousness.) However, the successive emergence of new appearances in the flow of consciousness and the retentional and protentional horizon connected with this emergence do not constitute a sufficient motivation for the continuous, synthetic coordination of appearances *with the same appearing object* or for their integration into a harmonious course of perception. For this purpose, a continuous synthesis of identification is required. As an essential moment of the perceptual process, however, this synthesis of identification is, in its primordial performance, an achievement of sensuous, and not of logical-categorial or intellectual consciousness. It is for this reason that Husserl speaks in the sixth of the *Logical Investigations* of an "identity through fusion" (*LI* II/2 [VI], § 29) in which "identification is performed but no identity [is] intended" (§ 47). In his lecture on the thing we find a further elaboration of this distinction between the sensuous performance of the phenomenal "synthesis of coincidence" (*DR*, §§ 26, 30, 52) and the subsequent logical-categorial reconstruction of this synthesis (§§ 26, 29, 44). The sensuous unity formed is "a certain unity of the homogenous flow" (§ 30) that results from the arrangement of manifold appearances under a sensuous type (§ 52). In the performance of this "synthesis, continuously connecting the manifold perceptions," we become conscious of a *uniform* thing, whether changing or unchanging, "and this continuous synthesis must be present as a basis in order that the logical synthesis, the synthesis of identification, [may] produce the evident givenness of the *identity* of the objects appearing in the diverse perceptions" (§ 44).

Looked at more closely, however, this continuous, sensuous synthesis is not a formation of unity introduced, as it were, from the outside and applied to a manifold of appearances homogenous in content. Rather, it is already essentially prefigured in the content of every single appearance. The continuum of appearances is the realization of the possible further course of perception, as this course is implied in the horizon that belongs to inauthentic appearance (§§ 30, 54f.). Yet not all of these emptily anticipated perceptual and phenomenal possibilities have the same motivating force. They do not all press on in like manner toward their actualization. On the one hand, this differentiation in the field of possibility issues from the connection of the inauthentic appearance with the appurtenant authentic appearance and with the retained, already elapsed continuum of appearances (cf. § 32). On the other hand, it results from the specific interest of the perceiving subject (cf. §§ 33, 36). (We shall for the moment disregard the fact that the concrete actualization of these two lines of motivational force is further mediated by kinaesthetic circumstances or by the sequence of kinaesthetic data.)

Husserl understands the subjective interest that regulates the course of the perceptual process primarily as a scientific, cognitive interest directed toward a maximum (or adequate) cognizance of the thing, and not as an interest directed toward aesthetic enjoyment or practical-technical application. Among the different possibilities of appearance connected by means of adjacency and similarity with the authentic appearance, priority is given to those which more closely determine the uniform object and which, accordingly, may lead to the satisfaction of the cognitive interest that is oriented toward the maximum differentiation and self-givenness of the object (§§ 36ff.). The continuous synthesis of perception is thus *a process of fulfillment* in which the empty intentions conjoined with an authentic appearance are fulfilled by newly emerging intuitive appearances that bring the uniform object to a more comprehensive state of self-givenness (cf. §§ 29f., 32f., 54). This nexus of appearances, bearing on the process of fulfillment, necessarily has the form of a sensuous synthesis of agreement. It does not, however, always have the form of a "closer determination" of the object or the form of a "progressive corroboration" of the intention (§ 18). The nexus of fulfillment can also lead to a modified determination of the object, to a disappointment of the intention, a conflict between what has been supposed and what is actually given; whereby, to be sure, it is "evident that the conflict presupposes agreement and that the disappointment presupposes fulfillment" (§ 29).

We cannot now enter more closely into a differentiation of the various forms of the process of perceptual fulfillment; and we would like also to reserve a more exact analysis of the structure of the synthesis of fulfillment for a later chapter (cf. below, chap. 6, § 2). It is important, however, not to confuse the cognitive form of fulfillment with the fulfillment of the mere expectation of the further course of experience, inasmuch as this latter mode of fulfillment likewise functions in the process of perception. The latter nexus of intention and fulfillment results immediately from the form of continuous, synthetic unity within which every phase in the course of perception actualizes the prefigurement borne in the foregoing phase. Here it is a question of the following:

> [To the] *arbitrary* series of alteration . . . , and to these series *as such* would belong interconnections among intentions, that is, indications which at any given moment run alongside the phases from phase to phase; one is drawn forward within the

familiar complex in a line of constant belonging together. Furthermore, the movement might lead in this direction or that [and] it might realize givenness in better or worse fashion. [§ 32]

Should, however, a cognitive interest come to be conjoined with the form of synthetic unity belonging to the multiplicity of appearances, then the series of alteration ceases to be arbitrary and the appurtenant forms of unity are "particular."

> There lies within them something which we call [an] . . . *increase . . . in the fullness of givenness*, a steadily more complete . . . attainment to the givenness of perception. . . . The incomplete [attainment] is . . . already a consciousness of givenness. . . . But it is not equal to the consciousness of givenness as complete; . . . it points beyond itself; it is an intimation of what is really meant; . . . it carries [with it] intentions which point in the direction of more complete representations or, respectively, in the direction of the "object itself" [§ 32].

Nevertheless, the goal of adequate self-givenness is not a "real" possibility but a merely "ideal" one; as we have already seen, the fully determined thing-in-itself is a Kantian idea. Husserl names the following as reasons for the essential impossibility of actually attaining adequate self-givenness of the thing within the process of appearance: (1) it is impossible to reduce infinite space to the finitude of the field of vision; (2) spatial objects, and even the sides of things, are represented in an infinitely extensible continuum of adumbration; (3) spatial bodies (*qua* movable) can withdraw from the field of appearance and later enter it once again (§ 35; cf. also §§ 30 and 32). Thus, from the essential inadequacy of every appearance of a thing, there follows the infinity of the experience of the thing; and infinite experience of the thing implies a course of perception harmonious in respect of fulfillment and progressing without end, a course of perception in which, however, the sudden ingress of experiential conflict and the resultant "explosion" of the object are in principle never excluded (§ 84; cf. *Id* I, § 46; and *Ms. M III 2 1 3*, 55ff. [1913]).

Continuous multiplicities of appearance, harmoniously conjoined in fulfillment, are "unities of cognition" and, as such, they also have "their uniform objective correlates" (*IP*, 13). This process of perceptual fulfillment is a process of "gradual *constitution*" in which "the object of experience is continuously constituted" (ibid.; cf. also 75—this is the first part of the lecture on the thing, of 1907). The perceptual continuum does not, therefore, attain to synthesis merely in regard to an identical object, and the nexus of synthetic fulfillment is not merely an act of progressive cognizance of the thing. Rather, in phenomenologically pure consideration, the thing, in its actual being, is nothing else than the objective correlate of this uniform, synthetic process of perceptual experience. Understood within the transcendental-phenomenological attitude, perceptual experience is accordingly not a progressive discovery of an objective reality independent of consciousness and firmly determined in itself, but a progressive determination and validation of the being of individual things. The thing is the objective unity progressively being built up in the multiplicity of continuous perceptual appearances; or, more precisely, it is the (noematic) correlate of the (noetic) identificational synthesis unifying these manifold appearances within a continuous process of fulfillment. Likewise, we now understand much better why the teleologically functioning idea of the thing-in-itself, if it is to be understood phenomenologically, must be derived from the (infinite) progress characterizing our experience of the thing. We also understand why the partiality of the appearance of the thing may not be derived from the objectively determined side of the thing. "Aspect of the thing," "surface of the thing," "progressively determined visual phantom," as well as "thing-in-itself," are concepts whose sense is phenomenologically disclosed only with regard to corresponding structures in the experience of the thing. In virtue of this phenomenological correlation between seeing and what is seen, between appearance and what appears, there results the possibility of forming a noematic concept of appearance as well as of considering a purely noematic description of the process in which a thing is constituted (cf. Gurwitsch and Bernet).

§ 3. The Kinaesthetic Motivation in the Constitution of Thing and Space

We have already spoken of the fundamental difficulty involved in constituting spatially transcendent objects in a nonspatial, that is, a phenomenologically reduced, transcendental consciousness. Husserl obviates this difficulty, firstly, by ascribing to the representational data of sensation not only a qualitative but also a pre-empirically extensional determinateness (*DR*, §§ 20f., 46). Secondly, he places these sensational data into a

motivational nexus of association along with a corresponding multiplicity of kinaesthetic data and, ultimately, along with the bodily [*leiblich*]
mode of being of the perceptual subject.

In accordance with their terminological introduction by A. Bain,
kinaesthetic sensations were taken by nineteenth-century psychology to
consist in muscular sensations (cf. *DR*, xxiv). Even with Husserl, the
kinaestheses remain related to the bodily organism in a manner which
must still be determined more exactly. This relation obtains, however,
without our being permitted, within the bounds of a phenomenologically pure consideration of the matter, to lay claim to the physiological
structure of the bodily organism. "Kinaesthetic sensations," along with
the "representational sensations," belong to the content of "the animat-
ing 'apprehension.' " They do so, however, in such a way that, in contrast with the sensational data, they "make representation possible
without themselves representing" (§ 46). Prior to the constitution of the
bodily organism and the localization of the kinaestheses within the bodily
organism, little more can be said in a strictly phenomenological fashion
than that these kinaesthetic data form a system of subjective capability
that "is actualized in the momentary kinaesthetic situation" and therewith motivates a situation of corporeal appearances within the field of
perception (*CES*, § 28). In pre-phenomenological, objectifying language, one can say that the kinaestheses, as sensations of the bodily organism, converge in various systems of possible movements on the part
of the bodily organs (eyes, head, hands, and so on). With these movements correspond various forms of possible (visual, tactile, and so on)
fields of appearance, and they correspond in such a way that every modification of the kinaesthetic system (eye-movements, and so on) effects a
modification in the system of appearances (a different focus in the visual
field).

Husserl attempts to slip past the naturally objectifying presuppositions of such a description by beginning his analysis with a description of the representational and kinaesthetic "sensations" understood as
phenomena belonging to pure consciousness. Nevertheless, his discussions in the lectures on the thing overstep these narrow bounds again
and again. The case is similar to that in the description of primordial
time-consciousness, where this description must help itself along with a
naturally inspired set of concepts quite ill-suited to its object, since "we
have no names for all of that" (*PITC*, 371). However, Husserl does not
ascribe too much importance to this difficulty, for he does not take it to
imply a presupposition of empirical reality. Actually, he takes it to be
merely a matter of terminology. He observes that the phenomenological

analysis of the constitutional function intrinsic to the ultimate, "absolute" time-consciousness has no choice but to help itself along with a terminology properly befitting the immanent temporal objects constituted by this consciousness (ibid.). But one might also appraise this difficulty as a sign of the fact that there is no absolutely constituting, transcendental consciousness subsisting independently of the intentional correlate constituted within it. For a method which understands itself to be seeking out the origin by way of a constitutional analysis, the phenomenological contemplation of intentional correlation would then be an ultimate datum. The case is much the same for the phenomenological determination of the kinaestheses and of the bodily organism always implicitly presupposed with them. Here, too, the difficulty is not so much that a phenomenologically pure contemplation of the kinaestheses could not hold good apart from the countersensical presupposition of empirical-physiological facts. Rather, the question arises as to whether a phenomenological consideration of the matter can and must push its inquiry even beyond the constitutional nexus between kinaestheses and bodily organism. Husserl writes the following: "Thus, the kinaesthetic sensations function, on the one hand, to constitute the . . . appearance . . . of the bodily organism and, on the other hand, [they are] localized in the bodily organism" (§ 83; cf. also § 47).

Husserl would like this assertion to be understood in the following manner: Kinaestheses are primordially ultimate data which, in addition to the appearance of things ("bodies"), also motivate the appearance of the bodily organism as an "organ of perception." In virtue of the kinaestheses being experienced as bodily-organic capabilities, the bodily organism itself attains the status of an organ of perception, a "functioning bodily organism" (*Ms. D 2*, 3a [1933]). This insertion of the kinaestheses into one's (own) bodily organism occurs after the fact and, indeed, on the basis of special experiences such as the intersection of different kinaesthetic systems (for example, in touching an eye which itself sees) or the intersection of different experiences within one and the same system (for example, in touching a hand which itself touches). On the other hand, one might understand the above cited assertion to mean that a reciprocal and hence further irreducible relationship of dependency obtains between the kinaestheses and the bodily organism. Not only are the kinaestheses constitutive for the experience of the bodily organism, but the functioning bodily organism is also constitutive for the experience of the various kinaesthetic systems. From this it would also follow (entirely in the sense espoused by Merleau-Ponty) that the transcendental-constitutional perceptual consciousness always belongs to a bodily organism.

We do not want to dwell any longer on these general questions and shall rather pass on to a concrete consideration of the constitutional achievement proper to the kinaestheses. Just as in the case of a process of appearance, the kinaesthetic consciousness has the form of a temporal continuum of succession. The continuum of the kinaesthetic flow [*Ablauf*] is normally a continuum of alteration, and Husserl takes motion to be the basic form of alteration. Kinaesthetic sensations are "sensations of motion." For its part, however, the sensed motion can be the motion of the bodily organism functioning as an organ of perception as well as the motion of the perceived thing. Among the kinaesthetic sensations of motion related to the bodily organism, one must still distinguish between the receptive sensation of the bodily organism and the sensation of the spontaneous "I can" (move myself thus and so . . .). The "kinaesthetic freedom" of the "I can" (*Ms. D 13 I*, 8a [1921]) refers not only to the possibility of voluntary movements of the bodily-organism, but also to the possibility of engendering the appearances of the thing which are motivated by those movements. This specifically sensuous form of "freedom" determines a "will" which can place itself in the service of a cognitive interest. In this case the "I can" strives to produce those kinaesthetic circumstances which would permit the optimal givenness of the perceptual object (65a [1921]). Kinaesthetic freedom consists in actively intervening in the phenomenal world. It combines the comportment of a bodily organism and the appearances of things in an indissoluble association. Even "receptive" and "habitual" kinaestheses are ultimately subordinate to the disposition of the "I can." Involuntary movements of the bodily organism and objectively conditioned modifications of appearances can always "be redressed, annulled," by the appropriate kinaestheses (55b [1921]). Habitual kinaesthetic processes are familiar forms of free comportment belonging to the bodily organism.

They contribute to the circumstance whereby an entire system of kinaesthetic capability stands on call at the disposal of the "I can."

> By means of . . . being run through frequently [they are] fused [. . . so as to form] a familiar, habitual system of movements. . . . By practice, a mastery over this system has evolved; "I can" thus [accomplish] every intended movement; which implies that this movement is able to be executed by me at any time. [53a f.]

This holds for every individual system of kinaesthetic mobility and, by the same token, also for "the complete system of kinaestheses at the disposal of consciousness" (*CES*, § 28). Husserl reconstructs this "complete system of kinaestheses" as a graduated formation of ever more comprehensive kinaesthetic systems. Thus, in the framework of visual perception, he distinguishes between the oculo-motor system of one eye alone and of two eyes together, the cephalo-motor system of head-movements, and the systems of the bodily organism at rest, in motion, and afoot (*DR*, §§ 47, 49, 63, 73). Each of these systems has its own series of typical modifications and the hierarchical ordering of the various systems is determined under the aspect of the progressive expansion of the visual field or the gradual construction of the spatial object.

The specifically phenomenological character of this analysis consists in each kinaesthetic system being described in accordance with its constitutional achievement. Furthermore, the phenomenological exploration of this constitutional achievement on the part of the kinaestheses always takes place with respect to the object constituted in the kinaesthetic performance. Such an exploration takes the form of a contemplation of an intentional correlation. Insofar, however, as the intentional object is co-constituted by the apprehension of sensational data representing the object in its material determination, and insofar as the kinaestheses accordingly bring forth an essentially non-independent constitutional achievement, the kinaestheses and the systematic ordering of the kinaesthetic systems can be explored only within the motivational nexus that combines them with adumbrations of a qualitative sort and with hyletic fields of materially determinate content.

We have seen that the spatial thing is constituted in a regulated nexus of manifold appearances and that these appearances are (noetically) determined as the apperceptive animation of the representational data of sensation. Husserl now traces this multiplicity of appearances back to the ultimate constitutive multiplicity, that of the sensational data. Prior to every intentional apprehension, these manifold data of sensation are conjoined to form primitive hyletic unities. Such a formation of unity is essentially an achievement of "passive synthesis" which assumes, above all, the form of association. The passively formed unities are pre-intentional complexes of sensations, which, nonetheless, are implied in every intentional perception of a thing. If one holds to Husserl's definition of perception as an intentional act apprehending pre-intentional contents of apprehension, then, accordingly, this passive forming of unity may not be designated as a perceptual process nor may the hyletic unities constituted within it be designated as perceptual objects.

Various interpreters of HusserI, however, shied away from imputing to all perceptual experience the thus prescribed apprehension of an apprehensional content. They were of the opinion that such apprehension was characteristic only for higher-level, linguistically elaborated, "explicative" acts of perception. They further held that in addition to such acts there were other, more primitive forms of perception that Husserl had already begun to describe in his analyses of passive synthesis and the formation of hyletic unity. Be that as it may, one must in any event distinguish clearly between two different forms of hyletic unity: (1) on the one hand is the open, universal horizon, into which are inserted all sensations of one and the same type; (2) on the other hand are the particular unities inside of this encompassing horizon. Husserl calls the encompassing horizon a "sensuous field." There are, in fact, different types of such fields but every one is formally organized in just the same way. Accordingly, the formations of particular hyletic unities within the various sensuous fields always obey the same rules.

Sensational data, or "representational data," are characterized by their pre-empirical extension and by the qualitative covering [*Bedeckung*] that belongs to this extension. Hence, the sensuous field, as a nexus of manifold sensational data, is also a pre-empirical system of positions [*Lagen*] with a qualitatively discontinuous covering (§ 48). The system of positions and its materially determinate, qualitative occupation [*Besetzung*] are thus phenomenologically correlative concepts.

> The loci [*Orte*] are differentiated within themselves, but the
> qualities [are differentiated] only by the loci. On the other
> hand, loci and complexes of loci owe their contrast to the qual-
> ities, that is, to [the] . . . discontinuities in these qualities.
> [§ 53]

Accordingly, the formation of unity among sensations, a formation which underlies the continuum of appearances (§ 55), is a process of both qualitative fusion and transformation within the system of loci.

> In every multiplicity of appearances or images [i.e., sensa-
> tions[1]] in which the representation of an object is . . . unfolded
> . . . in a systematic and uniform fashion, the unity pervades
> [both] the pre-empirical extension and [the] coloring [that is,
> the qualitative covering]. The multiplicity within the pre-
> empirical extension implies everywhere a transformation within
> the visual multiplicity of loci . . . on the basis of that transfor-
> mation . . . the colorings, too, . . . attain . . . to unity; or, on
> the basis of that transformation all of the thus and so colored
> images attain unity. [§ 53]

In the following text-fragment from his later work, Husserl pregnantly summarizes the results of the foregoing considerations.

> Appearances have a scope in which to play, [they have] an ho-
> rizon of potentiality. . . . The potentiality of the appearances,
> the being-able-to-let-them-take-their-course, as well as their
> way of playing within a certain scope, is a mediate potentiality
> and derives its sense from the immediate potentiality of the
> kinaesthesis. [*Ms. D 12*, 11b (1931)]

The kinaestheses motivate not only the various types of "scope in which
appearances play," or the "sensuous fields" belonging to the various
types of sensation; they also motivate the course of the "appearances" or
"images." This dual line of motivation leads us to distinguish, even for
the kinaestheses themselves, between different kinaesthetic *systems*, on
the one hand, and the continuous *course* of kinaesthetic data within a
determinate system, on the other (cf. *DR*, § 51). If we first direct our
attention toward the connection between the *fluxes* belonging to the kin-
aesthesis and those belonging to the appearances, we shall at the same
time gain a better understanding of the motivational nexus binding the
kinaestheses and the data of sensation or the appearances. The correspondence between the course of the kinaestheses ($=k$) and the course of
the representational data of sensation or images ($=i$) is first expressed in
the fact that k and i are given together already within each appearance.

> The appearance in each phase and the unity of appearances in
> its temporal extension, both have two essentially different com-
> ponents, the i-component and the k-component. The i-compo-
> nent furnishes the "intention toward"; the k-component
> [furnishes] the motivation for this intention. [§ 54]

More precisely, this motivational nexus has the form of the "if-
then" relating kinaesthetic circumstances and the corresponding course
of certain representational data of sensation (*Id* II, § 18a). However,
there is no question here of a "foundational unity" since the givenness
of a determinate k is not necessarily, that is, not essentially and eternally
bound up with a determinate i.

> Every arbitrary alteration of k is an unambiguous condition for
> an alteration of i. [k conditions i] in such a way that the same
> stretch of time that is filled with the one dependency is also

filled with the other. . . . This dependency is mutual. . . . On
the other hand, we know that the connection between k and i
is not a firm one, as if . . . this condition were inward and indissoluble. [*DR*, § 51; cf. also § 49]

The connection between k and i is thus a matter of a factual, not an
essential co-existence. In spite of the aforementioned "mutual dependency," the k-component distinguishes itself within this co-existence insofar as it possesses the form and motivating force characteristic of a
potentiality belonging to the i.

If in the k-position of the eye I have within my visual field a
certain pictorial distribution, and if I would like to have a different [distribution], . . . then I know straightaway which eye-
movement I have to execute. [§ 51]

Although the k-course and the i-course coincide temporally, and
although they "correspond reciprocally and unambiguously with one another in respect of their fullness," there is no "consciousness of unity
pervading the series of k's" (§§ 51f.) that would correspond with the
formation of unity among the multiplicity of i's. This is connected with
the fact that the kinaesthetic sensations have no representational function and hence, even if they are apperceptively apprehended, do not
serve to constitute a specifically kinaesthetic object. This does not, however, exclude the possibility that the (arbitrary) k-courses arrange themselves within the "firmly delimited multiplicity" belonging to a particular
k-system (§ 51). Underlying the continuous, but "nowise stable" motivational unity of the multiplicities growing from the courses of k and i, is
the "stable and indestructible association" between " 'k as such' " and
the "identical multiplicity of loci in the pre-empirical field" (§§ 51f.).
This distinction between stable and modifiable kinaesthetic circumstances is the proper motivation for the above mentioned distinction between the stable system of loci of the i-multiplicities and the unities
constituted through the modification of this system by the actual course
of i-multiplicities.

If we now turn to a consideration of the gradations among various kinaesthetic *systems* and corresponding sensuous fields of sensation,
we must first of all recall the motivational nexus that conjoins with one
another all kinaesthetic systems and all fields of sensation. The "scope"
within which the appearances or sensations have their free play is an
ordinal nexus, a system of fixed loci with alterable covering. The mani-

fold points in this system of loci are all ultimately aligned toward the central point of optimal givenness. Moreover, this null-point of phenomenal orientation is determined from the standpoint of the kinaesthetic "I can" belonging to a bodily organism.

> [I]n order to be able to have an open horizon of unperceived things existing in themselves for me, I myself must already exist as a bodily organism for myself and thus constitute the null-point or null-member of the world and of things, whichever things you like. [*Ms. D 3*, 10a (1920)]

The bodily organism, conceived as a "null-point of orientation," is an "organism" with a potentiality for perception that is built up from diverse perceptual organs or diverse kinaesthetic systems. Corresponding with this gradation of kinaesthetic functions is a gradation of phenomenal fields as well as a gradation of appearing objects. The most primitive form of movement belonging to that bodily organism which functions as an organ of sight is eye-movement. Viewed more exactly, this basic kinaesthetic system breaks down into the kinaesthetic systems of one eye alone and of two eyes together (cf. *DR*, § 49 and app. IV). The kinaesthetic system of one eye alone and the corresponding visual field exhibit a parallel structuring, namely, a "null-point . . . , directions right, left, up, down" (350). The visual field of one eye alone is a two-dimensional continuum of possible movements. As a result of the "accommodation" proper to the kinaesthetic system of two eyes together, we have in the corresponding visual field a coordination of images by pairs, the images being combined into double-images which allow the phenomenal representation of the "relief" that belongs to a thing. Pre-thingly [*vordinglich*] or pre-spatial unities are constituted in the kinaesthetically motivated transformation of the visual field or in the continuous course of manifold images or fields of images. The continuous multiplicity of kinaestheses in the movements of the eyes, for example, motivates the constitution of an identical oculo-motor image (cf. § 63) and, at once, of a uniform oculo-motor field (cf. §§ 59f., 67).

These oculo-motor unities are, to be sure, unities within multiplicities; but they are not yet things, nor are they yet spaces for things. The same holds for cephalo-motor unities (cf. § 57). Although the consideration of various types of head-movement and movement of the torso, along with the reciprocal coordination of these movements, represents an important expansion of the oculo-motor field, the new "field of objects" constituted within a continuous multiplicity of oculo-motor fields is still not space, and the "objects" arranged within this field are "still not things" (§ 63). At the very best, that is, if we include not only the "turning of the head around its axis" but also a determinate series of further movements of the bodily organism (such as motivate no appearance of depth), cephalo-motor space is "a spherically enclosed space" or "an homogenous Riemannian space composed of two dimensions" (309ff.). But this "space" or field of objects still lacks depth. The continuous multiplicity of cephalo-motor fields of objects constitutes three-dimensional Euclidean space only when depth is added, that is, when we bring into consideration the kinaesthetic systems such as "walking" (318ff. and app. IV). Within the field of objects, these systems motivate the phenomena of concealing, turning, and, especially, expanding (cf. §§ 63, 67, 73; pp. 311ff.). Along with infinite space, including the dimension of depth, the closed unity of the three-dimensional objectivity of a thing is also constituted.

We cannot here reproduce the contents of the extremely careful analyses which Husserl devotes to these phenomena. They take the form of a gradual constitutional analysis in which the unities already constituted within a continuous multiplicity function in turn as multiplicities constituting a higher unity. This gradation in the constitution of things and space is motivated by the gradation of the corresponding kinaesthetic systems. The ultimate, that is, the most primitive multiplicities that constitute visual space, are the visual fields of one eye alone. These visual fields are systems of loci covered with diverse "images" or representational data of sensation. Husserl never tires of pointing out that the terms involved in describing the field of sensation, "terms such as line, point, locus, figure, magnitude, etc., [. . . may] never [be understood] in the thingly [dinglich] and empirical-spatial sense" (§ 48). However, Husserl goes still further and designates these pre-empirically extended data of sensation as really immanent contents of consciousness. Yet it has seemed highly problematical to many an interpreter to ascribe extension and qualitative coloring to really immanent contents of consciousness. From this critical stance sprang the suggestion of defining the representational data of sensation or the adumbrations of things as noematic correlates of the activity of consciousness (cf. Asemissen, Claesges). With this, there arises the possibility of a specifically and exclusively noematic analysis of perception. In such an analysis it is not the sensation underlying an apperceptive apprehension but the noematic appearance and its horizonal reference to further possible appearances that functions as the ultimate constitutive multiplicity. This noematic appearance, or the thing in the "how" of its appearing at any given moment, is a member of a so to speak monadological system of interdependent perceptual possibilities, a system which can be conceived as a pre-spatially extended field of consciousness (cf. Gurwitsch). Husserl's early, noetically oriented analyses of the structure of sensuous fields can be transferred relatively easily to the characterization of the field of noematic appearances. Indeed, Husserl himself struck out upon this path in later manuscripts, preserved in his literary remains but presently still unpublished (cf. the list of sources in Bernet, 1978a, 264 fn.).

5

The Phenomenology
of Intuitional Presentiation

§ 1. Phantasy, Picture-Consciousness, Memory

Since the 1890s, and particularly in connection with the preparation of his *Logical Investigations* (1900/01), Husserl was occupied with the domain of *intuitive acts*. He contrasted the latter with the conceptual presentations belonging to the domain of significations, which received primary attention in the six investigations published as part two of the *Logical Investigations* (cf. below, chap. 6). As early as texts dating from the 1890s, Husserl had discussed the distinction between "intuitional and conceptual presentations." Among the intuitional presentations he counted "the perceptual presentations, the physical-pictorial presentations, the phantasy presentations (presentations of memory and expectation)." In contrast with the consciousness of signification, in which an object or a state of affairs is *signified*, it is generally characteristic of intuitional presentations that in them "an object appears, and this is either the presented object *itself* or a *picture* [*Bild*] of the latter" (cf. *Ms. F I 19*, 174 [probably written in 1894]).[1]

As is well known, the subtitle of part two of the *Logical Investigations* is "Investigations Concerning the Phenomenology and Theory of Cognition." It is Husserl's view that the higher-level, conceptual and categorial acts of intending [*Bedeuten*], in which cognition comes to pregnant expression, are *founded* in the sensuous, intuitive acts of perception and their modifications. The phenomenological clarification of the consciousness of signification, of conceptual thinking and knowing, must therefore also determine the forms of intuitional consciousness in respect of their cognitive achievement. Since one is dealing with the "lowest stratum of intellective acts," in the case of the various kinds of intuitional consciousness, Husserl sees their analysis as *fundamental* for the phenomenological clarification of cognition, or, as Husserl preferred to say some years after the publication of the *Logical Investigations*, for the "phenomenology of reason" in the strict sense.[2]

One of the chief tasks for the analysis of the domain of intuitive acts consists in setting off the diverse forms of presentiation [*Vergegenwärtigung*] from the basic form of intuitional consciousness, namely, perception (cf. above, chap. 4) by bringing into relief the intentional characteristics of these various forms. The at first rather special-looking task to whose solution Husserl devoted his efforts again and again for many years, allowed him at last to catch sight of unsuspected depths and interconnections in the intentional life of consciousness, matters whose importance for his later doctrine of the constituting, transcendental subjectivity can scarcely be overestimated.

Husserl was first inspired to concern himself with intuitive acts by *Brentano*.[3] He mentions more than once the latter's "unforgettable course of lectures on 'Selected Psychological and Aesthetical Questions' " in which Brentano "strove nearly exclusively after an analytical clarification of phantasy presentations in comparison with perceptual presentations."[4] In those lectures, after detailed discussion of the philosophical tradition from Aristotle on down to his own day, Brentano arrived at the following determination: "Phantasy presentations are nonintuitional or *inauthentic* [*uneigentlich*] *presentations* which approximate to intuitional presentations. . . . The border is admittedly blurred."[5] According to Brentano, the approximation to the intuitional presentations of perception is based on the fact that "the phantasy presentations contain, as it were, an intuitional nucleus" (Brentano, 84), albeit most phantasy presentations are in fact not intuitions but concepts with an intuitional nucleus (cf. 83). Brentano had exhibited the importance of the *inauthenticity* of phantasial presentations, as well as of the presentations of others' psychical phenomena and of one's own past and future psychical phenomena (cf. 83f.), as over against the authenticity of perceptual presentations. At the time of the conception of the *Logical Investigations*, Husserl defined this same contrast by distinguishing the act-character of *pictoriality* [*Bildlichkeit*] or "picturing [*verbildlichend*] apprehension" from the act-character of the self-giving of the object in perception.[6]

Regarded purely from the viewpoint of consciousness, an object of phantasy, memory, or expectation would be characterized in contrast with an object of perception in its givenness, by the fact that it does not appear as being "present itself," "bodily [*leibhaft*]" or, as it were, "in its own person," but rather merely hovers before me, merely is as if it were there, appears to me "in a picture" (a mental image, a memory-image). Husserl will always preserve the pair of opposites "bodily," and so on, and "as if," in respect of the modes of appearance of perceptual as over against presentiational consciousness. However, after the *Logical Investigations*, the path of his thinking led him from the incipient theory of the pictoriality of intuitional presentation—by way of a concretely executed analysis of the deep-seated distinctions between picture-consciousness and pure phantasy, or memory, and by way of the inclusion of internal time-consciousness (1904/05)—to the doctrine of the reproduction of acts, that is, to an insight into the essence of the intentional implication of another consciousness (one's own and then also another's in the actually performed consciousness).

Husserl usually proceeded in his concrete analysis in such a way as, by means of initial observations of diverse but related kinds of consciousness, and guided for the most part by ordinary linguistic usage, to create an "horizon of comparison which we must have at our disposal from the outset in order to be able step by step to submit each of these kinds of intuition [perception, phantasy, picture-consciousness, memory] (each of which unveils its peculiar eidetic characteristics only in contrast with the parallel kinds) to an eidetic cognition" (*Ms. A VI 11 I*, 67b [1911/1912]). Without being able in the framework of this study to enter into the individual steps of thought and their frequent *aporiai*, we shall attempt to bring together some of the essential results, often situated years apart, as links in a phenomenological theory of intuitional presentation.[7]

Regarding the matter quite generally, one must distinguish in this analysis between the moment of the *intuitiveness* (with its possible degrees of vividness, adequacy, clarity, obscurity, emptiness) and the moment of the positing (that is, of the doxical modalities) of the acts here in question.[8] What became decisive for Husserl's doctrine was the "intimate connection between intuitive acts and time-consciousness," a connection which he had recognized since the time of his lectures in the winter semester of 1904/05 (cf. *PITC*, 394). For only with the return to the fundamental, temporally interpreted distinction between impression (presentation [*Gegenwärtigung*]) and reproduction (presentiation [*Vergegenwärtigung*]), did Husserl succeed in making intelligible the distinction between the immediate intuitability of what is bodily present [*leibhaft*] (in perception) and what is not bodily present (in phantasy, memory, expectation) (cf. *Ms. A VI 11 I*, 61–95; *PBE*, nos. 12, 13, 14 and passim). On the side of positing, one must distinguish between actuality (positionality) and inactuality (neutrality). Husserl defines both pairs of distinctions, presentation and presentiation, as well as actuality and inactuality, as intersectional (cf. *PBE*, no. 13 [1910], and no. 16 [1912]). Thus, in respect of the domain of intuitional presentiation which interests us here, he speaks of a *positing* presentiation (memory, co-presentiation, expectation) and a *nonpositing* presentiation (pure phantasy) (cf. no. 12 [probably from 1910]).[9] The distinction that presented so many difficulties at the time of the *Logical Investigations*, that between pure phantasy and normal picture-consciousness, is finally universalized terminologically as the distinction between reproductive phantasy (or presentiation) and perceptive phantasy, that is, presentiation [*Vergegenwärtigung*] in a picture, in pictorial representation [*Darstellung*] (cf., e.g., nos. 16 and 18a [1918]).

Let us now attempt to gain a somewhat more precise idea, successively, (a) of the distinction, founded in internal time-consciousness, between impression and reproduction, that is, of the reproductive modification; (b) of the aspect of positing and neutralizing, that is, of the qualitative modification; and (c) of the peculiarity of picture-consciousness in contrast with reproductive presentiation.

(a) In his lectures of 1904/05 Husserl arrived at the conclusion that pure phantasy and memory, as pure, simple presentiational consciousness, must be sharply distinguished from perception, as presentational consciousness, but also from ordinary picture-consciousness which requires the mediation of something appearing perceptually in the present. For the purpose of more deeply clarifying this pair of opposites, presentation and presentiation, Husserl began an analysis of internal time-consciousness in the final portion of his lectures. In connection with the intuitive acts, it is a question of forming a concept of the fundamental distinction between "time-perception" as the originary time-consciousness constitutive for "being-present," and "time-phantasy" which is constitutive for "not-being-present" (being-past, being-in-the-future, and in general, being presentiated) (*PITC*, 16 / C, 36f.; cf. above, chap. 3, § 2).

In the years following his lectures from the winter semester of 1904/05, Husserl elaborated ever more clearly the more complex—in comparison with impressional presentation—intentional structure of presentation. He recognized that presentations "have a second, differently structured intentionality, one which is proper to them alone and not to all immanent experiences" (*PITC*, 52 / C, 75). This concerns the fact that a presentation is not merely consciousness of an object but is in itself, in "inner consciousness" or time-consciousness, also reproductive consciousness of the corresponding impression, of the corresponding originary course in which consciousness of the now presentiated object is primordially constituted (in the past, in the future, or as pure possibility in phantasy). In a note probably written in 1911/12, Husserl sums up the terms of this universal structure or "*eidetic law*" of *intentional modification or implication* among intuitional presentations, casting it in a perspicuous "formula." It is the case that "$R(P_a)=V_a$. For example, the presentation of a house [V_a] and the reproduction of the perception of this house [$R(P_a)$] exhibit the same phenomena" (128 / C, 177f.; cf. *PBE*, 311). Normally, that is, whenever I do not perform a "reflection in phantasy or memory," my intentionality is directed toward the presentiated object. However, it is not a matter here of a "simple" intentionality but of a "peculiar mediacy" (*EP* II, 116) that is no longer interpreted as pictoriality but points to the fact that for me, for example, the past can not "directly" attain to givenness *again* but can do so only upon being mediated by a reproductive consciousness of that past experience of mine which was constitutive for the remembered event.

The insight into this structure of the intentional implication of another consciousness in the presently actual consciousness may have been decisive for Husserl's revision of the original content-apprehension–schema, with the help of which he had previously wanted to establish the distinction between perception and phantasy (presentation). About 1909 he was able to write the following:

> I had the schema "content-of-apprehension and apprehension" and that certainly makes good sense. But, first of all in the case of perception as concrete, immanent experience, we do not have a color as a content of apprehension and then the character of the apprehension which creates the appearance. And similarly in the case of phantasy we do not again have a color as a content of apprehension and then an altered apprehension, the one which creates the phantasy appearance. Rather: "consciousness" consists *through and through* of consciousness, and a sensation as well as a phantasm is "conscious-

ness." There we have in the first instance perception as *impressional* (originary) consciousness of the present, consciousness of what is itself there, and the like; and [we have] phantasy (in the sense in which perception is the opposite!) as *the reproductively modified consciousness of the present*, consciousness of what is as if it were itself there, of what is as if it were present, [consciousness of our] phantasy of the present. [*PBE*, 265f.]

We may say in general that Husserl understood the reproductive structure of presentation in such a way that a "*presentiated present*," with all its modes of the flow of consciousness, was taken by him to be intentionally implied in this structure at all times, be it a past, future, possible, merely phantasized, or alien present.

(b) In order more concretely to clarify these diverse kinds of intuitional presentiation, the aspect of *positing*, the "qualitative modification," must be drawn into the analysis. Within the domain of reproductive modification Husserl arrived at the distinction between a positing presentiation and a nonpositing, inactual or neutralized presentiation (in pure phantasy). In section 111 of *Ideas I* (1913) we may read the following, concise characterization of phantasy: "Stated more precisely, phantasizing is, as such, the neutralizing modification of [a] 'positing' presentiation, that is, of memory in the broadest possible sense" (*Id* I, 224). In order adequately to understand this relation among phantasy, memory, and neutralizing modification, it must be kept in mind that phantasy had been defined as an act of presentiation, that is, as a reproduction of consciousness in the actually performed phantasial consciousness.

The doctrine of the neutralizing modification forms a universalization of the doctrine of "qualitative modification" found in the *Logical Investigations* (cf. *LI* II/1 [V], §§ 39f.). Qualitative modification is introduced in the *Logical Investigations* with respect to the class of objectifying acts, that is, as a modification taking place inside the acts of the "quality" "presentation [*Vorstellung*]."[10] In relation to these objectifying acts, Husserl sets forth the possibility of the transition from the *positing* act of presentation to an act of *mere* presentation of the same material, and the reverse (cf. *LI* II/1 [V], 435, 448). It is thus not a matter of a transition from one act-quality (class) to another, for example, the transition from a perceptual presentation to the complex act of joy which belongs to a new, founded act-quality (class). It is a matter of a "qualitative modification," that is, precisely, a possible modification of the quality "presentation," inside of the same act-quality. Instead of performing a presentation primordially, actually, as a positing, believing act, it is possible to perform it as a mere presentation, as a nonpositing act, leaving the issue of belief undecided. This qualitative modification is not able to be iterated. "If the 'believing' has been transformed into [a] 'mere presenting,' then we can at best return to the believing; but there is no modification which repeats itself and continues in the same sense" (452).

Ideas I introduces the neutralizing modification as a universal modification of consciousness as such. At the lowest level is the primordial *doxa*, the primordial belief of the perceiving consciousness, to which all modifications of belief (deeming possible, presumption, doubt, question, and so on) are referred precisely as doxic modalities of the primordial belief. The non-doxic acts (the non-objectifying acts in the sense understood by the *Logical Investigations*, for example, wishing, desiring, rejoicing, and so on) also refer intentionally to the primordial *doxa*. The universalization consists in Husserl's understanding all acts as positing (thetic) acts (among which the doxic acts form the special class of acts which posit being) having their possible counterpart in *neutral* acts as counterparts to all "achieving [*Leisten*]" (cf. §§ 109, 117).[11]

Now Husserl understood *pure phantasy* as a neutralizing modification of a special kind of positing, namely, the positing *presentations*. The term "memory [*Erinnerung*]" serves him in the manuscripts (cf., e.g., *PBE*, 246, 396), as well as in section 111 of *Ideas I*, as a designation for the *positing* presentations, namely, pre-presentation, co-presentation, and re-presentation, in their reproductive structure. In Husserl's view, memories of the immanent experience, as possible parallels to it, correspond to every immanent experiencing as originary consciousness of the immanent experience (*Id* I, 225). This being so, the phantasy modification, as a neutralizing modification of memory, also shows itself to be of universal significance (224). Stated quite generally, it is accordingly the case in phantasizing that I do *not actually* experience all the immanent experiences, whichever they may be, but only presentiate them to myself (in imagination [*einbildend*]), perform them only inactually [*inaktuell*] in a neutralizing manner, that is, without a positing of belief, on the condition of bracketing or leaving undecided every achievement of consciousness. I phantasize myself into an experiencing (whether I thereby draw myself into the phantasy-world or not); I feel *as if* I were experiencing, seeing, hearing, speaking, doubting, questioning, willing, desiring, and so on. The whole affair, be it a coherent phantasy-world, be it an incoherent sequence of individual phantasy situations, is given—in the modification of the as-if, without a performance of the believing or positing consciousness—as unreality (cf., e.g., *PBE*, nos. 15, 18a).

In contrast with this, it is essential for the *positing* presentations, that I perform them in the consciousness of the actuality of belief. In the case of a memory, for example, it is not simply so, that an imagined sequence of immanent experiences is presentiated free of all positing. Rather, the reproductively performed immanent experiences are given in the consciousness of the "again," which is a "believing consciousness" (cf. nos. 11, 12, 13). Above all, this also means that forward-pointing and backward-pointing intentions adhere inseparably to these experiences, and the intentions serve to arrange them in the total nexus of the stream of my past consciousness (cf., e.g., app. XXIX [probably written in 1910]). Analogous relationships would hold for presentations relative to future experience (cf. e.g., no. 13 [1910]). This positing, believing consciousness does not imply, of course, that I cannot be deceived or err in relation to presentiated situations. On the contrary, deception is generally speaking possible in two respects, either in relation to the reproduced act (I had not read it, rather it was told to me), or in relation to the presentiated object (it was not x, but y). It is characteristic, however, for the positing presentations, that I play one positing off against the other, as it were; that I move on the terrain of *doxa* and all the possible doxic modalities; and, as long as I do not become aware of the deception which memory has suffered, that I believe or posit that it *was* so or, doubting it, that I ask myself whether it was *so* or whether it was not rather *so* (cf. no. 15, and esp. app. XXXVII [1912]). Ideally, it would be possible to reproduce the sequence of immanent experiences from the remembered past or from the anticipated future down to the presently actual now. In the case of pure phantasy, however, that is, phantasy free of the consciousness of being mixed with now or once actual experience, such a continuity makes no sense. For the world of phantasy is thoroughly a world of the as-if, without an absolute spatial and temporal position in objective space and time (cf., e.g., app. LVI; no. 19a; *EJ*, §§ 38–42).

We now have to point out a phenomenon bearing on all reproductive, intuitional presentations and submitted to detailed considerations by Husserl beginning with his lectures on "Phantasy and Picture-Consciousness" in the winter semester of 1904/05 (cf. *PBE*, no. 1, §§ 24, 32; chap. 7; apps. IX [1905], XLIV [probably 1908], L and LI [probably 1912 or somewhat later]). This is the phenomenon of the *overlapping* [*Verdeckung*] or the *conflict of intuitions*, which is connected with the fact that in the stream of consciousness nothing is thinkable in isolation from the rest of the stream. Husserl speaks of the "stream of presently actual positing," "presently actual apprehensional intentions which organize themselves again and again into new [intentions], impart a force of coherence to everything which is inserted into them, and, to be sure, leave nothing outside of themselves." Whatever then is given in isolation, such as a phantasy, "yet in truth *covers up* [*verdeckt*] something in actuality" (485). Husserl brings out the point that "space is only intuitable once." "Spatial intuition 'covers up' spatial intuition." In the example of phantasy, I am turned toward a phantasy object, I look at a spatial world within a definite orientation.

> At the same time, however, I can direct my glance at the perceived spatial world with its orientation. If I do that, the other [world] vanishes: And this vanishing is not a mere darkening, but a being pressed down to an "empty" presentation. [ibid.]

An *intuitable "at the same time"* of present [*Gegenwart*] and nonpresent [*Nichtgegenwart*] (a nonpresent posited in the past or the future or merely phantasized) is impossible. Attention to the one *clashes* with a simultaneous attention to the other (cf. no. 1, § 32; app. IX). My actual point of view in the here and now, which opens up the visual field of perception to me, cannot *at the same time* be the point of view of the nonpresent. Rather, the latter is a past, a future, or a merely imagined point of view reproduced in presentation, a point of view that opens up to me a presentiated visual field which in turn covers up the actually present visual field precisely to the extent that my attention is devoted to the nonpresent. It is very important to notice that in these relationships, "however much it may lose its 'actuality,' 'withdraw from me,' " the perceptual world does not vanish from my consciousness when I perform a presentation. "It is always there perceptually" (*EJ*, 205 / C & A, 175f.). If in performing a presentation I were completely to lose consciousness of the perceptual world, then I would no longer be presentiating but presenting by way of *dreaming*, hallucinating, suffering a trance or a vision; and what were thus intuited would then have the character of the "itself-there," of bodily present actuality, such as is the case in perception; it would "also [be] fitted out with the character of 'belief,' " and no longer merely that of the "as if again" or the "as if" within the consciousness of semblance [*Schein*] (cf. *PBE*, no. 1, § 20; 150f.). A *unity* of simultaneous intuition in relation to perceived and remembered or phantasized objects is thus not possible. In intuition I am turned either toward the present or toward the nonpresent. However, there exists "among all immanent experiences of *one I*, a temporal unity," and so, "on the basis of being constituted together in the flow of *one* inner time-consciousness, the possibility exists of producing an intuitable connec-

tion among all the objects constituted therein" (*EJ*, 206f.). This unifying
I-relation, elaborated by Husserl in connection with his analysis of intuitional presentations, will be discussed in somewhat greater detail in
chapter 8, "The 'I' and the Person." It belongs thoroughly to the analysis of the essential moments of intuitional presentations.

(c) The "permeation [*Durchsetzung*]" or "interpenetration
[*Durchdringung*]" of intuitions "with conflict [*Widerstreit*]" is Husserl's
name for a phenomenon differing in kind from overlapping [*Verdeckung*]
and yet somehow akin to it. He finds this phenomenon actualized in ordinary *picture-consciousness*, that is, in presentation which is no longer
purely reproductive but is rather *perceptually founded* (cf. *PBE*, nos. 1, 16,
17; apps. IX, L; as well as most of the texts in this volume which have to
do with picture-consciousness). Inasmuch as he himself wavers a great
deal, it is not an easy matter briefly to summarize Husserl's doctrine of
picture-consciousness. An essential point forms the demarcation of picture-consciousness from fiction-consciousness (illusion), from which
Husserl's early analysis of picture-consciousness, with its accent on con-
flicting intentions, was probably too little clearly differentiated. Husserl
also oriented his analysis at first too much in respect of the idea of
depictability [*Abbildlichkeit*], such as would be found in a portrait. Later,
however, in discussing *aesthetic-artistic* representation [*Darstellung*], he
sought to understand "pictoriality [*Bildlichkeit*] in the sense of perceptual phantasy as immediate imagination" apart from the function of
depictability (514, no. 18b [1918]).

Just what is presentiating *in a picture*, understood initially as consciousness of a depiction [*Abbildbewußtsein*] (photographs, portrait and
landscape paintings, sculptures)? Husserl distinguishes the following
three types of objects [*Objekte*] which are implicit in picture-consciousness [*Bildbewußtsein*]: (1) The picture as a *physical* thing on the wall; the
canvas, or the photograph printed on paper, which hangs there, can be
torn, and so on, just like any physical object, and which is given perceptually; (2) the mental *picture-object* [*Bildobjekt*], which appears "perceptually," thus and so in its colors and forms, and yet is not apprehended as
reality. Insofar as I live within the picture-consciousness, this picture-
object is given to me in intuition. In it I apprehend the assimilating
[*verähnlichend*] traits *as such*, that is, as representing [*darstellend*]; (3) the
picture-subject [*Bildsujet*]; for example, the living person or the landscape itself. Fundamental is the *relation of similarity* between that which
appears and that which is depicted.

The nonpresent subject does not thereby appear yet a second
time in addition to the appearance of the picture-object (except when

the subject chances still to be present outside of the pictorial space as well!). Rather, it appears, it is depicted [*bildet sich ab*] or represented [*stellt sich dar*], *in* the "present" picture-object itself. In the appearing picture-object I "view" the subject *immanently*; *in* the photographic picture I "see" my friend. Thus, this double objectivity, consisting of the appearing picture and the depicted thing, does not stem within the picture-consciousness from two *separated* apprehensions making their appearance merely *comparatively* in a relation of similarity. Rather, according to Husserl, two apprehensions *penetrate* one another in a foundational relationship within the pictorial presentation. They do so in such a way that the objectifying apprehension constitutive of the picture-object *simultaneously* furnishes *the foundation for* the presentation which, by means of the picture-object, constitutes the other, nonpresent object (the subject), that is, the foundation for the inherently dependent or founded *representation of similarity* [*Ähnlichkeitsrepräsentation*] which produces the relation to the subject (cf. no. 1, esp. § 14). The conscious relation to the subject is consciousness of the *presentation of something which does not appear, within that which does appear*, a consciousness which arises on the basis of similarity (ibid.).

In his lectures of 1904/05, Husserl primarily analyzed the relationship of conflict between the appearance of the picture-object and the physical picture-thing [*Bildding*]. On the terrain of the schema "content and apprehension," he sets forth the fact that the sensuous contents seem to be *the same* for the picture-thing as for the appearance of the picture-object, whereas it is excluded that *two* appearances could come forth *simultaneously* on the basis of the same contents. Because the world, constituted in perception during the waking life of picture-consciousness, is continuously co-present for consciousness, and because the picture-thing, as a physical thing, belongs itself in this uniform perceptual nexus, there now emerges a *conflict* between the picture-thing and the picture-object, insofar as the sensuous contents get robbed, as it were, from the picture-thing by the *pictorial* apprehension, that is, insofar as they are claimed for the constitution of the picture-object. With its presentiating relation to the subject, the appearance of the picture-object "triumphs" in this conflict but does so at the cost of reality. The picture-object has the character of *irreality*, of *mere semblance* in the midst of the perceptually appearing surroundings of the picture (cf. no. 1, esp. the summarizing account in §§ 14, 25). On the other hand, Husserl also strongly emphasizes in these lectures the relationship of conflict "between the appearance of the picture-object and the presentation of the subject which gets intertwined with it or rather thrust over into it"

(§ 25), a conflict which rests precisely upon the relationship of greater or lesser similarity between the representation [*Darstellung*] and what is represented [*Dargestelltes*]. In other texts, Husserl also points to the "empirical conflict" between that which appears and that which is required by empirical experience ("human beings in photographic colors do not exist") (cf., e.g., app. I, § 13; apps. VII, VIII).

Husserl makes clear in numerous texts that, in the case of a picture, the consciousness of semblance or irreality cannot be a matter of fiction-consciousness in the sense of an *illusion*. The decisive factor is the following: The *fictum* proper to an illusion appears directly within the unity of a reality (for example, a waxen figure which I perceive as this or that person). It is an appearance with a positional character that now comes into conflict with other positings such that in this conflict of positings the *fictum* is exposed as an illusion, as a mere semblance: "It was not this or that person but only a waxen doll." By contrast, the character of irreality in the case of the picture is not the result of a conflict of diverse tendencies of belief, but rests upon my phantasizing into a perceptual appearance something which is not immediately present at all. Properly speaking, the picture does not "appear" within the unity of reality, "but within a space of its own which in itself has no direct relation to real space."

> With the normal picture, . . . [indeed,] already with the picture-object, where this stands out decidedly from the picture-subject, I have no consciousness of reality whatsoever, not even an "uninhibited" [consciousness of reality]. I have no inclination whatsoever to take it for real. I take it much as [I would take] a reproductive mental image, which I might rather vividly phantasize into reality, whereby it [scl. the mental image] also covers up real things, albeit in a peculiar manner. It also "appears," then, among the things and in the same space, and yet not in the manner of a reality. It is in this way that the *fictum* appears in the case of picture-consciousness, without having the character of a reality [and] without laying "claim" upon reality, a claim which would first have to be annulled. [480f.; cf. also no. 17]

Picture-consciousness *is* presentation, but not purely reproductive like phantasy. Rather, it is a perceptual presentation, penetrating a founding perceptual consciousness "very much as in the case of the signing [*signierend*] or symbolizing function: The symbol appears for itself but is the bearer of a relation to something else [which is] designated therein.

Similarly, in the case of the authentic pictorial function, the 'picture' is constituted in its own objective apprehension [and is the] bearer of a relation to that which has been depicted" (82).

An essential phenomenon remains to be mentioned. All the intuitional presentations that we have discussed can be *iterated*. They can be implicated in one another in manifold ways, for example, as the memory of a phantasy of a picture or, to take the example Husserl was fond of citing, as more complicated pictorial presentations (cf., e.g., app. XVIII [probably 1898]; *Id* I, § 101 and passim; cf. also § 112).

> He who is practiced in conscious reflection (and [who] has already learned at all to see the data of intentionality), will without further ado see the stages of consciousness which are present in the cases of phantasies within phantasies, or memories within memories or within phantasies. [*Id* I, § 112]

In the *Ideas*, Husserl writes thus especially in connection with his critique of the "Empiricist" conception of consciousness which he himself had not completely avoided in earlier years.

> Our assertion of the possibility of iterated, reproductive (as well as depictive) modifications, might knock up against rather general opposition. That [situation] will be altered only when practice in genuine phenomenological analysis has become more widespread. . . . As long as one treats immanent experiences as [if they were] "contents" or physical "elements" which . . . are viewed as some kind of "little things" [*Sächelchen*]; as long as one believes accordingly that the distinction between "sensational contents" and corresponding "phantasial contents" can be found in the objective characteristics of "intensity," "fullness," and the like; [for just *so* long the situation] . . . cannot get better. [ibid.]

In closing, we may say that Husserl's insight into the intentional modifications or implications of consciousness within consciousness, which confront us in his analyses of intuitional presentations, came to be of quite fundamental importance for his concrete theory of the intentionally performing, world-constituting subjectivity. It acquired this importance because in every type of such acts it is possible "to exhibit the wondrously interlaced intentionality and thus at the same time to render initially intelligible . . . the peculiarity of its subjective being and its subjective performance" (*EP* II, 128). "Yet let us take notice," Husserl says in the same text from the course of lectures of 1923/24, "how transcendental subjectivity in general is given in stages of relative immediacy and mediacy, and exists [at all] only insofar as it is given in such stages, *stages of an intentional implication*" (175).

§ 2. Our Experience of the Other

An Overview of Husserl's Occupation with the Problem of Intersubjectivity

In his published writings, Husserl did not speak in detail regarding our experience of the other until the appearance of *Formal and Transcendental Logic* (1929) and *Cartesian Meditations* (1931). As a consequence, one was for a long time able to believe that he had devoted himself to these problems only in his old age. However, the publication in the *Husserliana* of texts from Husserl's literary remains, especially volumes XIII, XIV, and XV, *On the Phenomenology of Intersubjectivity*, has made clear that from quite early on, beginning about 1905, he attempted again and again to come to terms with these questions. In the *Logical Investigations* (1901), in his discussion of the linguistic expression and its signification, Husserl had expressly disregarded the communicative function of language and so suspended the concomitant problem of intersubjectivity (*LI* II/1 (I), §§ 7–9). However, when in about 1905 he established his philosophical research upon its own methodologically reflected plane by introducing the phenomenological reduction, it likewise became necessary for him, beginning from this fundamental standpoint, to take a stance in regard to the problem of our experience of the other and intersubjectivity. He had to pursue the question how, from the standpoint of pure, transcendental consciousness, account could be taken of our experience of the other and of a plurality of subjects. On the one hand, he did this methodologically by "extending the transcendental reduction to intersubjectivity," a step which he succeeded in taking in 1910 in his lecture on the "Basic Problems of Pheomenology" (published in *PI* I, no. 6). On the other hand, he did it by means of the intentional analysis of our consciousness of the other (the consciousness which the reflecting subject has of other subjects). Husserl did not occupy himself exhaustively with the question how these two spheres of problems are to be linked systematically with one another.[12]

In his analysis of the experience of other psychical beings, Husserl took his departure from the fact that this experience can be understood neither as an authentic perception (the others's psychical experiences are not authentically perceived), nor as an authentic, logical inference. He conducted this analysis in large part in an attempt to come to terms with Theodor Lipps's theory of empathy and his critique of the so-called "theory of inference by analogy" in respect of our experience of the other (cf. nos. 2, 13; apps. X, XVI; *PI* II, no. 12). He took the term "empathy" over from Lipps but never accepted it in the Lippsian sense of an instinctive projection of one's own immanent experiences into bodies outside of one oneself (*PI* I, 335ff.; *EP* II, 63 fn.). Even his original approach to the problem, which he had already developed prior to 1910, does not lean on the example of Lipps's point of departure from the so-called movements of expression (of joy, anger, and so on). Rather, it begins with the conception of an external body as a sentient body or one capable of sensation (*PI* I, nos. 3, 4). No later than about 1914, however, Husserl abandoned this approach to the problem. He did so upon gaining the insight that no fields of sensation whatsoever can be empathized *immediately* in an externally perceived body, but that such empathy is possible only by means of presentiating the other's "point of view," a point of view from which the organism [*Leib*] proper to it is not a merely externally perceived body [*Körper*] (329).

During the time around 1914 in which he occupied himself in great detail with the problem of our experience of the other (nos. 8–13), his primary concern lay with the question of how it is at all possible for there to emerge a consciousness of the distinction between one's own and the other's immanent experiences; and, on the basis of the external presentation of oneself (presenting oneself as situated in external space), he sought to prove the possibility of our experience of the other even prior to its actuality (no. 8). He later rejected this attempt as "too constructive" (254, fn. 3) and proceeded to solve the problem of our consciousness of the other by means of a constitutional intentional analysis beginning directly with the fact of our experience of the other. He continued to occupy himself with this problem subsequently, addressing it mainly in 1921/22 while preparing a never-finished systematic work (cf. *PI* II, 1ff.); in his course of lectures, "Introduction to Phenomenology," from the winter semester of 1926/27 (393ff.); and in the last of the five *Cartesian Meditations* (written in 1929 and now published in *Husserliana* I). In this fifth of the *Cartesian Meditations* he portrayed the problem in a systematic, although in part summary fashion. Still, he was not fully satisfied with his handling of the matter and took it up anew again and again during the 1930s (cf. *PI* III).

The Sphere of Ownness or the Primordinal[13] Sphere

For Husserl, the phenomenological problem of our experience of the other is to discern in which explicit and implicit intentional syntheses and motivations the other comes to be manifested within my (transcendentally apprehended) consciousness and to be certified as existing (cf. *CM*, 133; cf., e.g., *PI* I, no. 8). In order to gain an understanding of our thus examined experience of the other, Husserl proceeds in the *Cartesian Meditations*, but also either explicitly or implicitly in other texts devoted to the problem of our experience of the other, by seeking first, "by means of a peculiar sort of thematical epoché," "to disregard all the constitutional achievements of such intentionality as is related immediately or mediately to an other subjectivity" (124) and to place himself on the basis of a sphere proper to the transcendental "I." It is in departing from this "sphere of ownness" or "primordinal sphere," thus-called by Husserl, that the constitution of the *other* must be understood.

It is not easy to understand what this sphere of ownness or primordinal sphere is. Indeed, in Husserl's reflections on this matter, two concepts stemming systematically from different contexts are often intermingled. The two different concepts have in common the fact that both designate a sphere of the "I" which is negatively determined by means of excluding everything other, all other consciousness. In positive terms, however, Husserl considers the sphere of ownness or the primordinal sphere in two respects. On the one hand, he takes it to mean the sphere of the most primordial [*ursprünglichst*] self-givenness imaginable (133), the sphere of the "best originality [*Originalität*] conceivable" (*PI* III, 10); and "primordinality" would seem for him to stand initially for "primordinal originality" (cf. *PI* II, 389f.). The other, understood as alien consciousness and as the content of this consciousness, is not given in such originality.

> Were that the case, were that which is essential to the other's own self accessible in a direct manner, then it would merely be a moment of my own essence, and, finally, he and I would be one and the same. [*CM*, 139]

This concept of primordinality as defined by originality is characterized especially by the fact that my experiences of the other, the so-called empathies of the "I," also belong in this primordinal sphere thus defined (125, 131; cf. *PI* III, 6–8, 11f.). For the empathies of the "I" are, indeed, its own immanent experiences and, in contrast with alien immanent experiences, are themselves given to the "I" in the best originality conceivable.

As defined in this manner, the primordinal sphere or sphere of ownness is thus by no means a solipsistic sphere, for it also embraces the ego's immanent experiences of the other. What is excluded is alone the intentional correlates (noemata) of these immanent experiences. This sphere encompasses all immanent experiences of the "I" whatsoever.

> The primordinal, concrete subjectivity embraces all modes of consciousness, even the modes of empathy and those which understand the expression of persons in objective things [Sachen]. It encompasses them as originally experienced and able to be experienced. It encompasses the modes of consciousness in which nature, spirit in all its senses, human and animal spirit, objective spirit as culture, spiritual being as family, association, state, nation, humankind, are in force. [PI III, 559]

This "sphere of the original [Originalsphäre]," as Husserl also says, thus designates that which is *directly* accessible to the "I" within the entirety of its experience. It is the ensemble of everything which is itself given in the original within all the experiences of the "I," everything which is not merely intended indirectly. But it can make up no concrete part, that is, no independently possible part, no independent stage in the constitutional building up of experience. It is rather something in my experience that is "pervasive throughout this experience" (CM, 129). The sphere of the original may not, then, be thought of as an independent, founding stratum, if only because according to Husserl himself immanent experiences are inseparable from their intentional correlates (noemata).

According to Husserl, the ensemble of everything that is itself given "in the original"—and this includes "nature" as well, although not in its intersubjective sense but only insofar as it is originally experienced by the "I"—is the whole of everything which is proper [eigen] to the "I." It makes up that "which I am, in full concretion within myself or, as we also say, within my monad" (135, 125). If Husserl's concept of the monad is defined in this way by original self-givenness then for him the individual monad can be neither something independent, nor, in this sense, something concrete. Indeed, Husserl says that with the monad it is only a matter of a "relative concretion," that this "is what it is only as a *socius* of a sociality" (PI III, 193).

> It is not as if each monad were for itself . . . and thus had being apart from the other monads. Rather, each one—insofar as

within its being it has intentionally constituted the others, [that
is, insofar as it has experience of others,] (just as each one, in
its present, has constituted [the] past)—cannot be apart from
the others. [194; cf. 370f.]

According to this concept of the sphere of ownness or primordinality,
the monad is the dimension of that which is "given itself, primordially-
originally [uroriginal]" (app. XXXVII) to the "I"; it is the dimension in
which the others are "mirrored."

That is *one* of the concepts of primordinality or the sphere of ownness which play a role in Husserl's determination of the point of departure for his intentional analysis of our experience of the other. At the
same time, however, there is yet another concept at work here, a concept
that one could circumscribe as the "*solipsistic sphere*," thus contrasting it
with the first concept, which was characterized as the "sphere of the
original." In precisely the same passage in the *Cartesian Meditations* in
which Husserl says that our experiences of others (empathies) belong to
the sphere of ownness (*CM*, 125, 131; cf. *PI* III, 6f., 8, 11, 12), he also
explains in contradiction to this that in order to gain the sphere of ownness it is necessary to suspend "the constitutional achievements of our
experience of the other," that is, the intentional correlates of our experience of the other, "*and along with it all modes of consciousness referring to
the other*," that is, the immanent experiences [*Erlebnisse*] in our experience of the other [*Fremderfahrung*] (*CM*, 125 [our emphasis]; cf. *PI* III, 7,
8). The sphere of ownness or the primordinal sphere thereby gains for
Husserl the sense of a stratum of experience prior to our experience of
the other, a stratum of experience belonging to the "I," which is supposed to underlie and found the higher stratum, our experience of the
other. Guided by such a concept of the primordinal sphere or the sphere
of ownness, Husserl could also assert the independence of this sphere
(*CM*, 127) and define this sphere by means of its inseparability from the
"I" (124f., 134f.; *PI* III, 6), something that would not have been feasible
in terms of the first concept, the sphere of the original, since the others,
as intentional correlates of the empathies belonging to the sphere of the
original, are inseparable (*PI* III, 191). Whereas in the sense of originality
the sphere of ownness or the primordinal sphere is a dependent moment
pervading *all* experiences of the ego (*CM*, 129), in the sense of the solipsistic sphere it is an independent foundation, a "substratum" of experience, which brings to givenness only a bare "nature" under the
exclusion of all spiritual or cultural predicates (127, 136; *PI* III, 8).

Husserl did become conscious of this ambiguity, but not until he had written the *Cartesian Meditations*. In a text composed just a few months after the latter work, he writes the following:

> *The solipsistically reduced world is not to be confused with the primordinal world, nor the solipsistic reduction with the primordinal reduction.* For the latter is the reduction *from* that [portion] of the world which holds good by the measure of my experience, *to* that [portion] of the world which I experience and always can experience *originaliter*. I am thereby reduced to my primordinal "I" as a stratum of my concrete "I." To the primordinal belong all my empathizing, immanent experiences, not, however, the others who are, albeit legitimately, experienced therein. And [the case is] similar with all determinations of intersubjective culture. [*PI* II, 51]

In a text stemming from 1934, Husserl speaks of an "essentially founded ambiguity [characteristic] of the talk about primordinality."

> In the primordially methodological sense it signifies the abstraction that I, the ego of the reductive attitude, consummate in phenomenologizing when I abstractively eliminate all "empathies." If afterwards I say "primordinal ego," then it takes on the signification of the proto-modal monad into which the proto-modal empathy is also taken up. [635]

Thus, according to this text, the primordial sense of primordinality would be the solipsistic sense. But in the *Cartesian Meditations*, unseparated from this and simultaneous with it, the sense determined by originality is also introduced (*CM*, 125).

In fact, the solipsistic concept plays the dominant role in determining the point of departure for Husserl's analysis of our experience of the other. Husserl takes his departure from a mere substratum of experience, namely—leaving out of account the "psychophysical" experience of the self—from an experience of a mere "nature" or "body [*Körper*]"; where, in accordance with the primordinal epoché, "nature" and "body" do not have an intersubjective sense, they do not have the sense "nature for everyone." He then proceeds to ask how the experience of other psychical beings, as a higher stage of experience, is motivated on the basis of this substratum (cf. 122, 136; *PI* III, 13, 14, 15). To be sure, the concept of primordinality determined by originality is also applicable to this substratum, so that, from the viewpoint of this concept, the problem of our experience of the other consists for Husserl in the question of how the intentionality of such experience "presents a 'there-along-with' [*Mit-da*] which is itself not there [and] can never become an 'itself-there' [*Selbst-da*]"; in other words, how our experience of the other is possible (*CM*, 139) if it consists in an "appresentation [*Appräsentation*]"[14] which can never be converted into a presentation [*Präsentation*].

Our Experience of the Other, as Mediate Apperceptive Transference [*Übertragung*]

According to Husserl, the appresentation of other psychical beings is motivated by the primordinal stratum in the following manner. Fundamental for this motivation is the similarity shown to my bodily organism [*Leib*] by a perceived, external body [*Körper*].[15] Motivated by this similarity, I perform an apperceptive transference in which I apprehend the external body in analogy with my own bodily organism as such; that is, I apprehend the external body as a sensing and perceiving body.

> It is clear from the outset that only a similarity conjoining that body there with my body, and doing so inside my primordinal sphere, can supply the motivational foundation for the analogizing apprehension [*Auffassung*] of the former [body] as another bodily organism. [140]

This analogizing apperception [*Apperzeption*] on the basis of similarity is "not an inference, not an act of thinking," but occurs rather with one glance (141), just as without further ado, without recollection and comparison, we apperceptively transfer to the objects of our ordinary perception the sense which corresponding objects, to which the former objects are similar, have acquired for us in earlier experiences. For example, without further ado we see something as scissors for cutting, if only we have earlier experienced this purposeful sense [*Zwecksinn*] in corresponding objects.

In contrast with the transference of sense in the perception of things, the transference of sense in the perception *as a bodily organism*, of an external body similar to my bodily organism, is distinguished by the fact "that here the primordially instituting original is perpetually present in vivid fashion" (ibid.). My own bodily organism is always there along with the other. One's own and the other's organism always make their appearance in perception as a pair so that the transference of sense is performed in the special form which Husserl calls an "association by pairing" (142). According to Husserl, an "association by pairing" is an "associative coinciding *par distance*" in the perceptual field, in that two perceptually contrasted unities are phenomenally conjoined by way of their similarity (*Ms. F I 32*, 168a [1927]; for example, similar red flecks on one image). Our experience of the other's organism thus comes to pass in the following manner:

> If a body makes its appearance within my primordial sphere, set off against my body [but] *similar* to it, that is, so constituted that it must enter into a phenomenal pairing with mine, then it seems clear without further ado, that in the transference [*Über-schiebung*] of sense it must forthwith take over the sense "bodily organism" from my [bodily organism]. [*CM*, 143]

Yet what here "seems clear without further ado" Husserl makes problematical by means of two objections which stem originally from Theodor Lipps (cf. *PI* I, app. XVI). The first objection is the following:

> But is the apperception really so transparent, one simple apperception by means of transference [being] like any other one? What makes the bodily organism into an other [bodily] organism and not into a second bodily organism of one's own?

Husserl's provisional answer is the following:

> It obviously comes into consideration here . . . that nothing from the transferred sense of the specific organistic character [*Leiblichkeit*] of the other body can be originally actualized in my primordial sphere. [*CM*, 143]

We shall return to this matter. The second objection is the following:

> But we now encounter the difficult problem of making intelligible how such an apperception is possible and [how it] cannot rather be immediately annulled. How is it, as the fact of the matter informs us, that the transferred sense is taken over in ontical acceptance [*Seinsgeltung*] as a set of psychical determinations existing in that body over there, whereas these determinations can never show themselves as themselves within the realm of originality [*Originalitätsbereich*] of the primordial sphere (the only one at our disposal)? [ibid.]

The problem thus consists in showing how the psychic side of the other organism, stemming as it does from the transference of sense, remains posited as existing and is not annulled again, even though it can never attain the original givenness. According to Husserl, the other psychic determinations are proven or confirmed by the fact that they stand together with the originally perceived corporeality in a nexus of continuous, *reciprocal* motivation.

> When I apprehend an external body similar to my bodily organism, [and apprehend it] as bodily organism, then, in virtue of its similarity [with mine], this bodily organism exercises the functions of *appresentation in the mode of "expression."* This requires that a manifold inwardness also be posited that develops progressively in typical fashion, [an inwardness] that on its part demands a corresponding outwardness, which actually does then arise in accordance with the anticipation [*Vorerwartung*] from within. Wherever the appresenting apprehension thus ensues, and is confirmed in this manner within itself by means of the continuance of corresponding expressions, there the appresentation is maintained. [*PI* II, 249; cf. 284, 493][16]

Husserl may here be thinking of examples such as the following. On the basis of its similarity with my bodily organism, I apprehend an external body as being a perceiving and, like my own, a seeing organism. I now see that this organism is moving toward a trench and, along with this, I apprehend appresentationally that it sees this trench. I expect as a motivational consequence that it will come to a halt before the trench or leap over it; that is, that it comports itself in some fashion in relation to the trench and will not simply roll down into it like an inanimate object—and, as a matter of fact, it comes to a halt before the trench, originally perceptible for me. Thus, not only does the originally perceptible "outer" motivate an "inner" which is originally not perceptible, but the originally imperceptible "inner" motivates an originally perceptible "outer" as well, and, insofar as the latter becomes perceptible for me, it confirms the inaccessible, motivating "inner." However, Husserl is also thinking about other kinds of examples.

> Intervening in the world around us we may possibly engender events which, in accordance with the sense of empathy, must also show themselves in corresponding modes of appearance within the inner surrounding world [*Innen-Umwelt*] of the other, and then, in accordance with effective analogy, yield mo-

tives for the comportment of the other, motives which must
find expression, be it in the organistic character of the other,
be it in further expressions, in his actions, in phonetic [expres-
sions], etc. [249]

The "tenor [*Gehalt*] of psychic determinations" of the other is
further confirmed insofar as he purposefully produces a work originally
perceptible to me, just as I know similar sorts of works as purposefully
engendered by me myself (503f.). Husserl gives yet another illustration,
the following:

> [There] is an excellent [example in the] case where the other is
> interpreted as [intentionally] related to my "I" and to that
> which pertains to my "I" [*mein Ichliches*] and [where] I actually
> experience this. Thus, the unity within the multiplicity of inter-
> pretational experience here finds a point of fulfillment in my
> specific self-experience. . . . In any case, if we think of the
> most primordial genetic continuity between mother and child
> and of the importance of social I-Thou-life [*Ich-Du-Leben*] [it
> becomes clear that] this mode of fulfillment plays a special
> role. [504]

Thus, according to Husserl, the confirmation of the other as a
being with his own immanent experience has *in toto* the character of a
concordance of interpretations which are joined together to form the
"unity of a total, interpretational perception" (503).

> The character of the existing other is founded in this kind of
> provable accessibility of the originally inaccessible. Whatever is
> originally presentable and demonstrable, that [is what] I myself
> am, or [it] belongs to me myself as [my] own. Whatever is
> thereby experienced in the founded manner of a primordinally
> unfulfillable experience, an [experience that does] not present
> itself originally yet consistently proves what has been indicated,
> [that] is [the] other [or pertains to the other] [*ist Fremdes*].
> [*CM*, 144]

With this insight, however, Husserl's analysis of our experience of
the other has not yet reached its conclusion. An essential deepening ac-
crues to it by way of the further insight that other immanent experiences
are not other merely by virtue of the fact that they cannot be originally
perceived by me.

After all, I apperceive the other not simply as a duplicate of
myself and so [as endowed] with my sphere of the original and
a like sphere, in conjunction with which [I would also understand it as endowed] with the modes of spatial appearance
which, [seen] from [the standpoint of] my "here," are my own;
but rather, looked at more closely, [as endowed] with such
[modes of spatial appearance] as I myself would have, in like-
ness [*in Gleichheit*] should I go thither and were I there. Furthermore, the other is appresentationally apperceived as the
"I" of a primordinal world or of a monad in which his bodily
organism is primordially constituted and experienced precisely
as the functional center for his holding sway [*Walten*] [within
his primordinal world]. Thus, in this appresentation, the body
which makes its appearance within my monadic sphere in the
mode "*there*," [the body] that is apperceived . . . as the bodily
organism of the alter ego, [this body] indicates the same body
in the mode "here" as the body which the other experiences in
his monadic sphere. However, it [does] this concretely, with
the entire constitutional intentionality which this mode of
givenness achieves within it. What we have just exhibited obviously points to the process of association constituting the mode
"other." This is not an immediate [association]. [146f.]

Association in our experience of the other is *not immediate*. This is
to say that one's own immanent experiences are not transferred immediately to the alien body. This body, in the mode "there," awakens immanent experiences "as if I were there." In this mediate mode, however, it
can appresent neither psychical life nor anything whatsoever from my
sphere of ownness; for "my entire primordinal ownness has, as a monad,
the content of the 'here' and not that of any 'there' whatsoever, hence,
also, [not that] of that determinate 'there.' . . . Each excludes the other;
they cannot be at the same time" (148). That body there associates immanent experiences as if I were there, experiences which cannot be my actual immanent experiences since I am *here*. It is thus the primordinal
incompatibility of the subjective situation appresented by that body
there with my own situation, which constitutes that situation as other.
Hence, the other is not other simply because his immanent experiences
cannot be given to me originally, but primarily because he is experienced
in a subjective situation which in principle cannot be my own. He is another "point of view."

That is the axis of Husserl's thoughts concerning our experience
of the other at the stage of development reached by the *Cartesian Medita-*

tions. The analyses published from his literary remains (see *Hu* XIII, XIV, XV), however, are much more highly differentiated. Thus, for example, he distinguishes between authentic [*eigentlich*] and inauthentic [*uneigentlich*] empathy. In our inauthentic experience of the other only that which pertains to the body of the other is actually presented in intuition, while that which pertains to his soul is but emptily awakened, along with [the bodily], in mere association (empty appresentation). This, our inauthentic experience of the other, is the foundation for the consideration of human beings, and of living beings in general, from the standpoint of the sciences of nature. In contrast with this, the subject in an authentic experience of the other, which Husserl also designates as an "absolutely empathizing cognizance [*Kenntnisnahme*]" (*PI* I, 445), lives as if [he were] within the other, in that he intuitionally transposes himself into the motivations of the other's situation (fulfilled appresentation). This authentic experience of the other is the foundation for a consideration of the human being from the standpoint of the human sciences (no. 16, §§ 9–13; apps. LV, LVI).

On the basis of this analysis of our experience of the other, or empathy, Husserl goes on also to discuss the problem of the intersubjectivity of the word (no. 14; *CM*, § 55), as well as the authentic social acts that, as acts of addressing others [*sich an Andere Wenden*], he distinguishes from mere empathy (*PI* II, nos. 9, 10; apps. XXIII, XIV, and passim).

6

Judgement
and Truth

The whole of Husserl's early work is clearly aimed at solving the question now before us concerning the truth of judgements. The attainment of a specifically phenomenological access to consciousness and, built upon it, the eidetic analysis of intentional consciousness as well as of the various types of conscious achievement, are crowned by a phenomenological investigation of the acts of cognition. Here we are speaking of cognition in the pregnant sense of this word. It is true that in our analysis of sensuous perception and its constitutive function we have already become acquainted with one form of cognitive achievement. Yet only the higher-level acts of judgement and the acts of authentic thinking associated with them are acts of cognition in the pregnant sense; and only an epistemological investigation of the connection between significant speech and authentic thought is able to provide a foundation for the objectively oriented pure logic that we sketched at the outset of our study. The insight that these pregnant, categorial acts of cognition do not suffice to provide an ultimate foundation for the ideal concepts and objects of pure logic may well form the most original result of Husserl's epistemological investigation. This insight, relating acts of categorial "intuition" to the sensuous intuition of materially [sachhaltig] determined individuals, also relates logic to pre-predicative experience. All the same, we shall be able to enter upon a more precise investigation of this complex of epistemological questions only when we have gained a closer understanding of Husserl's theory of language, and, in particular, of his concept of the intentional act of significant speech.

§ 1.   Linguistic Expression, Signification, and Intentional Consciousness

The *Logical Investigations*'s doctrine of the (predicative) judgement as well as of linguistic expressions as such, rests upon a series of preliminary decisions which are less than self-evident for the present-day reader. These "basic principles" of the Husserlian theory of signification or meaning and the judgement, concern, on the one hand, the nature of linguistic assertions, and, on the other, the nature of the semantical tenor [*Bedeutungsgehalt*] of these assertions. For Husserl, linguistic assertions are *ex-pressions* [*Aus-drücke*], that is, outward portrayals or signs of an inward process of intention or thought. These linguistic signs owe their signification in its essentials to the (subjective) performance of intentional acts that relate the signs to the signified object of reference, the object about which the assertion says what it says. Both of these preliminary decisions not only imprint themselves upon the positive content of Husserl's theory of language and signification, they also mark out clearly the difficulties with which this theory has to struggle. If, for example, our understanding the signification of an assertion is conceived as an intentional act, then there lurks, on the one hand, the threat of psychologistically confusing the signification with the psychological performance of the "signification-lending [*bedeutungsverleihend*]" intentional act; and, on the other hand, the equally fatal possibility of identifying the signification of a linguistic expression with the intentional object of reference of this expression. Similarly, the definition of the linguistic signs as ex-pressions of significations becomes entangled in difficulties as soon as one passes on to a consideration of such linguistic assertions (for example, metaphorical expressions) as are, to be sure, significant, but for which no univocal (or isomorphic) correspondence can be established between the structure of the signs and the signification of the intuitional or rational thoughts.

Expression and Signification

The central interest of the *Logical Investigations* is devoted to the theory of logical signification in general and (predicative) judgemental signification in particular. Referring to the theory of language bound up with this phenomenological theory of signification, recent interpreters have placed the results of the latter in question or even rejected this theory's metaphysical construction. We will thus do well, briefly, to portray the peculiarity and especially the boundaries of Husserl's theory of language before treating the questions regarding the reality of (assertional) signification, its referential relation, and its truth-value.

In contrast with the later representatives of the phenomenological movement, Husserl still oriented his analysis of language wholly in respect of the phenomenon of the speaking subject that expresses the immanent contents of its consciousness in language. For Husserl, speaking is not an anonymous happening; neither is it a mere function of discourse, that is, a materialistic, relational system of linguistic signs, regulated by quasi-economic laws. According to Husserl's conception, the speaker *knows* in principle exactly what he *says*, and his chief concern is to express this (inner) knowledge unambiguously, to "put" his cogitative and cognitive achievements "into words [*ver-worten*]" in such manner as to admit of no misunderstanding. This yields the twofold consequence for Husserl, firstly, that a privilege is bestowed upon the exploration of those (systems of) signs that function as ideal-linguistically univocal expressions or as (for example, arithmetical) surrogates for significations *properly seated in thought* (cf. esp., *PA*, 340ff.); secondly, that this ideal-linguistic isomorphism of thinking and speaking is to be understood as a relationship of representation [*Repräsentation*] or portrayal [*Darstellung*], that is, the linguistic signs have but a secondary function, they actually serve no other purpose than the external documentation of internal processes of thought. In consequence of this beginning, it becomes impossible to assign the function of endowing language with sense to the outward, public employment of signs.

In the first of the *Logical Investigations*, which bears the title "Expression and Signification," one can grasp especially clearly the Husserlian reduction of linguistic assertions to relationships of ideal-linguistic representation and these, in turn, to the semantic intentions that are seated in thought and find expression in speech. Especially characteristic of this tendency is Husserl's treatment both of occasional expressions (the so-called "shifters") and of linguistic communication. If we confine ourselves to the latter problem, we find Husserl's investigations culminating in the contention that the essential linguistic achievement consists not in the communicative exchange of information between speaker and listener but rather in the "soliloquy," the monologue of the solitary thinker (*LI* II/1 [I], § 8). This astonishing assertion can be understood only when one considers (1) that Husserl is oriented in respect of an ideal-linguistic, representational relationship between the signification and the linguistic sign of the expression; (2) that in the *Logical Investigations* Husserl still conceives the activity of the listener in communication as an understanding of signification by means of "taking notice [*Kundnahme*]" of the semantics or signitive acts of thought given notice of [*Kundgabe*] by the person speaking (§ 7); and (3) that this relationship of communicative giving-notice and taking-notice presupposes the physical reality of the linguistic sign, the "existence of the word" (36). By contrast, for the "expressions in the solitary life of the soul, we content ourselves . . . with represented [*vorgestellt*] words instead of actual ones." Hence, the assertion that the essence of significant speech finds its purest expression in "soliloquy" rests upon the conviction that the linguistic sign is an outer garment connected with the signification only by association, while the ideal signification, by contrast, is the very nucleus of a linguistic expression.

According to this conception, the essence of language consists in putting oneself in the service of thinking with such efficacy that one takes no notice of language at all, that is, that one forgets the mediating function of language (cf. § 10). Hence, we encounter language in its purest form where it is no longer directed toward a listener as an "appeal" (K. Bühler) but rather, in the form of a merely inward presentation of linguistic signs, serves as a "support" (49 / F, 289; cf. also *LI* II/2, 89 / F, 730) or a "prop" (*LI* II/2, 53 / F, 710). Yet just what are these *cogitational* [*denkmässig*] *significations* upon which everything within (ideal) language is supposed to depend? The signification of a linguistic expression is that which the speaker wants to say through the employment of linguistic signs (phonemes, letters, and so on), as well as that which the listener "understands" by way of the (acoustical, visual, and so on) sensuous perception of linguistic signs. We shall return shortly to the question of how Husserl characterizes more precisely this interconnection of the act of understanding and the meaning which gets understood. We shall also try to discover just wherein the achievement or result of such semantic understanding consists. First of all, however, we must clearly determine to what extent signification may really be designated in its essence as an independent linguistic function such that it must be distinguished from the linguistic utterance or speech-act. This distinction between signification and expression does not result alone from the introduction of a relationship of representation which combines both of them; that is, it does not result alone from the definition of the expression as a representation or a representative of the signification. Meaning and expression are also distinguished in immediate linguistic contemplation by the fact that an identical signification usually admits of various linguistic formulations for its expression, and that, conversely, different linguistic assertions are understood as assertions of the same tenor of signification [*Bedeutungsgehalt*]. Thus, for example, every linguistic translation rests upon this essential difference between the (uniform) signification and the (manifold) expression. Not only Husserl, but modern philosophy of language as a whole, has understood this connection between the identity (of the signification) and the difference (of the linguistic expression), against the background of its worship of presence. Different linguistic signs bring the same signification to present [*anwesend*] givenness. Only recently have thinkers like Derrida gone on to place in question the priority of identity over difference and of presence over absence. These thinkers have thereby been able to take account of the importance of the sense-instituting function of the difference among linguistic signs as well as of the possible absence of the object of reference.

Identical Signification and Individual Semantic Intention

However, the difference with which the identical signification is contrasted does not merely concern a multiplicity of signs. It also concerns a multiplicity of individual instances of givenness of the identical signification, that is, a multiplicity of temporally merging acts of understanding a uniform signification. Every assertion implies the fundamental possibility of later reactivating its tenor of signification, and in this recognitive repetition the identity of the signification is constituted. The intersubjective communication of an identical tenor of signification may then be understood in analogy with the intrasubjective recognition, namely, as the presentation [*Vergegenwärtigung*] of the tenor of signification borne in the linguistic assertion of an other person. Hence, the signification of a linguistic expression always has the structure of an identity within difference. Along with the various determinations of difference, the respective semantic identity may be characterized in regard to its ability to be translated, to be repeated, to be communicated. The semantic tenor of an expression is able to be translated because it is not bound exclusively to its material realization within a given phonetic or graphic system. It is able to be repeated because it is "transtemporal," that is, it can be consummated in semantic intentions variously individuated in time. Finally, the semantic tenor is able to be communicated because in principle it can be identically consummated as a logical "idea" by an infinite multiplicity of different, rationally thinking subjects. However, Husserl devotes his most exhaustive analyses to intrasubjective identity and difference, that is, to the synthetic connection between the identical, transtemporal signification and the temporally individuated, manifold, semantical intentions. Before concerning ourselves with these analyses in greater detail, however, we must make up for an omission in the foregoing account by undertaking a more precise determination of what Husserl calls the "semantic intention [Bedeutungsintention]."

A "semantic intention" is for Husserl an intentional act that, to state the matter schematically, has the function of bringing the linguistic sign and the signification into communication with one another in such a way that the linguistic sign is understood primarily as the representative not of the signification alone but of the significantly intended object of reference. In Husserl's own words, the semantic intention is "the understanding [Verständnis] . . . , this peculiar act of immanent experience, related to the expression, illuminating this expressing, lending signification to it, and, along with the signification, lending it objective reference" (LI II/1 [I], § 18). This citation contains implicitly, at least, the nucleus of the entire Husserlian theory of signification, namely, the two preliminary decisions, (1) that understanding is a mental (or phenomenological) process of thought associated with the physical reality of signs, and (2) that in understanding the signification of a linguistic sign, one understands that about which one is speaking, that is, one is referred intentionally to an object. The second of these two preliminary decisions is no less problematical than the first. For how, on the basis of this presupposition, would one understand those significant expressions that have in reality no corresponding intentional object whatsoever? Does this second presupposition not entail that the linguistic sign be a representative of the signification as well as of the object; that is, does the expression not then have two objects of reference, namely, its (mental) signification and its (extramental) object? Let us put the question in general terms. Is it admissible, on the basis of an analysis of certain kinds of linguistic expression (especially names) and of a certain kind of linguistic function (the expression of intentional experiences), to infer that every linguistic expression is significant if and only if it can be associated with the intentional presentation of an object-about-which [Gegenstand-worüber]? We shall return to some of these questions later. For the time being, we may simply observe that the attempts to answer them since Husserl's time have not been altogether satisfying, nor have those attempts even always succeeded in making decisive progress. We should like first of all, however, to turn our attention to the phenomenological analysis of the connection between the manifold semantic intentions and the uniform, identical signification.

In the *Logical Investigations* the connection between the uniform-identical signification and the manifold-individual semantic intentions is conceived throughout as a relationship between a species and its particularization. These specific individualities in which the ideal signification is particularized are the individual semantic intentions or, more precisely, the "intentional essence" of these individual acts. The identity of the signification is the "identity of the species. . . . The manifold individualities for the one, ideal signification [*Bedeutung*] are, of course, the corresponding moments of the significational [*Bedeuten*] acts, the semantical intentions. The signification is thus related to the momentary acts of signifying . . . just as the species 'redness' is related to the strips of paper lying on the desk, all of which 'have' this same 'redness' " (§ 31). Thus, as the species for a multiplicity of semantic intentions, the identical signification is an act-species, that is, its identity bears upon the performance of acts of speech. Accordingly, manifold assertions have a uniform, identical signification *insofar as* they are related to the same object in the same way, that is, in an identical determination. Yet may one really say that the identical signification is *particularized* in the manner of an eidetic universality within the really immanent tenor of manifold, significant acts of speech? Conversely, is the reference of an individual speech-act to its identical signification really bound to the logical operation of an eidetic universalization or ideation? Both possibilities seem implausible and yet in the *Logical Investigations* Husserl answers both these questions in the affirmative. One principal reason for this is surely the assimilation of the identical signification of an *assertion* to the status of the *eidos* "signification as such [*Bedeutungswesen*]" or to the status of a signification-in-itself, such as becomes the object of investigation in *logical* apophantics. The way an individual assertion refers to its identical signification is understood in analogy with the way an entity of pure logic, a logical law, for example, is *"applied"* within a psychological process of thought. Conversely, the identical signification of a momentary assertion should be *"apprehended"* in *just the same way* as is the ideal being or unconditional validity of a logical law, namely, by way of ideation or eidetic vision resting upon a synthetic nexus of acts drawn into comparison with one another. There are, however, at least three different critical arguments which can be marshalled against this doctrine of the connection between the identical signification and the individual semantic intention. Indeed, these arguments can be gathered in part from the later writings of Husserl himself (cf. Bernet 1979).

1. The identification of the signification of an assertion with the signification as regarded by pure-logical apophantics is questionable *from the standpoint of the philosophy of language* because even in an ideal language, in the language of logical apophantics itself, for example, it does not follow from the determination of the object of reference as an essence, that the signification of a momentary assertion about this essence will also be an essence. Since neither the distinction between ideal and ordinary language nor the distinction between assertional signification and logical-apophantical signification was familiar to the younger Husserl, at least, it is not surprising that this first critical point receives scant mention in Husserl's work.

2. It is, of course, possible to universalize the signification of an assertion to the level of a generic essence. Yet this essence is not the identical assertional signification, rather it already presupposes this signification. Perceptual and phantasy judgements of like wording (for example, "The pencil is red") have no common ideal signification which then gets particularized in a specific manner within the two diverse judgemental significations. Rather, each of the two different acts of judgement has a different, but in itself identical, judgemental signification. It is possible to extract a common nucleus from both these judgemental significations, and this nucleus can be universalized so as to form an essence. This essence ("being-red" or "redness of the pencil"), however, is no longer a judgemental signification. Husserl had already achieved these insights in a text stemming from 1908.

> Empirical signification [i.e., an assertional signification whose object of reference is not an essence but a fact] is not an idea (in the sense of an *eidos*) which could be gathered from an actual act of signification and an act of phantasy signification, just as "red" is an idea which can be gathered from a factual perceiving of red and a quasi-perceiving of red, namely, [a] phantasizing of red. [*VBL*, 214]

A priori significations, by contrast, that is, assertional significations related to essences or to eidetic truths, continued to be treated by Husserl as essences since their validity remained unaffected by the distinction between the actual and the phantasy performance of a judgement. By 1918, in the so-called "Bernau manuscripts on time," Husserl had acquired a more precise understanding of temporal individuation. Only thereafter did the identification of *a priori* significations with eidetic universalities, and, in particular, of course, the identification between the individuation of the identical signification into manifold semantical intentions and the process of specific particularization, begin to waver (cf. Husserl 1968, 9f.) In a text stemming from 1920 and incorporated into *Experience and Judgement*, Husserl comes out quite decidedly against the designation of the assertional signification as an essence and now speaks more distinctly about the "irreality" rather than the "ideality" of the signification.

> In order to comprehend the proposition [i.e., the judgemental signification] "2 < 3" . . . we do not have to compare acts of judgement which judge, "2 < 3"; we do not have to perform a generalizing abstraction, and, accordingly we never at any time come upon the proposition as a generic entity, as if, correspondingly, an individual proposition were to be found in every act of judgement, a moment proper to [this very act]. For itself, every judgement intends the proposition: the proposition, and, from the very beginning, this intended [proposition] is the irreal [proposition]. . . . Intending is an individual moment of every positing, but that which is intended does not have an individual existence and is not able to be particularized further. [*EJ*, 315 / C & A, 262f.]

3. If, then, every individual, significant act of speech intends (at least implicitly) the identical signification, then not only is this irreal meaning not an *essence*, but it is also not the essence of an *act*. Thus, the irreal signification may no longer be grasped as an identical mode of asserting and understanding, but rather as that *which* is said and understood, or as the thought [*der Gedanke*]. Husserl took account of this finding and, in a course of lectures held in 1908 ("Concerning Basic Problems in the Theory of Meaning and Judgement" [*VBL*]), introduced the noematic concept of signification for the first time. It is striking that this new concept of signification is oriented foremost toward the situation of the *listener*, the one who understands *what* the speaker is saying and who thereby understands what he is speaking *about*. By contrast, the noetic concept of signification had taken its departure primarily from the situation of the *speaker*, that is from the way the speaker, in consummating an assertion, is directed toward an object. The noematic concept of signification has the decisive advantage over the noetic concepts of setting out to explain the possibility of communicative understanding by appealing not to the intention of the speaker but to a quasi-objective givenness of the signification. Hence, the noematic concept of significa-

tion exhibits a distinct kinship with what Frege had called the "thought [*Gedanke*]." The cautious interpreter, however, will not be lured into hastily proclaiming the dissolution of the boundary between the phenomenological theory of signification and that of linguistic analysis. Rather, he will carefully inquire how it is still possible for Husserl to define the distinction between signification and object, if he does not, like Frege, understand the object of reference as the truth-value of the meaning (Frege's "sense") but rather as an intentional object. Every assertion seems suddenly to be referred to two different sorts of object, namely, the signification and the object proper. Is Husserl not then in danger of falling victim to the very same (pictorial) duplication of the structure of the intentional object which he had so convincingly refuted in his critique of Twardowski? (cf. esp. *LI* II/1 [I], § 13; [II], § 45; *Id* I, § 129).

Signification and the Intentional Object of Reference

Before we pursue further this question concerning the relation between the noematic signification and the intentional object, we shall do well to call to mind the principles underlying Husserl's definition of the referential relation of speech-acts to objects-about-which. According to Husserl's conception, this referential relation is in essence an achievement of the semantical intention. The semantical intention is an act of thinking which is intentionally directed toward an object and at the same time interprets or apperceives the linguistic sign as a representative of this intentional object. The relation of a linguistic sign to an object is thus mediated essentially by an intentional act of presentation [*Vorstellung*] which is associated with the linguistic expression. However, insofar as Husserl conceives the semantic intention as an individual consummation of an *ideal-identical* signification, his way of defining the referential relation does not imply a relapse into a psychologistic theory of signification. On the other hand, his definition of the semantic intention (and hence also the intentional theory of meaning pure and simple) may still be regarded as psychological insofar as the denotation and connotation of the speech-act's object of reference are ultimately derived from the speaker's intentional presentation of the object. This can be seen particularly clearly in Husserl's treatment of the so-called objectless expressions like "golden mountain," "quadrilateral circle," "2+2=5," and so on. Twardowski was of the opinion that such expressions are related merely to a mental content having no corresponding object in reality.

Compared with this, Husserl's solution is seductively simple. In his view, every intentional act has an intentional object as its goal (cf. esp. *LI* II/1 [V], § 11a), and the object of an hallucination is an unreal, fictive intentional object, while the object of a perception is a real intentional object.

> [E]veryone must acknowledge it: that the intentional object of the presentation is the same as the actual and, as the case may be, the external object of this presentation, and that it is countersensical to distinguish between the two. . . . If I represent [to myself] . . . a round square, then precisely this transcendent [thing] named here is meant, thus (but in other words) [an] intentional object [*Objekt*]; it is thereby a matter of indifference whether this object exists, [or] whether it is fictive or absurd. [425]

The thesis that every intentional act is directed toward an object does not, therefore, prejudice the question regarding the actual existence of this intentional object, for the intentional object, quite simply, is an object *qua* intended. As we shall see, it is perfectly consistent with this definition of the intentional object when Husserl understands the actually existing intentional object phenomenologically as the intentional goal of a distinguished kind of intentional belief, namely, as the object of an intuitively fulfilled intentional act.

This Husserlian definition of the intentional object may thus rightly be called "psychological" insofar as everything that can be said about this object is derived from the phenomenological analysis of intentional consciousness. (The introduction of the concept of the noema changes nothing in this regard, for the concept of the noema, or the intentional correlate-in-the-how [*Korrelat-im-Wie*] of belief, is a phenomenological datum derived from the reflective givenness of the intentional act.) Husserl's students and successors, especially Ingarden and Heidegger, repeatedly pointed to the fact that the determination of real Being as the intentional correlate of an intuitively fulfilled intention or as the intentional object of an act of cognition, leaves unanswered the ontological questions concerning objective actuality-in-itself [*Wirklichkeit-an-sich*] or Being that does not happen to be Being for a cognitive subject. We cannot here enter into the old dispute regarding Husserl's transcendental idealism. Indeed, we want to confine ourselves to the task of outlining the consequences implied for the philosophy of language by this subordination of the ontological point of view to the epistemological or intentional-analytical point of view. Of central interest in this regard is the determination of the intentional object on the basis of the phenomenological description of the intentional act. This is to say, that if one understands this intentional act as a semantic intention and the intentional object as an object-about-which of significant expression, then the first consequence will be that the object referred to by significant assertions cannot be determined independently of the actual consummation of significant acts of speech. Thus, the objects and states of affairs about which we speak are not the causes of the significant assertions that refer to them. Rather, it is only within the context of significant speech, within the intentional horizon of various, reciprocally related acts of speech, that objects and properties, states of affairs and logical relations, and so on, are constituted. As we shall see, this does not mean for Husserl that objects are constituted *only* in significant speech or that significant speech forms a satisfactory guarantee of the existence of the objects to which it refers. It remains the case, nonetheless, that the structure of the objects of reference is derived "pragmatically," as it were, from the activity of speaking or from the intentional act associated with it. This contains the further consequence not only that significant speech about an object that does not exist is possible, but that the activity of speaking first becomes intelligible as such against the background of the potential absence of the object referred to. As long as one confines oneself to Husserl's definition of "empty" speech, it remains true for Husserl (as for Derrida) that the object of speech is constituted against the background of its possible absence and within the differential context of significant acts of speech.

According to Husserl, the linguistic expression is related to an object of reference precisely to the extent that the physical expression or, respectively, the act of speech, is animated by a semantic intention that intends this object. In this manner, the determination of the intentional object is derived entirely from the determination of the intentional act, that is, from the determination of the semantical intention. It follows from this that the distinction between an actually existing object and a merely fictively existing object is irrelevant for the (phenomenological) analysis of its function as an intended object. Nevertheless, as we have already seen, the semantic intention referring to the intentional object is not an independent, phenomenological datum, for it necessarily refers to an ideal-identical signification. Does this not mean, however, that the semantic intention is an intentional act with two different intentional objects, that the semantic intention is related intentionally to the (noematic) signification as well as to the object of reference? Or can one possibly avoid this unusual doubling in the structure of the intentional object by identifying the signification and the referential object with one another? But is this identification admissible? May one really say that our understanding of a significant expression is exhausted in our looking toward its intentional referent? Husserl decidedly rejects this fusion of the signification and the object as well as the referential theory of signification which follows from it. "The object, however, never coalesces with the meaning" (§ 12). In the first of the *Logical Investigations*, Husserl substantiates this assertion not by means of a phenomenological intentional analysis of the conscious givenness of signification and object in the semantic intention, but by means of "linguistic analysis," as it were, alluding to kinds of linguistic expressions for whose comprehension the distinction between signification and object forms a necessary presupposition. There are expressions which, though they have each different signification, refer to one and the same object; and there are other expressions which have, indeed, one and the same signification yet which refer to different objects. Examples of the latter class are offered by the indexical expressions (such as "this," "here," and so on). Examples of the former class are offered by equivalent expressions such as "the victor at Jena" and "the vanquished at Waterloo." We cannot here embark upon a more exact analysis of this linguistic-analytical argumentation. We must, however, allude to the fact that Husserl prefers to orient himself in respect of a restricted class of expressions, specifically, names or definite descriptions. We must also allude to the fact that the object of equivalent expression does not permit of being determined independently of the truth-value of these expressions or of the actual (whether real or ideal) existence of the object. Furthermore, in the above example, Husserl would seem to derive his understanding of the expression "the victor at Jena," from his historical knowledge concerning the life of Napoleon, that is, from a prior knowledge of the object (cf. Tugendhat [1976] and Atwell).

It does not follow, however, from these shortcomings in Husserl's "linguistic-analytical" arguments concerning the distinction between signification and object, that Husserl was *eo ipso* unable to keep signification and object apart. Nor does it follow that the Husserlian theory of signification has ultimately to be filed in the class of realistic or referential theories of signification such as are commonly held to be rather primitive. The specifically phenomenological point of view in the discussion of the question concerning semantic reference is oriented less in respect of linguistic usage than in respect of the intentional analysis of the consciousness which lends signification to linguistic expressions. As long as one clings to the noetic concept of signification, there is no essential difficulty connected with the distinction between signification and object. The individual semantic intention is a specific particularization of the ideal signification, while the latter is defined as an identical mode of the intentional relation to the object. Within this model, the distinction between signification and object is the essential precondition for being able to say "correctly," "the expression designates (names) the object *by means of* its signification or, respectively, the act of signification [*Bedeuten*] is the determinate mode of intending [*Meinen*] the respective object" (§ 13). What is the status of the distinction between signification and object, however, when the identical signification itself comes to be designated as an intended (noematic) "objectivity"? One is tempted to base a possible answer upon the observation that in the initial consummation of a significant act of speech, the semantic intention is not directed toward the signification, but is rather referred thematically to the intentional object by way of the unthematically conscious signification. Accordingly, the object of reference would be the straightforward object of an expression, while the signification would be the intentional object of a reflection which, after the fact, thematizes the consciousness of signification that had been merely implicit in the initially consummated speech-act.

This answer cannot satisfy us, however, since phenomenological reflection upon the consciousness of signification must at once show how the objective relation of the initial act of speech was mediated by the unthematical consciousness of the noematic signification. Thus, in phenomenological reflection upon the semantic intention, we find ourselves anew before the problem that this semantic intention refers to two different kinds of intentional objectivity. A first attempt at solving this problem can be found, as early as 1908, in a text which develops the noematic concept of signification for the first time, namely, the course of lectures "Concerning Basic Problems in the Theory of Signification and Judgement" (*VBL*). There the object is defined as the pole of a "predication of identity" encompassing a multiplicity of (noematic) significations (*VBL*, 61f.; cf. also 80). Husserl required some time, however, before stating clearly what this view entails, namely, that within phenomenological reflection the object appears as an inner moment of noematic signification itself. Thus, he says that the "intended object is a moment of sense intrinsic to the proposition [*Satz*] itself and not something transcendent to it" (*Ms. B III 12*, 53b [1921]). However, Husserl did not work out this theory of noematic reference in a consistent fashion. Indeed, he bequeathed to us two crucial questions. There is the question concerning the noematic determination of the object of predicative propositions (Is it to be determined as an object named by the subject or as a state of affairs [*Sachlage*]?). There is also the question concerning the connection between the phenomenological and the ontological determination of the object of reference (the connection between the object *qua* "moment of sense" or semantic object-pole [*X*] and the object *qua* actual, transcendent object). In neither case did Husserl provide us with an unambiguous answer.

§ 2.   True Judging, Rational Thinking, and the Intuitive Givenness of the Object of Cognition

Several phenomenological thinkers, among them Heidegger in particular, have reproached Husserl's work with the charge that by constantly entering upon new, detailed, *epistemological* analyses, it obstructs our view of the basic ontological questions. In the present context, however, the debate between Husserl's and Heidegger's conception of phenomenology interests us only insofar as it helps give clear expression to the fact that, according to Husserl's conception, the question about verified cognition has at the very least a methodologically conditioned priority in relation to the question about the Being of beings. For Husserl, Being is first of all cognized Being, and, as an intentional correlate, cognized Being necessarily refers to the conscious activity of the subject of cognition. In addition to the epistemologically motivated forgottenness of the question concerning Being, Husserl was often reproached both with wanting to found his epistemological question upon the dogmatically presupposed separation of subject and object, and with seeking to solve the question of cognition on the basis of an intuitionism naively oriented toward the process of seeing. In the ensuing discussion of Husserl's question concerning judgemental truth, we shall see that the latter two reproaches against Husserl's beginning with the epistemological problem have only a limited legitimacy. Furthermore, the fact that our comments on the question of truth are oriented toward the problem of judgemental truth should not be understood as if, in the blindness accredited him for the question of ontological truth, Husserl also perforce reduced the concept of truth to the logical or epistemological concept of *judgemental* truth. We shall see that assertions, or the rational thinking that finds expression in them, do, indeed, represent for Husserl the field of distinguished cognitive achievements. Yet we shall at the same time see that these distinguished acts of cognition are necessarily founded in acts of sensuous intuition or, in other words, in the very appearing of sensuous objects.

It is the phenomenological analysis of *intentional consciousness* that Husserl departs from in his attempt to determine not only the understanding of signification in a linguistic expression but also the referential relation of this signification to an object. From the standpoint of its beginning in an analysis of intentionality, the phenomenological theory of signification sees itself forced to break with certain dogmas of the traditional, realistically inspired theory of signification. We have already seen that the phenomenological definition of intentional reference breaks away from the extensional description of the object of reference. What counts as significant speech is not reducible to speech about actually existing objects referred to by corresponding significations. For Husserl, the determination of the signification is not guided by the determination of the object of reference. Rather, the determination of the object referred to by a linguistic utterance is guided exclusively by the determination of the semantic relation to an object. Furthermore, Husserl understands this semantic reference of an assertion, or a speech-act, as the momentary, conscious consummation of the signification as an individual intentional act with an ideal semantic content. Our question, then, runs as follows: How, within this framework, is Husserl nonetheless able to take account of the distinction so important for a philosophical theory of cognition, the distinction between speaking about actually existing objects and speaking about not actually existing objects, or, respectively, the distinction between true speech and false speech?

Intuitively Fulfilled Categorial Acts as Cognitive Acts in the Strict Sense

The key concept in Husserl's doctrine of truth is clearly the concept of intuitive fulfillment. In the sixth of the *Logical Investigations* in particular, this concept receives detailed consideration. It is only in relation to the phenomenological process of fulfillment that the status and function of the concepts of cognition, evidence, and truth can be determined with greater precision: A fulfillment is a cognitive act in which an empty intention or assertion is brought into synthetic connection with a corresponding intuition such that by way of this synthesis the intention is confirmed and corroborated or, respectively, disappointed (cf. esp. *LI* II/2 [VI], §§ 6, 8, 11). This complex interconnection among different forms of intentional consciousness can be broken down schematically into the following three elements: (a) the act to be fulfilled or the (partially) empty act; (b) the fulfilling act; and (c) the act conjoining both these acts synthetically. With all three elements it is a question of relatively independently demarcated immanent experiences or psychical activities in which consciousness is intentionally related to objects. The synthetic nexus (c), which conjoins the fulfilling act with the act to be fulfilled, has the form of a synthesis of identification (§ 8). The *identity* constituted in this synthesis concerns the two conjoined acts ([a] and [b]) in accordance with the moments responsible for their intentional function (their "intentional essence"). The two acts coincide (at least partially) in respect of their intentional relation to the object.

They refer to the same object. However, the synthesis of identity of the two acts becomes epistemologically relevant only when both acts possess a different cognitive value (cf. §§ 13, 16). This *difference* between the two acts concerns their "cognitional essence" (§ 28), that is, it concerns the manner in which each of these acts *intuitively* (or emptily) presents its intentional object (the same intentional object) or brings this object to intuitive (or partially intuitive or non-intuitive) givenness. In the *Logical Investigations* Husserl understands this intuitive givenness of the object as an act that intentionally refers primitive, that is, pre-intentional contents of consciousness to the object, and which, through this mode of apperception, assigns to these contents the function of intuitionally representative data or appearances of the object (§§ 14b, 22). Husserl also says that the intentional act "represents [*repräsentieren*]" its object by dint of this apperception of primitive sensational data. The cognitional difference between the fulfilling act and the act to be fulfilled, hence, the difference between two intentional acts which intend the same object, thus derives from their mode of intuitive representation [*Repräsentation*] or from the range and richness of the sensational material apperceived in both acts at any given moment. Formally conceived, the process of fulfillment is thus a complex act that brings two acts into synthetic relation in respect of both the identity of their intentional object and the difference between their intuitive representations of this object.

Let us now consider somewhat more closely the case of the synthesis of fulfillment in which an empty assertion is epistemologically proven by means of the intuitional self-givenness of its object. The assertion, "The black bird flies off," is thus fulfilled in synthetic connection with our perceiving the asserted state of affairs. But can one account for the bird's *being* black, its determination *as* bird and as *the* bird, by means of the spectacle which presents itself to our eyes? Furthermore, might not what we see be expressed linguistically in other ways than the one we have hit upon? Both questions lead us to the insight, firstly, that a sensuous perception can fulfill a (predicative) assertion only in limited measure, and, secondly that an assertion owes its semantic tenor [Bedeutungsgehalt] only partially and indirectly to the linguistically expressed perception. In Husserl's terminology, this means that in perceptual judgement the linguistic signs in the authentic sense express not the perception itself but the judgemental signification. This signification is consummated in a categorial semantic intention and it is through this signification that the assertion acquires its reference to the perceptual object (§ 4). The consequence of this is, in turn, that the aforesaid semantic intention is fulfilled not by a purely sensuous intuition but by a categorial intuition.

Yet before we investigate more closely this synthetic nexus of categorial semantic intention and categorial intuition, we must bring to mind, at least in broad outline, what it is that makes up the essence of a *categorial act* as such. According to Husserl, categorial acts are acts of conjoining, relating, distinguishing, and so on. They are thus complex acts, that is, intentional acts with complex material. These acts relate diverse, pregiven, intentional objects to one another and bring them into synthetic unity under a categorial point of view, for example, that of the part-whole relationship. As a complex or synthetic act, the categorial intention presupposes both the acts brought into synthetic unity and the intentional objects of these acts. The performance of the synthetic act is "founded" in the performance of the synthesized acts (§§ 46, 48). As a thus founded, intentional act, the categorial act refers to a higher-order intentional objectivity first created by the categorial act itself (§ 43). However, it is extremely important that one not understand the performance of the categorial act as an action that modifies real objects by means of physical manipulation (§ 61). Rather, the achievement of the categorial act consists in the merely intellectual formation and articulation of a pregiven stuff or in the merely logical transformation of a stuff already formed categorially. Yet if the categorial act is not a sensuous, physical activity, neither is its intentional object a sensuous, physical object. It is not an object, in other words, which one can see with one's eyes or upon which one can sit. Contrasting them with real, empirical objects, or sensuous objects, Husserl calls categorial objects "higher-order" objects or "ideal" objects (§ 46). One must not, however, permit oneself to be misled by this terminology into regarding all categorial objects as essences. A state of affairs which I assert, that a dove is now sitting on my window sill, for example, is no less an ideal, categorial object than is the concept of a particular number or the formal-logical concept "object-as-such." If, with Husserl, one calls all categorial objects "ideal," then one must distinguish between empirical-ideal (or "sensuous-mixed") and *a priori*-ideal (or "pure") categorial objects (cf. § 60).

According to whether the intentional object of a categorial act is intuitively given or merely represented by a sign, one distinguishes between intuitive and signitive or empty categorial acts. Signitive categorial acts are the semantic intentions conjoined with emptily assertive acts of speech; but they are also the calculative operations carried out in accordance with an arithmetical calculus. Emptily assertive acts of speech are distinguished from technical calculation, however, in not being a surrogate for operations of thought that are incapable of intuitive performance. Rather, such acts of speech gain cognitional relevance only when they are fulfilled by a corresponding categorial intuition. In this categorial intuition, the categorial referent of the speech-act is no longer merely intended, emptily asserted; rather, it is itself given in intuition. In the sixth of the *Logical Investigations*, Husserl conceives this intuitional self-givenness of a *categorial* object largely by analogy with the self-givenness of a *sensuous* object, and he postulates a categorial form of intuitive representation. However, in the foreword to the second edition of 1920, Husserl remarks expressly that he "no longer approves of the doctrine of categorial representation" (v). It was the fatal error of this doctrine to define categorial representation as the *categorial* apprehension of a *sensuous* apprehensional content. Yet apart from this logical difficulty, it is not even clear in phenomenological terms, at least with respect to the pure categorial objects or formal categories, what could serve the latter as an intuitional representative (in the sense of sensuous self-givenness). Husserl's most convincing answer to the question of the intuitional givenness of categorial objects must be sought in his doctrine of eidetic variation. This is so even though this doctrine does not satisfactorily take into account either the distinction between "sensuous-mixed" and "pure" essences or the distinction between a generalizing and a formalizing grasp of essences (cf. *Id* I, § 13). Nevertheless, and this is already true of the *Logical Investigations*, Husserl resists the temptation to conceive categorial intuition in strict analogy to sensuous intuition. Indeed, as an essentially synthetic act, categorial intuition is distinguished in principle from the immediacy of sensuous seeing. Simply by being a *categorial* act, categorial intuition is a synthetic and therefore founded act. In addition, categorial intuition is also a founded act insofar as, being a cognitive act, it is a dependent moment in the synthesis of fulfillment.

Nor is a categorial intuition, as a cognitive act, anything like an "*intuitus originarius.*" Rather, it is a possible moment in the complex process of a "continuous enhancement of fulfillment," a process which is founded in sensuous experience (*LI* II/2 [VI], § 24).

Yet what does one really mean in saying that categorial intuition is to be designated as a cognitive act only insofar as it is a moment in the synthesis of fulfillment, that is, only insofar as it stands in synthetic connection with an act in need of fulfillment? It means in the first place that merely having the object intuitively given does not yet constitute a cognitive act. The intuitional givenness of the object is epistemologically relevant only once it has justified a cognitive pretension or satisfied a cognitive interest. Only in synthetic agreement with a corresponding empty representation, a "lack" (§ 21), does an intuitive act become a cognitive act. For Husserl, as for Kant, mere intuition is epistemologically irrelevant, or "blind," if it has not been subsumed under a corresponding empty intention and thereby been "classified." Correlatively, the empty intention is a merely "empty" presumption if it lacks intuitional confirmation, differentiation, and "approximation" to the intended object "itself." The fact that this empty intention, which is to be fulfilled in intuition, is by and large only partially empty (or already partially fulfilled) changes nothing in regard to the general characterization of the synthetic cognitive nexus of emptiness and fullness. It can therefore be left out of consideration in the present discussion. By contrast, it is of decisive importance that it is the synthesis of fulfillment typical of *categorial* acts that is first able phenomenologically to found the strict concept of cognition, that is, the cognition of something *as* something. If, with Husserl, one defines the empty categorial intention as a signitive intention, and this, in turn, principally as a categorial semantic intention, then the intuitionally fulfilled speech-act, that is, the assertion which has been justified by the intentional givenness of its object, proves to be the authentic paradigm for the act of cognition in the strict sense. The synthetic nexus of fulfillment, connecting a semantic intention and a corresponding categorial intuition, can also be described as a synthesis of the intentional objects of these acts. Talk of the cognition of an object *as* something is particularly well suited to this objectively oriented description of the synthesis of fulfillment which, following Kant, may be called a "recognition of the object in the concept" (cf. § 8). It is striking that this concept of cognition would not even be susceptible of phenomenological formulation, did Husserl not have at his disposal the structure of a merely emptily intended, that is, possibly nonexistent intentional object. As we have already remarked, the epistemological reality of the referent can be conceived and proven only against the background of the possible absence or unreality of this referent. We shall later see that this thesis is not the only point in which Husserl's doctrine of judgemental truth deviates from the standpoint of an extensional or realistic theory of signification.

The Truth of Judgements and the Laws of Authentic Thinking

Cognition, and for Husserl this means essentially *scientific* cognition, is a complex act of satisfied cognitive interest or justified cognitive claiming or pretension. Yet what is it toward which this interest is directed, and what does the cognitive intention claim or posit? If we continue to confine ourselves to the case of linguistically mediated acts of cognition, then the pretension lies in insisting that matters really stand just as we assert that they do. Regarded with greater precision, however, this pretension can be understood in still different ways, namely, (1) as an assertion about the actual existence of the object of reference; (2) as an assertion that certain properties actually belong to the object asserted to be of such and such a complexion; and (3) as an assertion that the object is not merely thus and so but rather is *exclusively* thus and so and is not additionally otherwise. Since, as we have seen, Husserl understands reference in respect of the semantic intention, and since every intentional act not only designates (denotes) its object but at the same time also determines (connotes) it, the first and second pretensions listed above cannot be separated from one another. A valid act of cognition is thus either an assertion which says nothing more of the object than what is at the same time given in intuition; or it is an intuitively fulfilled assertion which says everything that can be said positively about the corresponding object. As assertions fully fulfilled in intuition, both assertions are regarded by Husserl as *evident* acts of cognition. For the first assertion, however, evidence means intuitive "confirmation through a corresponding and fully adapted perception," whereas the second assertion is evident in the sense of the "most complete [or "ultimate" (§ 39)] synthesis of fulfillment" (§ 38). Evidence thus exhibits varying degrees of completeness; and even evidence in the sense of an intention fully satisfied in intuition is, generally speaking, the result of a complex, and that is to say gradually progressive process of fulfillment.

In the *Logical Investigations*, Husserl defines the goal regulating the process of steadily enhanced fulfillment as ultimate or adequate evidence. The telos implied in our cognitive interest is thus the complete "agreement between what is meant and what is given as such" (§ 39), "adequation to the 'thing itself' " (§ 37). This consummation of the "ultimate synthesis of fulfillment" is a synthetic act of phenomenological consciousness that forms the legitimate origin of the concepts "evidence in the strict sense," "truth," and "Being." In this connection, wholly oriented toward the process of fulfillment or the act of cognition, "Being" means nothing other than the object's "truly-being" or actually "subsisting" (§ 39). If one defines truth, in an initial sense, as the objective correlate of the ultimate synthesis of fulfillment, and defines the consummation of this synthesis as evidence, then evidence is the synthetic experience of the "full agreement between what is meant and what is given as such," that is, it is the "immanent experience of truth," the intuitive proof that an object of cognition "truly is." If, by contrast, one orients truth, in a second sense, not toward the gradually fulfilled agreement between what is meant and what is given, but toward the agreement between the act of intending and the act of intuiting, then truth is no longer synonymous with actually-being, but rather with the idea of evidence, that is, that which belongs essentially to the experience of the ultimate synthesis of fulfillment. This second determination of the connection between truth and evidence thus corresponds with the discussions found in the *Prolegomena*. The only exception is that in the epistemologically oriented context of the sixth of the *Logical Investigations* the immanent experience of evidence is not defined from the standpoint of the concept of ideal truth, and it is not defined as an "application" of this concept. Instead, the concept of truth comes to be founded in the phenomenological description of the experience of evidence or of fulfillment.

These comments from the sixth of the *Logical Investigations* are by no means unproblematical, nor are they Husserl's final word concerning the problems of evidence and truth. In particular, the orientation of the strong concept of evidence toward the concept of the *adequate* synthesis of fulfillment appears to be questionable. Since the demand for adequate self-givenness of the object cannot be satisfied in large areas of scientific cognition, including the area of logical, *a priori* cognition, one must ask whether the function of the principle of evidence as a possible methodological norm for phenomenological science is not thereby undermined (cf. Ströker). One can also ask in general whether the orientation of scientific cognition toward the telos of adequation does not rather destroy than found the idea of a rational progress in cognition (cf. Bernet, 1978b).

We cannot here enter further into these questions. Instead, we should like to meditate briefly upon those positive aspects of the Husserlian theory of truth that promise still to bear fruit. It is a primary characteristic of Husserl's concept of cognition and truth that the intuitionistic demand for the self-givenness of the object is not understood sensualistically. Husserl understands the epistemologically relevant form of the intuitional self-givenness of the object as a result of subjective, synthetic activity not, for example, as the mere possession of "little things [*Dingelchen*]" which function in consciousness as causally conditioned representatives of the thing-in-itself. Intuitional representation of the thing is essentially apperception of a hyletic stuff and actually establishes truth only in the synthesis of fulfillment, namely, when a connection has been established between the intuition and a cognitive intention. Accordingly, "adequation to the thing itself" (§ 37) does not mean agreement of representatives in consciousness with the represented and in itself fully determinate thing-in-itself. It means rather an agreement, within phenomenologically determined consciousness, between the intention and the givenness of the ultimately differentiated object. We shall not dispute the fact that in the sixth of the *Logical Investigations* Husserl was not yet able fully to free himself from the old concept of adequation (*adaequatio rei et intellectus*). Yet the true sense of his remarks points clearly in the direction of an agreement, in fulfillment, between various subjective acts. It thus points at once in the direction of a concept of truth oriented primarily toward the coherence of cognitive life. In any case, it is perfectly clear that the old problem of the "bridge" between subjective, cognitive activity and objective thing no longer presents itself for Husserl, and that even "verification" in the sense of the comparison of linguistic assertions with the "actual" constitution of the thing as it is "in itself" cannot count for him as a criterion of truth. Truth rather concerns the agreement among various intentional acts or their intentional objects. The phenomenological analysis of truth is especially dedicated to formulating the ideal conditions for the possibility of this agreement. If we can now investigate in greater detail the general conditions for this agreement in the case of judgemental truth, this may not be taken to mean that judging is for Husserl the most primordial site of true cognition. It is, of course, correct that categorial acts are cognitive acts in a distinguished sense; yet not all categorial acts are speech-acts. Furthermore, in the definition of truth as "agreement between what is meant and what is given as such" (the first concept of truth), "being-true" is a predicate belonging not to a judgement but to a state of affairs.

Husserl defines the concept of judgemental truth by taking as his point of departure the immanent experience of agreement between the significant speech-act animated by a cognitive interest, on the one hand, and, on the other, a corresponding act of categorial intuition in which the object of reference is given. Phenomenological exploration of the ideal conditions for possible judgemental truth thus has the form of an exploration of the conditions for the possible intuitional fulfillment of speech-acts. This, in turn, means nothing other than exploration of the conditions for the performance of categorial intuitions (§§ 62f.). The latter conditions fall under two types according to whether one has in mind the compossibility of categorial forms or their applicability to determinate sensuous stuffs. One must therefore distinguish between analytic and synthetic conditions for categorial intuition or for "actual and possible fulfillments of signification." On the basis of the intuitional givenness of the sensuous stuff, the synthetic conditions determine whether, in view of the "respective particularity" of this stuff, a categorial form may be used, or whether a given "categorial formation" of this stuff is "actually able to be consummated" (190). By contrast, the analytical conditions abstract from the particular material determination of the sensuous stuffs. That is, they treat these sensuous stuffs as "determinate but arbitrary" (189) "variables" (195), maintained "in identity with themselves" (189) in categorial formation and transformation. The positive task of exploring these analytic conditions concerns the formulation of ideal laws which regulate the "ideally closed circle of possible transformations of any given form into ever new forms" (190). Thus, for example, according to these analytical laws the transformation of the proposition "g is a part of G" into "G is the whole covering g" is valid, whereas its transformation into "G is a part of g" is not valid. The assertion, "g is a part of G, and G is the whole covering g," satisfies the synthetic laws of possible categorial intuition only if the sensuous objects designated by g and G can be brought actually, and that is to say empirically, into the relationship of part and whole. However, we shall still see that the actualization not only of these synthetic laws, but also of the universally valid analytical laws, necessarily presupposes the possibility of the intuitional givenness of individually determined, sensuous objects.

Categorial acts which contradict the analytic and synthetic conditions for their possible intuitive performance cannot be true. Yet such categorial acts, which are necessarily able to be performed only signitively, need not as a consequence be non-significant in the sense of nonsense. Signitive categorial acts such as linguistic expressions are significant if they obey the grammatical laws; but the possibility of their being true arises only when *in addition* they obey the laws of possible categorial intuition. If we call the signitive categorial acts "inauthentic acts of thought," and the intuitive categorial acts "authentic acts of thought" (193), then the authentic acts of thought are necessarily subject to the laws of possible inauthentic acts of thought but the inauthentic acts of thought are not necessarily subject to the laws of possible authentic acts of thought. "The domain of significations is much more comprehensive than that of intuition" for there is an "unlimited multiplicity of complex significations . . . which are, indeed, consolidated into uniform significations, but significations to which no possible, uniform correlate of fulfillment can correspond" (192). Thus the only true assertion is the assertion whose semantic intention, or inauthentic act of thought (193), can be intuitively fulfilled by a corresponding categorial intuition, by a corresponding authentic act of thought. The truth of a linguistic utterance, or of a speech-act, is derived from the possibility of performing a corresponding authentic act of thought. This comes about in such a way that, firstly, the semantic intention (in the unity of fulfillment) corresponds unambiguously with the authentic act of thought; and that, secondly, the semantic intention, conceived as an inauthentic act of thought, finds "unambiguous expression" in the linguistic sign, the "word" (cf. 191). Centered in the authentic act of thought or categorial intuition, this graduated sequence of unambiguous correspondence or isomorphism of "word," "signification," and "intuition," implies additionally an unambiguous correspondence between authentic thinking and its objects.

> The ideal conditions for the possibility of categorial intuition as such, are correlatively the conditions for the possibility of objects of categorial intuition, and [they are at once the conditions] for the possibility of categorial objects pure and simple. [189]

With these remarks does not Husserl accommodate himself unreservedly to the canon of a realistic theory of signification which, having received its classical expression in the *De Interpretatione* (cf. 16a) of Aristotle, is oriented toward the unambiguous representations of the "thing" in certain "states of the soul," and of these, in turn, in the linguistic "word"? Surely this question may be answered only with a qualified affirmation, for in Husserl's system it is not the thing but authentic thinking which constitutes the supporting pillar for the multilevel complex of representations. In Husserl, the accent shifts, therefore, from the semantic [*bedeutungsmässig*] internalization of the external thing to the linguistic externalization of the inwardness of thinking. The truth-value of a speech-act is derived from a corresponding act of authentic thinking. In view of the equivalence between the conditions for possible categorial intuition and the conditions for possible categorial objects, the truth-value of categorial objects can be seen similarly to be derived from a corresponding act of authentic thinking. The adequation of the signification to the object is but a correlative formulation of the connection of fulfillment between the signitive semantic intention and the corresponding categorial intuition.

Without entering further into a discussion of these questions we would like nonetheless to consider some of the consequences of this Husserlian system of isomorphic correspondence or representation of expression, signification, intuition, and object of cognition (cf. Bernet 1981). One consequence of this representational nexus, centered as it is in the concept of categorial intuition or authentic thinking, concerns the relationship between *language and thinking*. To be sure, authentic acts of thought do, under the proper conditions, fulfill semantic intentions; authentic acts of thought and fulfilled semantical intentions are "parallel," but they are "not identical"; the latter follow "faithfully after" the former (*LI* II/2 [VI], § 63). The authentic acts of thought, upon which the truth-value of cognition essentially depends, are *prelinguistic. Linguistic* acts of cognition can be valid insofar as they "follow faithfully after" or give "unambiguous expression" to these prelinguistic, intuitive acts of thought (ibid.). This demand for a relationship in which acts of prelinguistic thinking are unambiguously represented by the "system of . . . significations . . . expressing them" (ibid.), is problematical insofar as such a demand applies at best to the ideal language functioning as the "garb" of thinking. It certainly cannot account for the language in which signification is first instituted, the ordinary language of our ordinary dealings with linguistic signs. The introduction of a prelinguistic criterion for truth has the further consequence that this criterion becomes to a certain extent private. It does so insofar as the performance of an authentic act of thought or a synthesis of fulfillment is an intrasubjective event which can be made accessible to the intersubjective linguistic community of scientific investigators only secondarily. In the aftermath of Heidegger, attention has often been drawn to the fact that Husserl's derivation of the determination and the Being of actual objects from the performance of authentic acts of thought implies a problematical, preliminary decision in respect of the *ontological question*. Much as in the case of linguistic expressions, the forms and the Being of objects are but mirrorings of the determinations of corresponding acts of cognition. This relationship of representation, too, is one-sided. The Being of that which objectively is, is determined with a view to the purely theoretically determined subject of cognition. It is determined, therefore, as being-known [*Erkannt-sein*]. Just as in the case of the ideal language, one can here ask whether this limited, epistemological understanding of Being, represents a merely preliminary restriction or whether it does not rather represent an anticipatory decision concerning the question of Being.

Sensuous Experience as the Foundation of True Judgement

Husserl defines judging, but also thinking, as a categorial act. Categorial acts are synthetic acts in which pregiven stuffs are given logical form or in which the resultant logical forms are transformed. This formational activity, however, is not an absolutely independent and spontaneous activity of the understanding, for it presupposes the necessary pregivenness of ultimately sensuous stuffs.

> It lies in the nature of the case that everything categorial ultimately rests upon sensuous intuition, indeed, that . . . thought . . . apart from a founding sensuousness, is an absurdity. [§ 60]

If we recall that intuitively fulfilled categorial acts were designated as cognitive acts in the strict sense, then the question arises concerning the extent to which the pregivenness of sensuous stuffs founds not only the essential determination of these acts as categorial acts but also their truth-value.

Talk of the foundedness of all categorial acts, whether signitive or intuitive, has a double sense according to whether one understands the concept of founding logically or phenomenologically. Taken in its logical sense, the foundedness of categorial acts signifies that as synthetic acts these acts imply the performance of the partial acts unified by them. Hence, as synthesizing acts, categorial acts are founded in acts of simple relation to the members which are to be synthesized just as the uniform whole is founded in its manifold parts. It is to be observed, withal, that these synthesized members can already be, perchance, (nominalized) categorial objects; that, however, the process of categorial complications has an absolute beginning; and, thus, that all categorial objects are ultimately founded (logically) in sensuous stuffs. If, placing ourselves in a phenomenological attitude, we contemplate the performance of the synthetic act, then it strikes us that the members that are to be synthesized also enjoy a chronological priority over the performance of the synthesizing act. Taken in this second sense, talk of the foundedness of categorial acts thus signifies that categorial acts are able to be consummated only when the appurtenant partial acts have already been performed.

Let us now pass on to consider that special class of categorial acts capable of bringing fulfillment to signitive acts such as semantic intentions. In this case, talk of the founding of categorial acts in the pre-givenness [*Vor-Gegebenheit*] of sensuous stuffs acquires a new and narrower sense. In addition to the logical compatibility of the categorial forms employed, there belongs to the intuitional performance of a categorial act, and especially to the intuitional performance of a *synthetic* categorial act, the adaptation of these forms to the particularity of the stuffs to which they are applied. Only when these stuffs are *intuitionally* or perceptually given in the particularity of their material determination is it assured that one does not incorporate them into an unsuitable categorial nexus. The possible performance of a categorial intuition and the possible truth of a categorial speech-act are thus founded in the perceptual givenness of sensuous objects functioning as stuffs of a logical formation.

Thus, for example, the truth of the perceptual judgement, "The pencil is red," is *founded* in the perception of a red pencil. (Yet the perceptual judgement, or its meaning, is not *contained* in the perception, since no perceptual givenness corresponds with the categorial form of the predicative synthesis of identification,) What is the status of this necessary foundedness in the sensuous perception of stuffs, however, when we move on from synthetically true judgements to analytically true judgements, such as, "G is the whole covering g, and g is a part of G"? Still, mere variables function here as stuffs; and variable stuffs, that is, stuffs regarded independently of their particular material determination, "arbitrary" stuffs, do not at all events fall into the realm of sensuous seeing. On the other hand, stuffs which function as arbitrarily variable, though thoroughly self-identical stuffs of categorial formation, are not for that reason necessarily to be designated as *eidetic* generalities, whether material or formal. (These "arbitrary nuclei, conceived as able to be held fast only in their identity with themselves" [cf. *FTL*, § 55], function as essences, in the sense of "modes of something-as-such," only when analytically true assertions have been generalized to the level of becoming logical laws.)

In the *Logical Investigations*, Husserl seems clearly to take the view that even the intuitional performance of an *analytical* categorial act is founded in the intuitional givenness of sensuous stuffs, and founded in such a way that in the actual performance of the categorial act there is presupposed, at the very least, a phantasy presentation of a sensuous object that suits the terms of the categorial form employed (*LI* II/2 [VI], § 62). In the *Formal and Transcendental Logic*, Husserl supplements these early investigations by showing that it is not only in their apprehension that analytically true assertions, especially formal-logical laws, refer to the intuitional givenness of sensuous objects. Rather, even in their application these laws refer ultimately and necessarily to materially determined individuals (*FTL*, § 82). If the pure-logical laws come to be understood as laws of possible truth, then their "idealizing presuppositions" (§§ 73ff.), related to their possible application in actual experience, require critical clarification. Thus, the formal logic of truth implies assertions which refer not only to materially determined individual Being, but also to the intuitive-sensuous experience of such Being. The critical justification of these (implicit) assertions is a task which can be accomplished not by formal logic itself but only by a transcendental logic of our living experience of the world. In his effort to found formal logic in a genetic phenomenology, Husserl went as far as to postulate a "prepredicative" "syntactical accomplishment" of this "founding experience" (cf. § 86). In the present setting, however, we cannot enter into a discussion of this later development in the problem of founding the judgement in experience.

The most important yield from Husserl's early analyses of judgemental truth is surely their hint at the necessary founding of acts of linguistic cognition in non-linguistic cognitive performances. Acts of true judgement are in the main mere linguistic realizations or expressions of acts of "authentic thinking," and these acts of authentic thinking are cognitive acts in the strict sense. According to Husserl's conception of the matter, however, authentic thinking is necessarily founded in sensuous intuition, and Husserl, therefore, does not hesitate to designate even these sensuous acts as cognitive acts. It is correct, to be sure, that such prelinguistic acts can be scientifically explored only in the medium of language. Yet Husserl, in contrast with a broad current in present-day philosophical thinking, refuses to conclude from this that all cognitive performances, *as a matter of necessity*, presuppose language from the very beginning and must consequently be designated as linguistic performances. An examination of this thesis in light of the more recent findings of cognitive psychology is an important desideratum for the actualization of Husserl's way of posing the epistemological problem.

7

Static and Genetic Constitution

Husserl's distinction between static and genetic phenomenology belongs to a relatively late phase of the development of his phenomenology. Prior to his establishing this distinction, his philosophical relationship to genetic problems of subjectivity was a changeable one. While he attempts in his first work, *Philosophy of Arithmetic* (1891), to clarify the psychological generation or genesis of the basic arithmetical concepts (unity, multiplicity, and number; cf. above, chap. 1), in his phenomenology or "descriptive psychology" of the *Logical Investigations* (1900/01) he wants to see all genetic considerations excluded. Stirred by Frege's criticism of his position, Husserl learned to understand logical and mathematical concepts as objective [*objektiv*], ideal objects [*Gegenstände*] existing in themselves and opposed to psychical objects. For him, their phenomenological clarification can consist not in an investigation of their subjective genesis, but only in an analysis of the mode of their primordial and, hence, intuitive givenness within consciousness. In the *Logical Investigations*, Husserl distinguishes phenomenology ("descriptive psychology") and (empirical) psychology straight off by means of the concept of genesis. Pure phenomenology describes immanent experiences while psychology provides their genetic explanation (1st ed., vol. II, pp. 4, 8). Yet already in the *Ideas* (1913), and in the second edition (1913) of the *Logical Investigations*, he drops this concept as a criterion for distinguishing phenomenology and psychology from one another and begins to employ it, although only infrequently, in the realm of pure phenomenology. However, at this juncture the concept of genesis has not yet acquired its proper signification, whereby it would designate a temporal generation and coming-to-be. Not until the period of 1917 to 1921 does Husserl outline for the first time the idea of a properly genetic phenomenology. To be sure, this phenomenology has nothing to do with an empirical, causal explanation. Rather, it involves an *a priori* comprehension of the motivational complexes of transcendental consciousness.[1] Nevertheless, Husserl's phenomenology is not from this moment on simply and exclusively genetic in its approach. Its first task continues to be a "static" analysis of immanent experiences and of the constitution of objects within consciousness. As a second step, however, a genetic analysis of constitution has to follow this "static" phenomenology.[2] Although he appears never to have fully succeeded in elaborating this difference in a consequent and consistent fashion, from this time onward Husserl seeks constantly to maintain the two-part division of pure or transcendental phenomenology into a static and a genetic mode, that is, he strives to preserve the distinction between static and genetic constitution. The beginnings for such a distinction are, indeed, clear and manifest in Husserl's work, albeit the boundaries are not always easily discernible. The reason for this lack of clarity seems to us to lie in the fact that Husserl did not elaborate clearly enough the methodology of genetic, constitutional analysis.

   Husserl's understanding of "genetic phenomenology" can best be understood in contrast with its counter-concept, static phenomenology. Static phenomenology begins from species of stable objects, both real objects (for example, natural things) and ideal objects (for example, mathematical propositions), and proceeds both noetically and noematically to investigate the complexes of immanent experiences in which these species of objects attain teleologically to givenness. In the course of such an investigation, and within the "phenomenological reduction," these objects are regarded purely as the objective correlates of modes of consciousness. The intention in thus regarding them is to clarify the sense and validity of these objects by means of regressing to their systems of manifestation [*Bekundung*] and authentication [*Beurkundung*] within the consciousness by which they are primordially given (cf. *PI* II, 40, 41). The analysis distinctive of static constitution has a twofold character. In the first place, it has stable objects, a stable "ontology," for its guide. In the second place, it inquires into immanent experiences.

   As mentioned, Husserl already employed the expression "genesis" at the time of his *Ideas* (1913). The concept of genesis as it was then understood, however, did not yet lead beyond the just outlined "phenomenology of ontological guides and immanent experiences." He made use of this word during that period of time in order to characterize constitutive phenomenology (or, as he would later call it, "static" phenomenology) over against ontology. Whereas ontology takes objective unities as stable identities, phenomenology contemplates the unity "within the flow, namely, as the unity of a constituting flow; it follows the movements, the courses in which such unity, and every component, side, and real property of such unity, is a correlative identity. In some measure, this approach is kinetic or 'genetic.' Every unity of cognition . . . has its 'history' or, correlatively, the consciousness of this real thing has its 'history,' its immanent teleology in the form of a regulated system of *essentially* appurtenant modes of manifestation and authentication which can be elicited from this consciousness, brought out by questioning it" (*Id* III, 129 / K & P, 117). According to Husserl's later conception, however, the analysis of this "system of manifestation and authentication," a system directed teleologically toward the primordial givenness of an object or toward the fulfillment of the corresponding intentions, is not yet genetic in the proper sense. To be sure, these systems are rules for the temporal courses of the multiplicities of consciousness, but such courses are only the subjective correlates of a stable identity, that is to say, they are the subjective correlates of the object that attains to givenness within them. In a properly genetic phenomenology, the concern will no longer be with analyzing these finished systems of correlation, but rather with inquiring into their genesis. "To investigate the constitution is not to investigate the genesis, the latter being precisely the genesis of the constitution" (*PI* II, 41).

At the time of the *Ideas* (1913), Husserl speaks in still another improper sense of "genesis." Phenomenology does not contemplate in a merely isolated or rhapsodic fashion the constituting multiplicities belonging to the consciousness of this or that objectivity. Rather, it brings these constitutive systems into coherent connection with one another. This interconnection of systems is a "graduated structure" in accordance with the principle of foundation. The constitution of certain objectivities presupposes the constitution of others. Thus, for example, the constitution of categorial states of affairs presupposes the constitution of sensuous objects of perception and the constitution of other psychical beings presupposes that of spatial things. Regarding this graduated order of constitution in which the "higher" presupposes the "lower" as the condition for its possibility, Husserl says the following:

> Using the image of a genesis, one can think of the graduated
> formation of constitution by imagining that experience is really
> consummated for the first time in the data of the lowest stage
> alone, that what is new in the new stage then steps forth, and
> that with it new unities are constituted. [*Id* III, 125 / K&P,
> 113]

Yet according to Husserl's own words, "genesis" is in this case only a fictive image. For in this graduated order "the conditioned is not [explained] by that which conditions" (*PI* II, 41), indeed, no temporal priority is even asserted for that which conditions.

Finally, Husserl speaks of genesis in still a third connection, one which already appears within his earlier phenomenology, specifically in relation to the constitution of *time*. Not only is temporality the universal form of genesis, but temporality itself builds itself up in a "constant, passive and fully universal genesis" (*CM*, 114 / C, 81; cf. *PI* II, 39, 41). In the *Cartesian Meditations* the constitution of internal time-consciousness is counted among the "genetic problems of the first and most fundamental order" (*CM*, 169, cf. 109 / C, 142, 75). As early as the lectures of 1904/05 Husserl had devoted himself to the problem of the constitution of time (cf. *PITC*) and he was able to refer to this problematic when he wrote to Paul Natorp in 1918 that he had, since more than a decade, overcome the stage of static Platonism and posed to phenomenology as its chief theme the idea of transcendental genesis.[3] Here Husserl speaks of genesis *after* having conceived of a genetic phenomenology, and he seems to be employing the word in its proper sense. Yet the situation is not without ambiguity, for he does not consistently maintain the designation of primordial time-constitution as genesis. Thus, for example, he can explain early on in the 1920s that it is not a question concerning genesis if we "pass over in our descriptions . . . from the original impressions . . . to the various modal transformations into retentions, recollections, expectations, etc., and thereby pursue a principle of the systematic arrangement of apperceptions . . . " (*APS*, 340).

Similarly, a passage from the *Cartesian Meditations* seems to assign to genetic phenomenology only those questions which go beyond the domain belonging to the formation of time (*CM*, 110 / C, 76). This difficulty in comprehending primordial time-consciousness under the rubric of genesis seems to follow from the fact that, as a steady transformation ("modification") of primordial impressions into retentions, this consciousness not only takes necessarily the form of a genesis but is, as form, a flow, and yet is something constant, something unchanging (cf. above, chap. 3, § 2). In any case, as long as time-consciousness is considered only in regard to its form, it possesses no becoming, no genesis, such as do its various contents, its apperceptions. Thus, insofar as it investigates the mere form of time, the phenomenology of time-consciousness is not a genetic phenomenology in the sense otherwise common in Husserl. Rather, inasmuch as it exhibits the foundation of genesis, it is the foundation of genetic phenomenology. On the other hand, insofar as it does not restrict itself to the mere form of time but also takes contents into account (as it in fact must do in consideration of Husserl's concept of protention), then it would indeed be a properly genetic phenomenology.

> Mere form is, to be sure, an abstraction, so that the intentional analysis of time-consciousness and of its achievement is from the beginning abstractive. It comprehends [and] is interested in nothing but the necessary temporal form of all particular objects and multiplicities of objects, or, correlatively, [it is interested in] the form of the multiplicities which constitute the temporal. . . . Yet [as regards that] which gives unity of content to the occasional object, or that which constitutes the differences of content from one object to the other—[and this means differences] for consciousness and resulting from its own constitutive performance—[as regards that] which makes possible, in consciousness, division into parts and relationships among parts, and like matters, [as regards all of] this the analysis of time alone, precisely because it abstracts from all matters of content, tells us nothing. So, too, it provides no notion of those necessary, synthetic structures of either the streaming present or the unified stream of the present that somehow affect the particularity of the content. [*APS*, 128]

According to Husserl, there is a concept capable of taking into account such interconnections of content insofar as the fundamental, merely passive formations of the unities of consciousness are concerned. This is the concept of association, a concept which displays the "universal principle of passive genesis" (*CM*, 113 / C, 80).

But let us now ask what really does make up the idea of genetic phenomenology according to Husserl! Its basic insight is surely the following: The "I" is not an empty "pole of identity," not a mere form in successive intentional acts or experiences (as the matter had been described in *Ideas I* [1913]). Rather, it is an "I" who possesses his capabilities (in the consciousness that "I can do this and that"), his attitudes, and his convictions. Only in such capabilities and convictions is there a world pregiven as a "horizon of ability" for the "I," a world from which the "I" can, by available means of manifestation and demonstration, bring any objects whatsoever to givenness. These capabilities and convictions point back to earlier experiences and positings. They are *habitualities acquired* by the "I."

> That there is for me a natural world, a cultural world, a human world with its social forms, etc., signifies that there exist for me possibilities of corresponding experiences—as able to be brought into play for me at any time, whether I am actually experiencing such objects or not; [it signifies] further that there are, corresponding with those worlds, other modes of consciousness, vague opinions and the like, as possibilities for me, and also that there belong to these modes of consciousness possibilities for fulfilling or disappointing them by means of experiences of a prefigured type. Therein lies a firmly cultivated habituality—a cultivated habituality acquired from a genesis governed by certain eidetic laws. [109f. / C, 75ff.]

For example, even in the fact that I am able to apperceive something as a spatial thing that is able to be brought to givenness in an array of appearances, there lies an acquired capability, an habituality that has a genetic origin and a history. This history is at once the history of the "I" and the history of its objects as being for it, as being valid for it with this or that sense.

> [W]herever it is considered, life is a living-onward that has life behind it as well as beside it, but not in a merely natural externality, much rather in the inwardness of an intentional tradition. We may also say that life is through and through historical; living-onward is a going forth out of a life from which it has its prefiguration of sense and Being, a prefigurement that, as historical, encloses its own historical lineage as something that can again be disclosed, which can be unveiled, which can be drawn out of it by questioning. [Lectures on "Nature and Spirit," from the summer semester of 1927; *Ms. F I 32*, 163a]

Husserl had probably become aware of a genesis such as this as early as 1915,[4] and, during the years of 1917 to 1921, under the title of genetic phenomenology, he worked out the problem of how to investigate such a history. Whereas static phenomenology illuminates already developed, "finished," constitutive systems by describing successions of intentional experiences regulated according to eidetic laws, experiences in which objects of a certain kind attain to givenness, genetic phenomenology inquires into the very origin of such systems. The concern of genetic phenomenology lies with the genesis of this constitution and so at once with the genesis of the kinds of object constituted therein. The object is no longer a fixed guidepost as it is in static phenomenology. It is rather something that has come to be. The phenomenology of genesis "pursues the history . . . of this objectification and therewith the history of the object itself as the object of a possible cognition" (*APS*, 345). What is in question here is not the factical history of isolated apperceptions but rather the universal form or type of this history, a form which Husserl regards as an *a priori* or essence.[5] It is a question of the eidetic laws of compossibility and succession, inasmuch as the latter have the basic character of a motivational nexus (cf. *APS*, 336ff. and *CM*, §§ 36f.).

Within genetic phenomenology, Husserl distinguishes two basic forms of genesis, *active* and *passive* genesis (cf. *APS*, 342f. and *CM*, 111 f. / C, 77f.). The achievements of productive reason belong to active genesis. These include the achievement of real, cultural products (such as artworks, tools), as well as that of ideal objects (such as predicates and predicative states of affairs, syllogisms and theories, sets and numbers). Husserl outlined the program for the genetic analysis of logical structures in *Formal and Transcendental Logic*. Judgements contain a sedimented genesis of sense in the form of "concealed intentional implications." If clarity is to be achieved regarding the concealed presuppositions of the various configurations of judgement, then this history of sense must be unveiled. Thus, for example, nominalized configurations of sense ("the red," "this, that *S* is *p*") point back within themselves to the corresponding, more primordial configuration ("red," "*S* is *p*"). According to Husserl, what is genetically primordial in this context is twofold. In the first place, the genetically primodial is the respectively more primordial configuration. In the second place, however, it is the activity of primordial acquisition in which the new logical structure is produced upon the foundation of the more primordial configuration. "The activity of primordial acquisition is the 'evidence' for these idealities" (*FTL*, 150 / C, 168). The lowest stratum to which the genetic analysis of the logical leads us is formed by judgements regarding individuals, while in their turn these judgements point back genetically to pre-predicative experience (§§ 85, 86). Such experience, proceeding by way of passive syntheses, is the passive, underground domain of the active production of judgements, just as in general every active genesis presupposes a pregiving passivity. For Husserl, this foundedness is the very definition of activity.

In turn, however, passivity has its genesis, passive genesis, whose universal principle is association. Husserl said in 1929 that phenomenology only "very lately has found ways of access to the exploration of association" (*CM*, 114 / C, 80). This corresponds with the fact that Husserl saw in association an essentially genetic principle which he could only deal with in his lately conceived genetic phenomenology (cf. the discussion of the concept of association in the 1st ed. of the *Logical Investigations*, vol. II, p. 29). For Husserl, "association" does not designate a merely empirical lawfulness in the complex of psychical data but is rather a "most highly encompassing title for an intentional, eidetic lawfulness in the constitution of the ego" (114 / C, 81).[6] Above all, he puts forward two forms of association, which are the following: (1) association as a principle for the formation of unity, a principle for the integration and configuration of various moments of coexistence and succession found within our consciousness of the immediate present (for example, groups of colored spots, series of tones); this integration and configuration is accomplished by means of a reciprocal, affective waking or strengthening, on the basis of the contiguity, similarity, and contrast of the intentions directed toward these moments; (2) association as a principle for the apperception of objects as objects of a determinate sense, apperception on the basis of the associative waking of earlier experience and the analogical transference of sense which proceeds from it.

This transference of sense is an associative "induction" or an inductive association in that it anticipates something that corresponds with the type of experience that has hitherto prevailed. On the basis of similarities, what is present is passively apprehended within a sense that was "primordially instituted" in earlier experience and that has since become habitual. "By means of association, the constitutive performance is expanded at every level of apperception" (*APS*, 118). Not only passive formations of unity but also actively produced configurations of sense become habitual acquisitions of the subject. These acquisitions can be passively wakened by association within a "secondary sensibility" and transferred to what is present. With this consideration before him, Husserl says the following:

> As Hume correctly teaches, habit is not only our nurse, rather
> it is the function of consciousness that shapes and constantly
> further shapes the world [and,] indeed, [in like manner shapes]
> all objectivity. "Habit" is the primordial source of every be-

stowal of objective sense, habit as induction, though of course accompanied by a corresponding fulfillment, which is the constant and primordial force constitutive of existence. [Lectures on "Nature and Spirit," from the summer semester of 1927, *Ms. F I 32*, 162a]

With this sketch of the passive and active genesis of various kinds of objectivity, however, Husserl's idea of a genetic phenomenology is not yet fully outlined. Such objects are for the "I" *in* acquired apperceptions, capabilities, dispositions, convictions; and in these habitualities the "I" itself *comes to be* as a determinate personality, as a distinctive individuality. The concrete subjectivity, the monad, has, "necessarily, the form of a unity of becoming, a unity of incessant genesis" (*PI* II, 34). In respect of this, the task arises, within a "phenomenology of monadic individuality," of pursuing a universal inquiry into the *a priori* eidetic laws "which supplement the laws governing immanent experiences and establish the requirement made by the individual unity and self-containment of a monad . . . " (ibid.). Since, however, the single monad is bound up with other monads in respect of its acts and its possession of a world, the genesis of any monad implies the genesis of its communalization with other monads. Thus, Husserl remarks as follows:

> But to trace the world that is valid for me back into its structures of validity is to clarify my genesis, the genesis of the bearer of validity and therewith the genesis of my co-bearers, those who themselves acquire for me a sense of Being by way of a genesis; and, as the genesis of these co-bearers commences, at the same moment there commences the genesis of the communalization of my comrades and the communalized genesis in its encompassing movement, a movement that branches out from my initial, solipsistic genesis and spreads out into wider domains. [*Ms. B I 14*, transcr. X, 25]

Finally, genetic phenomenology leads to the generative problems of birth and death and the interconnectedness of generation. Regarding these matters, the *Cartesian Meditations* explain that they "plainly belong to a higher dimension and presuppose such a colossal expository labor in respect of the lower spheres that they cannot become topics of investigation for a long time to come" (*CM*, 169 / C, 142).

Husserl's idea of genesis is of considerable importance for his own understanding of his philosophy as *phenomenological* or *transcenden-*

tal idealism. It was during the 1920s, with the emergence of his conception of a genetic phenomenology, that Husserl first laid claim to this title for his philosophy (see *FTL* and *CM*). To be sure, certain considerations within "static" phenomenology already pointed in the direction of a "transcendental-idealistic" position. Husserl's static phenomenology is guided by the thought that the question of what, and in what sense, any object whatsoever ultimately *is*, can only be decided by an analysis of its mode of givenness or manifestation within consciousness. Already by 1907 Husserl had arrived at the insight that things belonging to physical nature could in principle, even "for a divine intelligence," be given only in subjective appearances (adumbrations, aspects, perspectives). In primordial givenness, a thing of physical nature is nothing but an identical unit of a fundamentally inconclusive multiplicity of appearance (cf. above, chap. 4). As such an identical unit, it is a *correlate* of this subjective multiplicity, which is to say that *without* the latter it would be meaningless. About 1914 or 1915, Husserl writes the following: "Transcendental idealism purports: A nature is not thinkable apart from coexistent subjects capable of experiencing that nature" (*Ms. B IV 6*, transcr., 45).[7] However, since it analyzes the givenness only of "finished" objects within their corresponding systems of manifestation, static phenomenology cannot speak about a "producing" or "bringing forth" of objects. Since Husserl regards systems of manifestation within genetic phenomenology as having come to be, he also regards the objects that manifest themselves therein, insofar as their sense gets realized in this givenness, as having correlatively come to be, as "*formations of achievement* [*Leistungsgebilde*]" which have arisen along with the systems of manifestation.

> Precisely thereby every kind of being, real and ideal, becomes itself intelligible as a formation [*Gebilde*] of transcendental subjectivity constituted within this very achievement [*Leistung*].
> [*CM*, 118 / C, 85]

However, insofar as the sense of a being fails to get realized within the modes of givenness of the "I," this being cannot be dissolved into the coming-to-be of the subjective system of manifestation. Husserl took this thought into account with his idea of a "constitution of the other 'I.' " According to its proper sense, the other is *for itself*. For me, it is never itself given as such ("in the original"), but only "indicated." The other is a "true transcendency" (cf. *PI* II, 8f., 256ff.; and above, chap. 5, § 2). So, too, the transcendence proper to nature, *as intersubjective nature* over against the isolated "I," stems from this first, true transcendence.

8

The "I"
and the Person

The terms "I" (the pure "I") and "person" (the personal "I") denote two aspects of a unitary problem that became increasingly important, and underwent a progressively differentiating analysis, only after the *Logical Investigations*. At the time of the *Logical Investigations* themselves, Husserl rejected the concept of a pure "I," regarding it as a fiction. Furthermore, a treatment of the concept of the person was simply not to be found within his phenomenology of immanent experience. After years of perplexity as to "what constitutes the phenomenological character of the 'I' " (*PITC*, 253 [1905]), Husserl in *Ideas I* (1913) succeeded in arriving at a positive point of view in respect of the question concerning the pure "I." Determined by motives that we shall discuss below at greater length, he recognized the phenomenological evidence of the pure "I" within the domain of research made up by phenomenologically reduced, pure, immanent experiences. In the work conceived as a continuation of book one of the *Ideas*, that is, in the drafts from his last years in Göttingen, he had also laid bare a number of essential traits of the *personal* "I" (cf. *Id* II, passim). It is especially from 1916 onward, thus during Husserl's Freiburg period, that we come upon a deepened consideration of the question concerning that "which we call an 'I' in the proper sense" (*PP*, 215 / S, 164); and at the same time we find here a clarification of the relationship between the concept of the pure "I" and that of the personal "I."

On the basis of the phenomenological reduction first introduced in the period of about 1905 to 1907 (cf. above, chap. 2), it would at first appear as if phenomenological analysis had to do with immanent experiences "in a nowhere-land" (*EP* I, 166), or with the pure, immanent experiences "of no one at all" (*DR*, 40f.). On the basis of phenomenology itself, Husserl seems unable at first to extract any sense from the question how it stands with "me," with the "I," I who have these particular, immanent experiences, which, as a phenomenlogist, I investigate within the reduction in respect of their eidetic constitution. The most he can make of this question is to regard it as a problem concerning the constitution of the empirical, thingly [*dinglich*], transcendent "I" of the human being, *within* pure, immanent experiences (ibid.).

In the years prior to *Ideas I*, however, two quite different connections within the static analysis of immanent experience moved Husserl to take into consideration, within the phenomenological reduction, the subjective orientation toward an I-subject of these pure, immanent experiences. On the one hand, he considered the "I" as the principle of unity delimiting one stream of consciousness over against another stream of consciousness. On the other hand, he brought the "I" into consideration in order to define the pregnant concept of the *cogito* as an act of the "I." Whereas the concept of the pure "I," which was bound to the first, intersubjective, motivational nexus, could always be differentiated into an "I" and a "you"; the concept of the pure "I," established as the form of the *cogito*, is situated prior to all such differentiations. Numerous difficulties emerge along with this concept of the "I" defined as the universal form of consciousness. Throughout Husserl's works, a deep-seated ambiguity in the concept of the pure "I" results from the fact that Husserl drew the contents of this concept from the two, diverse domains delineated above.

1. As concerns the first motivational nexus, the reference to the "I" showed itself to be unavoidable as soon as, beyond the "one," absolutely given, (phenomenologically still unclarified "own") consciousness, *other* consciousnesses had also to be drawn into the fundamental problematics, regarding the constitution, performed by consciousness, of objectivities as "intersubjective unities" (cf. *PI* I, 135)—unities such as things, nature as such, the sciences. The problem posed here is no longer merely that of determining the unity of a stream of consciousness as a continuously *temporal* interconnection of immanent experiences. It is rather the problem of fundamentally determining the phenomenological *self-containment* of one (*my*) unity of consciousness over against other

unities of consciousness given in "empathy." As soon as presentiations [*Vergegenwärtigungen*] like empathy were drawn into the phenomenological field, "the ever and *a priori* possible question" (*Ms. B II 19*, 29b [1912]) just "*whose cogitatio, whose* pure consciousness" (*PI* I, 155) is the "pure consciousness" that gets thematized in the phenomenological reduction, took on its full poignancy; for "empathy does not belong to modes of consciousness of the sort that presentiate one's 'own' cogitationes" (221).

The task was posed of showing, in a purely phenomenological manner, that temporally unified, immanent experiences are *exclusively* the immanent experiences of a *single* experiencing subject. In this context, Husserl asks, "how is *this* pure consciousness characterized, this *pure I*-consciousness?" In order to answer this question, he sets out to establish "the solely decisive principle . . . for constructing the unity of the stream of consciousness" (186). In doing so, he discerns in compelling fashion the unity-function [*Einheits-Funktion*] of the pure "I" (cf. no. 6, §§ 36ff.; app. XXVI; nos. 10, 11). We can summarize Husserl's train of thought as follows: The stream of consciousness as a whole is not given but rather is "able to be brought to givenness in the form of recollections and post-factual reflections within the recollection" (219). As essential for determining the unity of a stream of consciousness, Husserl now sets forth the phenomenon of *possible I-identification* (the possible being-present of the same "I" within the actually performing consciousness and within the presentiated consciousness). It is the I-identification that decides whether the data of consciousness belong (refer) to my stream of consciousness or to another stream of consciousness. In the case of presentiations like empathy, this being-present of the "I" within the presentiated immanent experience is "not connected with the demand of identification."

> An identifying extension of the "I" by means of the addition of presentiations of the "I" and the *cogitationes* is possible only in the form of memory and expectation, or, if need be, of the empty possibilities. [319; concerning these various forms of presentation, cf. above, chap. 5]

One can see that what comes into view in these analyses as the "supreme subject who performs the coincidence as an act of identification" (303) cannot be the "empirical subject (the human being) endowed with this or that body and this or that set of determinate personality traits" (296). Rather, it can only be a subject which must be designated as a *pure* "I" "in indeterminate corporality (or none at all) and in indeterminate personality" (296). Over against the unity of *temporal* continuity, there now emerges the novel point of view of the unity of a stream of consciousess that is phenomenologically self-contained in relation to other streams, a unity grounded in the *pure I-identity*. In a manuscript stemming from 1914, Husserl writes the following: "It is not merely a consciousness-time-field [*Bewußtseins-Zeit-Feld*] as a stream of consciousness . . . rather: an evident identity is conscious, . . . [a] reference to a point of unity, [namely, to the pure 'I']" (*Ms. A III 4*, 58b).

If we take a brief look at Husserl's later work, we find his thinking confronted time and again with the already discussed stock of intersubjective problems regarding, on the one hand, the consciousness that is encountered primordially within phenomenological reduction and reflection and, on the other hand, the other consciousness that announces itself therein. Husserl is constantly concerned with the phenomenological delimitation of what is "my own," of the "sphere of originality" (or "sphere of ownness," "sphere of primordinality") as against the Being and life of all others (cf., e.g., *EP* II, 432; concerning experience of the other, cf. chap. 5, § 2). Again and again in this context he sets forth the function of the pure "I" and grounds "mineness in this centering of experience in the 'I' [that takes place] by way of a constantly self-actualizing coincidence within every emerging presentation" (*PI* III, 351, 193).

It is true in respect of this I-principle of unity, and this was set forth by Husserl as early as *Ideas I*, that it forms a transcendence within the immanence of the stream of pure, immanent experience (*Id* I, § 57). For the pure "I" is not to be encountered in a really immanent fashion among the pure, immanent experiences that flow by and away in consciousness. Rather, it preserves a numerical identity in contrast with the *cogitationes* which come and go. During the years following *Ideas I*, Husserl defined the pure "I" ever more decisively as a unity that does not itself belong in the immanent, temporal flow, a unity that rather is "atemporal," a "transtemporal, 'ideal' [that is, not really immanent] unity, nevertheless related to [the] immanent temporality" of immanent experiences (cf. *Ms E III 2*, 35; *Ms. L I 20*, 4a [1917–18]; *Ms. A IV 5*, 42a/b [1925]). Only as an "I" identi*fied* within the presentiating and presentiated act does it have a temporal duration (cf., e.g., *PI* I, 318) and form a unique objectivity (cf., e.g., *Id* II, 101).

2. As concerns the concept of the pure "I" attached to the universal concept of an act of consciousness in the pregnant sense of the *cogito*, we meet the following thesis in *Ideas I*:

> Among the universal, eidetic characteristics of the transcen-
> dentally purified domain of immanent experience, the fore-
> most position properly belongs to the relation of every
> immanent experience to the "pure" "I." Every "*cogito*," in an
> eminent sense every act, is characterized as an act of the "I"; it
> "goes forth from the 'I' "; the "I" "lives" in the act "in pres-
> ent actuality" [*aktuell*]. [*Id* I, § 80]

In the years immediately preceding *Ideas I*, Husserl introduced this concept of the "I" in connection with the phenomenon of *attention* that is
constitutive for the concept of the act in the pregnant sense. Ever since
the *Logical Investigations*, he had placed the phenomenon of attention
into an essential connection with intentionality as such. He conceived
attention "as a basic kind of intentional modification" (192, fn. 1 / G,
270). In a note from the spring of 1912, Husserl writes the following:

> [W]ith every intentional, immanent experience, the mode of
> living within this experience is eminent and signifies an actually
> engaged [*aktuell*] attention to the object of this immanent ex-
> perience. . . . This attending, as a being-directed, a being-
> turned-toward, . . . is . . . nothing other than an expression for
> the "performance [*Vollzug*]" of an intentional, immanent expe-
> rience. [*PBE*, 344]

For Husserl, presumably influenced by the psychological doctrines of
Th. Lipps and A. Pfänder concerning the "I" as the central point of
psychic life (cf. *Id* I, 192, fn. 1 / G, 270), such being-directed-toward, or
performing, points back to a center of radiation or a performing subject,
a source-point of the life of consciousness.

Again, early in 1912, Husserl wrote the following:

> With this change in self-directing attention, . . . it is as if the
> self-directing were an emitted ray and as if all these rays co-
> hered as emanations from a central "I." . . . "I," but that is as
> a rule the *empirical* "I." We shall here leave undecided whether
> it can comprise or signify something else, and, in general, what
> more this relation to the "I" comprises phenomenologically.
> [*Ms. A VI 8 I*, 18a]

Then, a few months later, in *Ideas I*, Husserl unquestioningly introduced
the "I" in its function as the source-point of the rays of attention.

> "Being-directed-toward," "being-occupied-with," "assuming-an-attitude-toward," "experiencing or undergoing something," necessarily shelters within its essence the fact that it is precisely a "from the 'I' thither," or, in the reversed directional ray, a "thither toward the 'I' "—*and this "I" is the pure "I,"* no reduction could find fault with it. [*Id* I, 160 / G, 223]

From certain self-critical texts it is clear that Husserl was thoroughly aware that all talk of an "I-center" was *figurative* or analogical, being modelled after the centering of orientation in the *body*. In a note which probably stems from 1914, for example, he asks the following:

> [I]f we abstract from the body and from the bodily determinate subject, if we leave out of play whatever is brought into play by these particular apperceptions, does something remain which makes possible the image of the I-center, the ray and counter-ray, etc.? [*PI* I, 248]

However, Husserl never quite demonstrated with clarity that, if, properly speaking, the bodily determinate subject fulfills its function as the center of the course of sensuous consciousness, then it is precisely not *the pure "I"* "in indeterminate corporality (or none at all)" that can be the subject to which falls the task of accomplishing the centering in the here and now.

As concerns this concept of the "I," bound as it is to the form of the *cogito*, let us also have a look at the later path of Husserl's thinking. As soon as Husserl deepens his transcendental theory of constitution by means of a systematic analysis of pregiven items [*Vorgegebenheiten*] constituted in passive association, he introduces the notion of the "I" as the pole of the affections, as the center of reception [*Einstrahlungszentrum*] (cf., e.g., *PI* II, 30). This corresponds in all respects with Husserl's doctrine of the "I" as the center of radiation [*Ausstrahlungszentrum*], or, as he will say increasingly after *Ideas I*, as the pole of the actions or of the intentional, immanent experiences which have the specific form of the *cogito*. Affection is defined as a "form of performance of intentional, immanent experiences, or as a mode of the I's participation in intentionality" (*Ms. M III 3 III 1 II*, 165 [1921–23]). Over against the active "I" stands the passive "I." "Whenever it is active, [the 'I' is] at the same time passive, both in the sense of [being] affective and in the sense of [being] receptive" (*Id* II, 213 [ca. 1916]). During the 1930s, going beyond the necessary I-relatedness in the sense of "streaming in [*Einstrahlen*]" that

takes place at the lowest stage of constitution, Husserl ponders the possibility of understanding these lowest intentionalities as *streaming out* of
the "I." He speaks of a "universal intentionality of drives" which goes
forth from the self-temporalizing "I" as a pole (cf. *PI* III, 595 [Sept.
1933]).

The pure "I," as it has been understood in the static analyses discussed up until now, is essentially distinguished by its *immutability* and by
the related possibility of "drawing it completely, . . . as an *adequate
givenness*, . . . from every *cogito*" (*Ms. F III 1*, 6a; *Id* II, 97, 111; *Id* I, 86).

> No accumulation of self-experiences, however vast, can teach
> me to know that the pure "I" is and [to know] what it is better
> than the isolated experience of a single, simple *cogito* can. It
> would be absurd to hold the opinion that I, the pure "I," pos-
> sibly do not exist or am something quite other than that which
> functions in this *cogito*. [*Ms. F III 1*, 240b; *Id* II, 104]

During the years following the publication of *Ideas I*, Husserl conceived, over against the static and, as it were, empty "I," both the much
more concrete concept of the *personal "I"* in correlation with its surrounding-world, and the concept of the *monad* (cf. above, chap. 5, § 2,
"Our Experience of the Other"). The development of the concept of the
personal "I" seemingly coheres very closely with Husserl's turn to a *genetic* understanding of the problem of constitution (cf. above, chap. 7).
During his Freiburg period, Husserl constantly thematized anew *the de-
veloping correlation between the personal "I" and the surrounding-world*
[*Umwelt*]. In this way he arrived at the principles of a theory, linked to
Kant but exceeding him in its concreteness, of transcendental subjectivity and intersubjectivity as rooted in the "constant and abiding *personal
'I,' *" or in the *community* of personal I's, and correlated with the objec-
tive world of experience (cf. *CM*, 101 / C, 66f.)[1]

With reference to the "self-constitution" of the "I" in the genesis
of apperceptions, Husserl states that, *as the subject of apperceptions*, the
subject is "itself concretely determined."

> It is not merely and generally an abstract I-point related to a
> surrounding-world of things; rather, it exists as a subject with
> capabilities (a subject having a determinate "I can"). [*Ms. A VI
> 30*, 39f.]

> The capabilities point back to *fields of possession* [*Felder der
> Habe*], and therewith is expressed a primordial and acquired

psychical possession from which stimuli go forth upon me, the
subject of freedom, stimuli which I, following them, have at my
disposal. [*Ms. A VI 9*, 2a (probably 1916)]

"What we call an *'I' in the proper sense* (apart from the communicative
relation to a 'you' or a 'we')," Husserl defines ever more pregnantly as a
"*personal individuality*," as the "*subject of personal motivations*" (*PP*, 215 /
S, 164; *Ms. A VI 9*, 2a). The following characterizations from the decade
of the twenties are typical in this sense:

The "I" in the proper sense is the I-pole with the habitualities
and capabilities which accrue to it from living and taking positions. [*PI* II, 275]

Yet the "I" is always constituted (and constituted in a manner
entirely its own) as a personal "I," the "I" of its habitualities,
its capabilities, its character. [44, fn. 1]

Husserl is endeavoring to develop a phenomenological "*concept of
the essence* of the person" (21). Although "the personal 'I' is *individual*,"
we can determine according to universal eidetic laws "what this 'I' is, an
'I' which can be comprehended only through living familiarization with
an actual *cogito*, with the interconnection of attitudes lying in the background (having become habitual) and with the motivational nexus; [we
can determine] what I actually encounter as an identically continuous
person, as 'I' " (21, 17). Here we can but touch on Husserl's manifold
descriptions concerning the concept of the personal "I" by indicating
several main themes. One essential thought which comes to the fore
again and again is that Husserl grasps the person as a "principle of *intelligibility*, thus, *rationality*" (cf., e.g., *PI* II, 17; *PP*, 225 / S, 172; *Ms. E III
2*, 21b; *Ms. A VI 25*, 10 ff.). The person is not simply an "associatively
and inductively constituted unity" in which "nothing of individuality" is
manifested (*PI* II, 19ff.; *PI* I, 434f.). Rather, the person is constituted
with an "individual peculiarity," an "abiding style" with a pervasive unity
of identity, a "personal character" (cf. *PI* II, 23; *PP*, 215 / S, 164f.; *CM*,
101 / C, 67). According to Husserl, these concepts, "personality," "individuality," "character," refer to "the field of convictions formed by the
'I' and defining the 'I' as an 'I' " (*PP*, 214 / S, 164); they refer to the
habitual peculiarities.

The individual peculiarity that distinguishes the "I" is manifested
in the attitudes of the "I," in its interests, its motivations, fixed opinions,

decisions, and convictions. Husserl attempts to understand the essence of the changing personal "I," in correlation with its surrounding-world, as a *"unity of consistency."* When the "I" abandons a conviction "it alters its 'direction toward.' " It is nevertheless "again, and necessarily, directed (and directed in the manner of the abiding 'I'), but it has over against itself 'another' surrounding-world . . . ; it is the same subject of the new world, but, on the other hand, it is that which has changed in respect of its convictions, wishes, etc." (*Ms. A VI 30*, 45b [between 1918 and 1921]).

> My surrounding-world is thus a constantly changing realm of abiding positions, and, correlatively, I myself am constantly changing as the subject which consistently posits these positings of the world. I myself change in the form of inconsistency.

However, the following is true:

> There persists throughout all the I's which change by way of inconsistency, and throughout all the ever new, habitual I's, or there is constituted within them, a *consistently abiding "I,"* and, as its correlate: *one and the same surrounding-world* (the universe of what holds good from the standpoint of my positing). [*Ms. A VI 30*, 46b]

During the decades of the twenties and thirties, Husserl thematized this correlativity of the personal "I" and the surrounding-world with respect to the following "possibilities."

1. With respect to Kant's problem of the " 'I' of transcendental apperception" and the concomitant "transcendental deduction." The idea of a consistent "I" appears to Husserl in the final analysis to be "too formal" (*Ms. A VI 30*, 37a), insufficient for a full, concrete determination of the *self-preservation*, the unity of the "I," which belongs to the genuine sense of the "I" of transcendental apperception (cf. *Ms. A VI 30*, 37a, 43f.; *Ms. A V 21*, 101a). The "I" of self-preservation must be defined concretely in connection with the "question of the universal structure of experience, or the constitution of a stable and enduring world." Husserl seeks to demonstrate that *"as an 'I,' the 'I' has unity in virtue of the world,* if it is an actual world, if it is the title for a realm of truths-in-themselves" (*Ms. A VI 30*, 38b). The world must have a certain structure and, on the other hand, the "I" must bear within itself "potentially the possibility of an acquirable, stable habituality," for "it is obvious that everything

which is for me under the title 'world,' is for me only from the standpoint of my intentionality" (*Ms. A VI 30*, 38). In a brief note bearing the title, the " 'I' of Transcendental Apperception," Husserl writes the following:

> [The] I-pole is not I. I am in my convictions. I preserve my one and selfsame "I"—my ideal I-of-the-understanding—when I can continue to strive, constantly and assured, for the unity of a total conviction; when a world of objects remains constantly preserved for me with the open possibility of determining it harmoniously and ever more closely. [*Ms. A VI 30*, 54b (probably 1926)]

2. With respect to the possibility of the dissolution of the world into a tumult, in correlation with the dissolution of the "I" of transendental apperception. Along with his doctrine concerning the factuality of the constitution of the world (cf. below, chap. 10), Husserl conceives the possibility of a disintegration of the personal "I." In one of the numerous texts dealing with these problems, one can read the following:

> Need there be steadfast and abiding I's as persons, or at least a steadfast and abiding personal totality in possible community . . . ; need I, need any person be? Does there lie in the evidence of the "I am" more than the evidence of the person in relation to a presumptive world, and why should there not be able to be a "variegated [*vielfärbiges*]" self? Is the opposite not in fact thinkable; can I not, as it were, commit *personal* suicide by way of dismantling the associative constitution of experience, while my life, even if it is objectively significationless, nonetheless remains as the foundation for this suicidal possibility, my life together with the I-polarization, although this I-pole has no personal, habitual signification. [*Ms. A VI 30*, 52b (probably from the decade of the twenties)]

3. Finally, Husserl explores the question concerning the *a priori* grounding of the possibility of diverse kinds of unitary surrounding-worlds in correlation with diverse kinds of "personal" subjects. Summarizing his efforts in a very general fashion, we may say that he investigates the surrounding-worlds belonging to humans—among them the world of early childhood, the world of the "mature" person as "normal," the world of "primitive" peoples, the world of the abnormal, the world of the sick—over against the surrounding-world belonging to animals.

From the 1930s in particular, one finds notes in which Husserl is seeking to grasp the specific difference of the surrounding-world belonging to humans, or of the person, as against the animal world. Above all, he emphasizes both human *self-relatedness* to the *universality of life*, and individual as well as social *history*, over against the "present-I [*Gegenwarts-Ich*]" of the animal.

> [The] human person does not live within the bare present; it lives within its whole life; its whole life, its personal Being, as personal Being that has been and, again, as future personal Being; the whole of past personality within the whole of personal temporality, within the whole of the personal, streaming duration of life, is thematic for the person, is a motivational field, a field of specifically human attitudes, valuations and volitions. [*Ms. A V 5*, 12a/b]

He asks whether in the case of animals we must not, by contrast, assume a "purely instinctive intentionality, instinctively directed toward harmony," in order to explain the constitution of the surrounding-world belonging to animals, an instinctive intentionality such that animals themselves would know nothing of this intentionality "which we ascribe to them in naive empathy" (*PI* III, 184).

> They have the past only as retentionality and they have the self-sameness of things only in the form of a primary recognition, [a recognition] which as yet has cognizance neither of going back to the past in recollection (as a quasi-perceiving-again), nor of the identifying of temporal and spatial positions which makes possible the individuality of things as existing. [Ibid.]

Husserl then attempts in the following manner to establish what would, by contrast, distinguish the *human* being and the surrounding-world belonging to *humans*:

> With humans there is accomplished a constant transformation of passive intentionality into an activity, [a transformation which stems] from *capabilities of repetition*. Is this correct as a rough distinction? [Ibid.]

In conclusion, let us allude to Husserl's determinations of the relationship between the pure, immutable, numerically identical "I," and the personal "I". On the one hand, a sharp distinction exists between the two concepts in respect of what they address. This distinction is reflected in the mode of phenomenological givenness.

> The pure "I" is not the person. . . . The person "I" is he who remains *identical within the alteration* in the life of my "I," my being active and affected; it is never given adequately in reflection. [*Ms. A VI 21*, 21]

On the other hand, there indeed exists and must exist an identity of the "I." "[The] pure 'I,' however, also lies enclosed within the personal 'I'; every act *cogito* of the personal 'I' is also an act of the pure 'I' " (ibid.). The identity within alteration, which is constitutive for the personal "I," remains ultimately grounded in the pure "I."

> The [personal] "I" remains unchanged as long as it "stays with its conviction, its opinion"; to alter its conviction is to alter "itself." But both in alteration and in non-alteration the "I" is identically the same, precisely as a pole. [*Id* II, 311]

The Lifeworld, Both as a Problem Concerning the Foundation of the Objective Sciences and as a Problem Concerning Universal Being and Truth

§ 1. A Remark Concerning Husserl's Use of the Word "Lifeworld"

Prior to 1920 Husserl can already be found making sporadic use of the expression "lifeworld [*Lebenswelt*]."[1] It is not until the 1920s, however, that it enters Husserl's philosophy as a technical term for a fundamental problem. Initially, "lifeworld" is used interchangeably with "natural concept of the world [*natürlicher Weltbegriff*]"[2] and "world of ['natural' or] simple experience [*natürliche oder schlichte Erfahrungswelt*]." In the course of the 1920s, however, it acquires a special signification distinguishing it from these expressions. The problem designated by the term "lifeworld" takes on great systematic importance in the lectures, "Phenomenological Psychology," from the years 1925 and 1928, published in *Husserliana* IX; "Introduction to Phenomenological Philosophy," from 1926/27, published in part in *Husserliana* IX and XIV; "Nature and

Spirit," from 1927, still to be published; and in the works on *Formal and Transcendental Logic* and *The Crisis of the European Sciences.*

§ 2. The Problem Concerning the Foundation of the Objective Sciences; in Particular, the Problem Concerning "Nature and Spirit"

Husserl's philosophical activity is motivated in large measure by questions concerning the foundation of the sciences. Originally impelled by problems concerning the foundation of mathematics and logic, it expanded to become a universal theory of cognition. In point of method, it ultimately understood itself as an "analysis of pure consciousness" and, in the course of clarifying this methodological self-understanding, was led rather early on to questions regarding its own relation to psychology, and thus at once to questions regarding the methodological foundations of psychology.[3] In spite of all the contrast differentiating phenomenological philosophy from psychology, Husserl's phenomenology claims to be able to adduce the conceptual foundations of psychology as well. Stimulated above all by ideas of Dilthey, Windelband, and Rickert, Husserl had already sought, prior to the publication of the *Ideas*, but then especially in the posthumously published second volume of this work, to clarify the fundamental concepts of the pertinent sciences. He attempted to do so by means of constitutive analyses of the world of nature and the natural-scientific (naturalistic) attitude, as well as of the world of spirit and the spiritual-scientific (personalistic) attitude. However, it was only during the 1920s that—within these philosophical discussions, oriented initially toward the multitude of the factual, empirical sciences—the question concerning the *unity and fundamental organization* of these sciences stepped into the foreground for Husserl. This was at once the question concerning the unity and inner structure of the *world* to which all of these different sciences refer. It was only through the fundamental centering of concern in this concept that Husserl's philosophical investigations, related reflectively to the empirical sciences, acquired a systematic unity and thereby approached the ideal which had guided Husserl for so long, the ideal of *one*, universal science embracing all the positive sciences and resting upon an ultimate philosophical foundation.

The ideal: Whether one call it philosophy or universal science,
there is, in the highest sense of the word, only one, single, genuine science. There will always be special sciences, of course,
with special domains of research, special methods, a special
theoretical technique and presupposing special personal apti-
tude. The division and apportionment of the special sciences
will not be arbitrary, it will not be simply practical and accidental, not, at least, if it should turn out, as we have predicted,
that the world of experience has its essential, universal structures in the form of abstractive divisions into domains, such as,
perhaps, [the division] into [the domains of] nature and spirit.
But all the sciences will now be organs, even if essentially
united, living branches on the one tree of the universal science.
[*Ms. F I 32*, 41a (Lectures on "Nature and Spirit," 1927); cf.
Ms. A IV 5, 10b]

Husserl was driven on to unfold the problem of the "natural concept of the world," or the "lifeworld," principally by the question concerning the relationship between nature and spirit, and thus between the
natural sciences and the human sciences (see *PP*, 54ff.; *Ms. F I 32*, 40a,
86a, 99a, 117ff.). More precisely, he was impelled by his attempt to come
to terms with the dualism of the Cartesian tradition, which understood
the body (nature) and the spirit (soul) as two separate realities, capable,
however, of being known in methodologically analogous fashion. Husserl had become convinced early on that a psychology cultivated on the
model of natural science would overlook the proper essence of the psychic. Over the years, the insight deepened in him that actual clarification
of the relationship between nature and spirit could be accomplished
only by stepping back *from* the guiding, factual, scientific concepts, as
products of methodological technique, *to* the world of primordial experience, in which nature and spirit are given "within a primordially intuitable interpenetration of one another" (*PP*, 55; *Ms. F I 32*, 40a). Only the
world of primordial experience can provide the guidelines for appropriate scientific interests.

Had one gone back to the full, primordial concretion of the
world, just as it is always experienced in naive primordiality,
and had one in one's methodological abstractions never forgotten this concretely intuitable world as the primordial field [of
experience], then the perversions of naturalistic psychology
and the naturalistic human sciences would not have been possible. One could never have hit upon the idea of interpreting the

> spirit as a merely causal annex of the material, bodily organism
> [*Leib*] or as a causal sequence parallel to physical materiality.
> One could never have regarded humans and animals as psycho-
> physical machines or even as parallelistic double-machines.
> [*PP*, 56f.]

In spite of all differences, this return by Husserl to the world of natural experience is reminiscent not only of the more recent attempts by the philosophy of natural language (Wittgenstein, Austin, Ryle), but especially of Richard Avenarius's idea of the "restitution of the natural concept of the world" over against the falsifications of dualistic metaphysics.[4] Husserl himself, however, does not aim at the restitution of this primordial concept of the world but rather at the foundation of the sciences which are related to this world.

> If the primordial source of all world-related sciences lies here,
> then . . . every primordially clear distinction among the sci-
> ences must be performed by way of a return to the world of
> experience . . . ; the domain of every special science must lead
> us back to a domain belonging to the world of primordial ex-
> perience. Here we behold the site of the origin of a radically
> founded distribution or division of possible sciences of the
> world. [64]

§ 3. The Scientific World and the Lifeworld

What at first was for Husserl a foundational problem in the theory of science, developed in his considerations into a "problem of universal Being and truth." In his last work, the "lifeworld" has come to designate a "universal problem" (cf. *CES*, §§ 34f.). This revaluation was carried out by way of a deeper meditation, conditioned by difficulties in the very subject matter, on the question of *what* the experiential foundation of scientific praxis might be. It was thus carried out by way of a revaluation of the concept of the lifeworld itself.

During the 1920s, the regress from the sciences to their experiential foundation signified for Husserl the return to "simple" or "pure" experience. At the time, this meant for him a return to *preconceptual* (prelinguistic, pre-predicative) experience. The world of simple experience, in which all sciences are ultimately founded, "is prior to all empirical thinking" (*PP*, 69); within this world, "every predicating, theorizing activity, like every other activity which lades the object of experience with any novel sense whatsoever, remains disengaged" (59). "Within the unity of experience itself, a thoroughly uniform, continuous, internally coherent world is experienced prior to all talking about, thinking over, founding, [and] theorizing" (*Ms. F I 32*, 39b, 40a). It is the world of bare, preconceptual perception and memory (*PP*, 58ff.), the world of bare intuition. It is what Husserl calls in the *Cartesian Meditations* the "primordinal world" or the "sphere of ownness," that is to say, the world which is itself experienced primordinally and which is able thus to be experienced by the individual subject in abstraction from the traditional, intersubjective system of communication (*CM*, § 44; cf. above, chap. 5, § 2). Within this perspective, the task for the inquiry into foundations is the following:

> To traverse the path which leads from mute, conceptless experience and its universal interweavings; first to typical, vague, primary universality, which is sufficient in everyday life; and thence to the genuine and true concepts, such as genuine science must presuppose them to be. [*Ms. F I 32*, 39b, 40a]

During the 1920s Husserl also called this unhistorical "world of intuition" the "lifeworld" (110b). As in certain tendencies within the so-called philosophy of life, the concept of life would here seem to form a contrast with intellectual, conceptual thinking. In the course of time, however, Husserl's definition of the kind of experience that could furnish a foundation for the sciences changed, and, with this change, the concept of the "lifeworld" changed as well. In the lectures on "Phenomenological Psychology" from 1925, Husserl stated the matter as follows:

> We go from [what] in our mind [are] the questionable concepts "nature" and "spirit," as concepts defining the provinces of [certain] sciences, back to the world situated prior to all sciences and their theoretical intentions, as a world of pretheoretical intuition.

Later, in his manuscript for this lecture, however, he adds the following note: "[Y]es, as a world of the presently actual [*aktuell*] life in which the world-experiencing and world-theorizing life is enclosed" (*PP*, 56). And in the lectures, "Introduction to Phenomenology," from 1926/27, after demanding not only an "epoché in respect of all science" but also a "radical meditation on the sense of that which is situated prior to all science as the universal ground of experience upon which science builds" (*PI* II, 396), he says the following:

> On the other hand, for us cultivated Europeans, the sciences
> are nevertheless there, a constituent of our multifarious world
> of culture, just as are our art, our scientific technology, etc.
> Albeit we may leave their validity unengaged, albeit we may
> place them in question, they are for us coexistent matters of
> fact [*Mit-Tatsachen*] in the world of experience in which we live.
> Whether they are clear or unclear, fully valid or invalid, the sci-
> ences, like all products of human work, be they good or bad,
> belong to the make-up of the world as a world of pure experi-
> ence. [Ibid.][5]

The experience which ultimately supports the sciences is thus no longer a mute, preconceptual intuition, but rather the experience of the actually present [*aktuell*], concrete, historical world, together with its cultural products and, hence, its concepts and sciences. This thought, initially expressed hesitantly by Husserl during the 1920s, was clearly conveyed in the *Crisis*. There Husserl maintains that objective science has its foundation in the lifeworld and, as a human achievement, be-longs, like all other human achievements, in the concrete lifeworld (cf. *CES*, 107, 127, 132f., 136, 139, 141, 460 / C, 104f., 124f., 129ff., 133, 136, 138f., 380f.). If Husserl's problem concerning the foundation of objective science was initially formulated as a problem concerning the foundational relationship between the scientific concept and the precon-ceptual intuition, in the course of his reflections it was transformed into the problem concerning the fundamental relation between the abstract world of objective theory and the concrete, historical world of subjective life in which "theoretical praxis" belongs as one mode of human praxis *among others* ("and, in fact, a peculiar and historically late" mode of praxis) (113, 135, 145 / C, 111, 132f., 142).

On the one hand, the thing that led Husserl to this transforma-tion of his problematic was no doubt already conditioned purely in terms of considerations within the theory of science. The foundation of the human sciences, in any case, cannot be a mute, preconceptual experi-ence. It can only be a living participation in the cultural world. On the other hand, during the 1920s, the problem of objective science came to be perceived by Husserl not only as a concern belonging to the theory of science but as a problem involving the relevance, the sense of science for concrete, historical life. Like many of his contemporaries, Husserl became sensitive to the "estrangement from life" characteristic of the objective sciences; that is to say, he became sensitive to the fact that these sciences had nothing to say with regard to the most important questions for human life, the questions concerning the sense and meaning of life. It was in this fact that he saw the deepest crisis of the sciences, in the literal sense, their separation from concrete, subjective life. It was for this reason that the problem concerning the relationship between the objective sciences and concrete, historical life, or between reality as constructed by objective science and the reality of the subjective lifeworld, stepped into the center of his interest (cf. *Ms. F I 32*, 109a ff.; *CES*, § 2).

Regarding this relationship, Husserl developed the following main thoughts: The objective Being of the sciences, as they have developed since Greek Antiquity and the Renaissance (especially Galileo), is the correlate of a quite particular *teleological idea*, namely, the idea "of the world existing stably and determinately in itself and of the *idealiter* scientific truths ('truths-in-themselves') that explain this world predicatively" (*CES*, 113, cf. 124f. / C, 111, cf. 121f.). It is the idea of true Being, existing *in itself* and independent from all that is merely subjective and relative. This Platonic notion was carried over and applied to nature by Galileo insofar as he imputed to nature an ideal, mathematical Being. Husserl also defined this guiding idea as an "hypothesis of Being-in-itself" (133, cf. 129 / C, 130, cf. 126). Under the guidance of this idea, the objectively constructed world of the sciences is the product of an idealization. In the course of his vocational activities, the objective scientist lives under the sway of this teleological idea. As he engenders his results (objective truths), this idea constitutes the horizon of his interest. This particular, teleological idea determines his "world," that is it determines what for him is real (correct in respect of his aim) and unreal (incorrect in respect of his aim) (cf. app. XVII / C, app. VII). It is, however, only "*one* of many practical hypotheses and projects" within the encompassing, intersubjective nexus of life (133 / C, 130).

> The scientific world . . . like all purposeful worlds, "belongs" to the lifeworld, just as do all humans and all human communities as such and their human aims . . . [along with] all products of [human] work. . . . Each of these worlds has its particular universality as determined by its vocational aim, each has the infinite horizon of a certain "totality." All these totalities, however, are fitted into the world that encompasses all beings and all existing totalities, just as are all their aims and all humans and human societies having aims. [460 / C, 380f.]

As "a purposeful structure that continues without end" (461/ C, 382), the scientific world is founded in a mode of "Being [*Sein*] that precedes all purpose" (462 / C, 382).

> The lifeworld is the constantly pregiven world, constantly hold-
> ing good in advance, but holding good on the basis of no pur-
> pose [or] theme whatsoever, in accordance with no universal
> aim. Every aim presupposes the lifeworld. [462 / C, 382]

Yet, although objective science presupposes the always pregiven lifeworld, which afterwards absorbs the work of science, the lifeworld is not the theme of science (462 / C, 382f.).

The lifeworld is the "actually concrete surrounding-world" (*Ms. F I 32*, 110a; cf. *PP*, 55), the reality proper in which we live and, for us, the always already pregiven, preexistent ground and horizon of all theoretical and extratheoretical praxis (*CES*, 145 / C, 142). As such an horizon and ground, the lifeworld does, to be sure, always inhabit consciousness: but, even in prescientific and extrascientific praxis, it is never as such an object of our attention and reflection. For we live our lives engrossed thematically in our current aims, be they momentary or enduring, aims which constitute their own, abstract "worlds" inside of the lifeworld; "normally there is no reason to make the lifeworld universally [and] expressly thematic for ourselves" (459 / C, 379).

Over against the objective world of science, the lifeworld is "the universe of being [*Seiendem*] which constantly is for us in an unceasing movement of relativity" (462 / C, 383). It is the world of that which is intuitively experienced, that which is relative to the experiencing subject (127 / C, 124f.) and which, even in ordinary life, is related to our human community as a community of human beings endowed with normal sensibility and normal mutual understanding (*Ms. F I 32*, 6a, 25b).

> The presupposition which always guides [our] life, [namely],
> that the experiential world is—whereby Being is referred in na-
> ive fashion to a presupposed, empirical normality—is now laid
> hold of in science almost involuntarily as something uncondi-
> tional; i.e., one presupposes a truth and a true Being [*Sein*]
> which reaches out beyond all distinctions between normality
> and anomalousness. However, since every actual individual ex-
> perience and every [actual] communal experience is relative,
> the presupposition of a true Being [*Sein*] and of correspond-
> ingly true in themselves, transrelative determinations of what is
> [*Seiendes*], is from the outset an ideal presupposition, a presup-

position transcending every actual and possible experience.
[*Ms. F I 32*, 6b]

The contrast between the subjectivity of the lifeworld and the objectivity
of the scientific world thus lies in the fact "that the latter is a theoretical-
logical substruction, the substruction of something fundamentally unable to be perceived, something fundamentally unable to be experienced
in its own being-itself [*Selbstsein*], whereas the subjective [character] of
the lifeworld is distinguished in each and every respect precisely by its
ability actually to be experienced. The lifeworld is a realm of primordial
evidences" (*CES*, 130/ C, 127).
    Although the logical substruction of objective science transcends
the intuitable, subjective lifeworld, it can nevertheless have its truth only
with reference to the evidences of the lifeworld. The theoretical praxis
and the instruments of scientists, both of which are experienced in the
lifeworld, remain the constant basis for acceptance.

> [T]hat which is subjective and relative does not function, shall
> we say, as an irrelevant route of passage but rather as the ulti-
> mate foundation for the theoretical-logical acceptance of Being
> [*Seinsgeltung*] in all objective verification: thus, it functions as
> the source of evidence, the source of verification. The visible
> instruments of measurement and marks of graduation, etc., are
> made use of as actually existing and not as illusory; thus, what
> in the lifeworld actually is, as something valid, is a premise.
> [129 / C, 126]

As a "primordial evidence" for science, the evidence offered by the subjective lifeworld possesses a "higher dignity" in the task of founding cognition than do the evidences of objective-logical science (131 / C, 128).
However, the lifeworld is not only the founding basis for the scientifically
true world. Rather, it simultaneously comprises this world of science
within its own, universal concretion.

> If we cease to be absorbed in our scientific thinking, if it dawns
> upon us that we scientists are, after all, human beings and, as
> such, constituents of the lifeworld, then, along with us, the
> whole of science enters into the—merely "subjective-
> relative"—lifeworld. [133 / C, 130f.]

Husserl thus carries on a critique, over against the objectivistic
orientation of the empirical sciences, analogous to the critique brought

to bear by Kant over against the pure thinking of metaphysics. Whereas Kant acknowledged for *a priori* thinking no cognitive value in itself (as metaphysics), but only a function within empirical cognition, Husserl sent the thinking of an objective "in-itself" yet a step lower by conceding to it, as an objective theory, no value in itself, but only an abstract, practical function within the subjective-relative lifeworld. In other words, he pointed to the fact that a false metaphysics still lay hidden even in the objective "in-itself" of empirical theory, that is to say, in the absolutization of this theory. The empirical sciences which Husserl had in mind in these reflections were, of course, primarily the natural sciences. However, they were not exclusively these, insofar as, according to Husserl, the "hypothesis of the 'in-itself' " "ruled over the entire *universitas* of the positive sciences in the modern period," while Galilean physics served as a model for the objective sciences as such (130 / C, 127).

§ 4. The Idea of an Ontology of the Lifeworld

Husserl now projects the idea of making the subjective-relative lifeworld, as such, the theme of a new kind of science. The aim of this science would be not only a clarification of the foundation for the validity of the objective sciences, but an understanding of the sense of worldly Being and truth as such.

> Can one not [turn to] the lifeworld, the world of which we are
> all conscious in life as the world of us all, without in any way
> making it into a subject of universal investigation, being always
> given over, rather, to our everyday momentary individual or
> universal vocational ends and interests—can one not survey it
> universally in a changed attitude, and can one not seek to get
> to know it, as what it is and how it is in its own mobility and
> relativity, make it the highest subject matter of a universal
> science, but one which has by no means the goal of universal
> theory in the sense in which this was sought by historical phi-
> losophy and the sciences? [462 / C, 383]

This new kind of science requires as its first step "an epoché in respect of all the objective sciences," that is, a kind of abstinence "in respect of the entire objective, theoretical interests, the total aims and actions which are peculiar to us as objective scientists or even simply as scientifically curious" (138f. / C, 135). The results of the objective sciences possess validity within the lifeworld and continuously add themselves to the stock of the lifeworld as superimposed layers of validity (cf. 134, 136 / C, 131, 133). The epoché demanded here by Husserl plainly means an abstinence from complicity in the performance of such validities; indeed, it means an abstinence from every attitude interested in this respect in truth or falsehood (138 / C, 135). Nevertheless, these validities, the objective sciences and the scientists, do not thereby disappear for the one practicing the epoché.

> They continue to be what they were before: matters of fact within the unified context of the pregiven lifeworld, merely that we, in virtue of the epoché, do not function as interested parties, as collaborators, etc. [139 / C, 136]

For the one practicing the epoché, these validities are neutralized; they are no longer co-performed by him, but rather remain present only as opinions of the scientists.

The thematic inspection of the lifeworld, however, requires the epoché not only in relation to the objective sciences, but in relation to *all* interests directed toward an aim and holding us perpetually enclosed within a special horizon (141, cf. app. XVII / C, 138, cf. app. VII). The lifeworld is given prior to all practical aims and can, according to Husserl, come concretely and universally into view only within an attitude that is free of all aims. The attitude that he demands here may have been regarded by Husserl in close proximity to an aesthetic freedom from aims and interests.[6] Certain it is that according to him this aim-free relationship to the world is made possible by an exclusive interest in subjectivity. Such freedom does not dim or diminish these aims, however. Rather, in virtue of its submitting itself to no aim whatsoever, it is able universally to mirror all aims.

This attitude, required for the new science of the lifeworld, seems not to be identical with what Husserl called the "personalistic attitude," the attitude "in which we are whenever we live with one another, speak to one another, shake hands with one another in greeting, relate to one another in love and aversion, in disposition and deed, in address and response; in like manner, in which we are when we regard the things surrounding us precisely as our surroundings, and not, as is the case in natural science, as 'objective' nature" (*Id* II, 183). For Husserl, indeed, the personalistic attitude designates a relation to the world more universal than the relation of the natural or objectivistic attitude, since the latter, "by way of an abstraction, or rather by way of a kind of obliviousness to itself on the part of the personal 'I,' acquires a certain autonomy, thereby simultaneously [and] illegitimately absolutizing its world, [that is,] nature" (183f.). Yet even in our daily, personalistically oriented lives, we are, according to Husserl, directed toward individual aims which leave the lifeworld unthematized in its concreteness and universality.

The surrounding-lifeworlds are relative to the various cultures but have a *universal structure*, which, although it comprises a subjective relativity, is common to the various factual cultures. Thus, there is a temporality, a spatiality, and a causality of the lifeworld, none of which are identical with the corresponding idealizations of objective science. It was in a universal structure or typicality such as this, that Husserl envisioned an *"a priori* of the lifeworld" which would be comprehended in an *a priori* science, in an "ontology of the lifeworld" (176 / C, 173; cf. *PP*, 64f.). Such an ontology would also have to comprehend the universal structures of subjective relativity and intersubjective praxis (for example, the structure "familiar world and foreign world" [cf. *PI* III, app. XI, XII, XIII, XLVIII; no. 27]). Husserl never systematically elaborated such an ontology.

According to Husserl, an *a priori* science of the structures of the lifeworld, such as we have described, is still possible independently of transcendental-subjective interests. This is to say that it is still possible on the basis of the lifeworld prior to assuming the attitude of transcendental reflection (*CES*, 176f. / C, 173f.). Yet, according to him, this sort of "naive" ontology of the lifeworld is ultimately unable to understand the sense of Being that belongs to the lifeworld, for the lifeworld is essentially relative to subjectivity. Final clarification is possible only in reflection upon transcendental subjectivity, upon the "universal, performing life in which the world comes to pass as the world constantly existing for us in streaming occasionality [*strömende Jeweiligkeit*], the world constantly 'pregiven' to us" (148 / C, 145).

> Only thus can we study what the world is, as the basic validity [*Bodengeltung*] of natural life in all of its projects and conducts, and, correlatively, what natural life and its subjectivity *ultimately* are, i.e., purely as the subjectivity that functions there as the consummator of validity. [151 / C, 148]

For the study of this natural life, the transcendental epoché and reduction are methodologically requisite. Thus, in the problematic of the lifeworld, Husserl saw a path to the transcendental reduction (cf. above, chap. 2).

10

First and Second Philosophy or Transcendental Phenomenology and Metaphysics

n this closing chapter we shall comment briefly upon Husserl's overall conception of philosophy. Husserl presents his transcendental phenomenology as a science of *essences*, as an eidetic or *a priori* science in contrast with the factual sciences, the sciences of facts (see *Id* I, 4 / G, 44; and above, chap. 2, § 2). Yet even at the time of the publication of the *Ideas* (1913), he did not regard phenomenological philosophy as restricted simply to essences or the *a priori*. In 1914 he wrote the following:

> By no means do I reduce philosophy to theory of cognition and critique of reason as such; much less [do I reduce it] to transcendental phenomenology. In my eyes, this latter is a science in its own right, the eidetic science of transcendentally pure consciousness and its correlates, which in a certain way encompasses all other eidetic sciences (the system of the formal and material ontologies) and yet does not enclose them within itself. The complete projection of the ontologies and the systematic execution of the transcendental phenomenology corresponding with them and leading back to the highest unity, are in my view the cardinal conditions for the possibility of a scientific philosophy, the complete eidetic foundation for such a philosophy. More particularly they alone make possible a scien-

tific metaphysics that no longer concerns itself [as does transcendental phenomenology] with mere ideal possibilities but
rather [concerns itself] with actuality. . . . Metaphysics is the
proper science of reality. Thus, I, too, want a metaphysics, and
one that is earnestly scientific, except that, in order to keep
pure the boundaries of strict science, I provisionally content
myself in my publications with a more modest task and concen-
trate my energies upon laying the eidetic foundation. [Letter to
K. Joel, 11 March 1914, in *Ms. F III 1*, 140a/b]

For Husserl, it is, on the one hand, in the special essence of consciousness that we find the foundation for the fact that transcendental
phenomenology, as eidetics, has to *precede* "metaphysics," the "absolute
science of factual actuality" (*Ms. F I 14*, 24a [1911]), and thereby constitutes the scientific foundation for this absolute science of the actual. As a
"Heracleitean flow," consciousness is able to be scientifically comprehended only on the basis of essences (cf. above, chap. 2). On the other
hand, he deems universally valid the epistemological principle that everything factual ultimately finds its full rationality only in the realm of
the eidetic or *a priori*.

All reason in the *a posteriori* has its principles *a priori*, and these
principles are the bases of the legitimacy of its objective and
unconditional validity. [*Ms. F I 10*, 95a (1906)]

In my view, the ancient ontological doctrine that the cognition
of possibilities must precede that of actualities is, provided that
it is correctly understood and utilized in the right way, a great
truth. [*Id* I, 159 / G, 232]

Indeed, all rationality of the factual is situated in the *a priori*. A
priori science is science of the fundamental principles to which
factual science must have recourse in order ultimately to be
grounded fundamentally. [*CM*, 181]

If, owing the transcendental reduction to my pure *ego* my true
interest lies in the unveiling of this factual *ego*, still, this unveiling can become genuinely scientific only by having recourse
to the apodictic principles that belong generally to the *ego* as
an *ego*, that is, by having recourse to the eidetic universalities
and necessities by means of which the fact is referred to its rational grounds, to the rational grounds of its pure possibilities,

and is thereby made scientific (logical). . . . "In itself," then, the science of pure possibilities precedes the science of actualities and first makes it possible as science at all. [106]

Transcendental phenomenology thus unfolds the *a priori* enclosed within a transcendental subjectivity and within the intersubjectivity constituted therein. Inasmuch as it does so, then, as a science of pure possibilities and on the basis of the relatedness of all conceivable Being to transcendental subjectivity and intersubjectivity, transcendental phenomenology is ultimately "universal ontology" understood as the doctrine of possible Being.

> This universal, *concrete ontology* (or, likewise, [this] universal and concrete theory of science, this concrete *logic of Being*) would thus be the intrinsically *primary universe of science* constructed upon an absolute grounding. . . . This total science of the *a priori* would then be the *foundation for genuine sciences of facts* and for a *genuine, universal philosophy in the Cartesian sense*, a universal science of what in fact is, constructed upon an absolute grounding. [181]

In accordance with this order of grounding—and corresponding with the Platonic origin of this conception—Husserl calls eidetic, transcendental phenomenology (universal ontology or the logic of Being), *primary philosophy*; and he designates empirical philosophy of the factual as *secondary philosophy*.

> The strictly systematically executed phenomenology in the just now expanded sense [that is, expanded to include empirical phenomenology], is identical with this philosophy which encompasses all genuine cognitions [that is to say, it is identical with the universal science drawn from a radical self-justification]. It breaks down into eidetic phenomenology (or universal ontology) as *primary philosophy*, and into *secondary philosophy*, the science of the universe of facts or of the intersubjectivity synthetically comprising all facts. [*PP*, 298f.]

According to Husserl, secondary philosophy or metaphysics seems initially to be nothing other than an ultimate grounding or clarification, on the basis of transcendental, *a priori* principles, of all the sciences of facts. In the spirit of this Kantian thought, Husserl writes the following in a supplement to his lectures on "Primary Philosophy" in 1923/24:

> In the phenomenological interpretation of the positive sciences of facts, there spring up the ultimately scientific sciences of facts, the sciences of facts that are in themselves philosophical and tolerate, besides themselves, no other special philosophies being attached to them. By means of the ultimate interpretation of the objective Being [*Sein*] explored in these sciences as a fact, an interpretation that accrues to these sciences in the application of eidetic phenomenology; and by means of the universal contemplation, also required in this phenomenology, of all the regions of objectivity [*Objektivität*] in relation to the universal community of transcendental subjects; the universe of the world, the universal theme of the positive sciences, acquires a "metaphysical" interpretation, which means nothing other than an interpretation behind which it would make no scientific sense to seek another. [*EP* I, 188, fn.]

Similarly, several years later, in 1928, he writes the following:

> Provided only that we think of it from the outset as methodologically grounded in an absolute fashion by eidetic phenomenology, the empirical phenomenology which comes after eidetic phenomenology is identical with the complete, systematic universe of the positive sciences. [*PP*, 298][1]

Finally, however, Husserl's philosophy of actuality, his "metaphysics," does not simply consist in this eidetic-phenomenological interpretation of the factual sciences. In the *Ideas*, after speaking of the " 'phenomenological reversal' of the ordinary factual sciences, made possible by eidetic phenomenology," he writes the following: "there remains only the question, to what extent, beginning from that juncture, something further could be accomplished" (*Id* I, 119 / G, 184). Similarly, in the above-mentioned supplement to the lectures on "Primary Philosophy" (1923/24), the passage cited is followed by the following remark:

> But behind this, there presents itself on the phenomenological terrain a problem that does not permit of further interpretation [presumably he means to say, "a problem which does not permit of further interpretation on phenomenological ter-

rain"]: the problem concerning the irrationality of the transcendental fact which enunciates itself in the constitution of
the factual world and the factual life of the spirit: thus, metaphysics in a new sense. [*EP*, 188]

In the same sense, and already in quite early texts, Husserl regards the
fact that actuality corresponds with the theoretical and practical ideals of
reason—the irrational fact of the rationality of the world—or the problem, to what extent actuality does and can correspond with these ideals,
as the object and theme of metaphysics (cf. *EP* II, 385, 394). The *Cartesian Meditations* characterize the content of this metaphysics in the following way:

> [I]nside of the factual monadic sphere, and as an ideal eidetic
> possibility in every conceivable monadic sphere, there emerge
> all the problems of contingent facticity, of death, of fate; the
> problems of the possibility of a "genuine" human life, [a possi-
> bility that is] required to be meaningful in a particular sense;
> among them also the problems concerning the "meaning" of
> history, and so ascending ever higher. We may also say that
> these are the ethical and religious problems, but posed on the
> terrain upon which everything simply must be posed that is
> supposed to be able to have a possible meaning for us. [*CM*,
> 182][2]

"Metaphysics in a new sense"—and we may surely also say in Husserl's
sense, secondary philosophy in a new sense—can no longer be a merely
transcendental, eidetic interpretation of the empirically factual. Husserl
appears to consider quite a different kind of methodological procedure
for the philosophical treatment of these ultimate questions concerning
the meaning of factual, human life. He points to the "postulates of practical reason" as being "perhaps the greatest of Kant's discoveries."[3]

During his last years, to be sure, Husserl places in question his
distinction between primary and secondary philosophy in respect to the
priority of eidetic possibility over actuality. A text stemming from the
year 1931 says the following in regard to the *eidos* "transcendental ego":

> We have here a noteworthy and unique case as regards the re-
> lationship between fact and *eidos*. The Being of an *eidos*, the
> Being of the eidetic possibilities and the universe of these pos-
> sibilities, is independent of the Being or non-Being of any actu-
> alization of such possibilities whatsoever; [indeed,] it is

independent of the Being of all actuality, that is, of all corresponding actuality. *But the eidos "transcendental 'I' " is unthinkable without the transcendental "I" as something factual.*

After speaking of the full ontology as teleology and of the factuality presupposed by this teleology, Husserl proceeds in the same text as follows:

> We come upon ultimate " matters of fact," primordial matters
> of fact upon ultimate necessities, the primordial necessities.
> But it is I who think them, I begin to inquire and finally come
> upon them from out of the world which I already "possess." I
> think, I practice the reduction, I, [the one] who I am, am for
> myself within this horizon. I am the primordial fact in this pro-
> cess; I recognize that, in additon to my factual capacity for ei-
> detic variation, etc., there result in the course of my factual
> inquiries certain primordial constituents as primordial struc-
> tures of my factuality; and [I recognize] that I bear within my-
> self a core of "primordial contingencies" in eidetic forms, in
> forms of potent functioning in which the mundane, eidetic ne-
> cessities are founded. I cannot transgress my factual Being and
> therein [I cannot transgress] the Being-with [*Mitsein*] of others
> intentionally comprised by it, etc., thus absolute actuality. The
> absolute has its ground, within itself; and within its groundless
> Being [it has] its absolute necessity as the one "absolute sub-
> stance." Its necessity is not an eidetic necessity that would
> leave open [the possibility of] something contingent. All eidetic
> necessities are moments of its fact, [that is, of the fact of the
> absolute; they] are modes of its functioning in relation to itself,
> its modes of understanding itself or being able to understand
> itself. [*PI* III, 385f.][4]

This reflection is found in a context in which Husserl takes his start from
the fact of the teleological alignment of transcendental intersubjectivity
as borne [*getragen*] by the divine will and directed toward completeness
in "true Being." Not only the "primordial fact" of the "I," but also the
fact of its historical world as such, appears here to form the starting
point for philosophy, even such that much of what Husserl says in this
context is reminiscent of Heidegger's hermeneutic of facticity (cf.
666ff.). Following this new beginning, however, Husserl did not succeed
in attaining to a systematic elaboration of the relationship between eidetics (to which he clung, unshaken, as the condition for the possibility of
transcendental knowledge), actuality, and empirical fact.[5]

Appendix

Chronology of Husserl's Life, Work, and Teaching

1859   (8 April) Edmund Husserl born in Prossnitz (Prostejow, Moravia) as the second of four children.

I. 1876–1887   Years of Studies.
Winter term 1876/77–winter term 1877/78, University of Leipzig:
Astronomy; lectures in mathematics, physics, astronomy and philosophy. First philosophical reading: Berkeley. Meeting with Thomas Masaryk, the later President of Czechoslovakia, who pointed the way to Franz Brentano in Vienna.
1878–1880/81, University of Berlin:
Studies of mathematics (with L. Kronecker, and C. Weierstrass whose private assistant he was during the summer term of 1883 and from whom he got "the ethos of his scientific aspiration") and of philosophy (with F. Paulsen).
1881–1881/82, University of Vienna:
Studies of mathematics.
1882, 8 October: Acceptance of his dissertation "Beiträge zur Theorie der Variationsrechnung" ("Contributions Towards a Theory of Variation Calculus");
1883, 23 January: Ph.D. promotion.

1884   Death of his father (24 April).
Winter term 1884/85–summer term 1886, University of Vienna:
Philosophical lectures with Franz Brentano.
Winter term 1886/87–summer term 1887, University of Halle a.S.:

Lectures with Carl Stumpf with whom Husserl studied for his Habilitation at the recommendation of Brentano.

1886–1895   Studies mainly in areas of formal mathematics and formal logic.

1887   Marriage with Malvine Steinschneider (6 August).

1887   Fall: Printing of the Habilitationsschrift *Über de Begriff der Zahl, Psychologische Analysen* ("On the Concept of Number, Psychological Analyses").

Acquisitions of philosophical books during years of studies (selection):

1880: Schopenhauer, Spinoza. 1884: Hegel, *Phänomenologie des Geistes*; H. Spencer, *Grundlagen der Philosophie*. 1886: E. Mach, *Beiträge zur Analyse der Empfindungen*. 1887: G. Frege, *Die Grundlagen der Arithmetik*.

II.   1887–1901   As a Privatdozent in Halle.

1887   Inaugural lecture "Die Ziele und Aufgaben der Metaphysik" ("Aims and Tasks of Metaphysics") (24 October).

1891   *Philosophie der Arithmetik. Psychologische und logische Untersuchungen*; review of Schröder's *Vorlesungen über die Algebra der Logik*.

1900   *Logische Untersuchungen, Erster Teil: Prolegomena zur reinen Logik*.

1901   *Logische Untersuchungen, Zweiter Teil: Untersuchungen zur Phänomenologie und Theorie der Erkenntnis*.

1901   First meeting of M. Scheler with Husserl.

1901   Early September, appointment at Göttingen, which had been pending for one year.

Topics of Husserl's Teaching at Halle (in chronological order):

—Introduction to the Theory of Knowledge and Metaphysics (lectures, 1887/88)
—Fundamental Problems of Psychology (lectures, 1888).
—Encyclopaedia of Philosophy (lectures, 1888/89).
—Logic (lectures, 1889; 1890; 1896).
—Ethics (lectures, 1889/90).
—Selected Questions from Philosophy of Mathematics (lectures, 1889/90; 1890/91).
—History of Modern Philosophy (lectures, 1890/91).

—Fundamental Problems of Ethics (lectures, 1891; 1893).
—Psychology (lectures, 1891/92; 1894/95).
—Philosophical Exercises in connection with Locke's *Essay Concerning Human Understanding* (seminar, 1891/92; 1898/99).
—Introduction to Philosophy (lectures, 1892; 1893; 1894; 1896; 1897/98; 1898/99).
—Philosophical Exercises in connection with Descartes's *Meditationes de prima philosophia* (seminar, 1892; 1896/97).
—On Free Will (lectures, 1892/93; 1893/94; 1894/95; 1896; 1897; 1899; 1900; 1901).
—The Proofs for the Existence of God (lectures, 1892/93).
—Philosophical Exercise in connection with Schopenhauer's *Welt als Wille und Vorstellung* (seminar, 1892/93).
—Theism and Modern Science (lectures, 1893/94).
—Ethics and Philosophy of Law (lectures, 1894; 1897).
—On Recent Investigations in Deductive Logic (lectures, 1895).
—Philosophical Exercises in connection with Mill's *Logic* (seminar, 1895).
—History of the Philosophy of Religion since Spinoza (lectures, 1895/96).
—Philosophical Exercises in connection with Hume's *Dialogues Concerning Natural Religion* (seminar, 1895/96).
—Introduction to the Theory of Knowledge (lectures, 1896/97).
—Philosophical Exercises in connection with a text of Schopenhauer's to be selected (seminar, 1897).
—Philosophical Exercises on Kant's *Prolegomena* (seminar, 1897/98).
—Kant and Post-Kantian Philosophy (lectures, 1898).
—Philosophical Exercises in connection with Kant's *Kritik der reinen Vernunft* (seminar, 1898; 1900/01).
—Theory of Knowledge and Main Points of Metaphysics (lectures, 1898/99).
—History of Philosophy (lectures, 1899; 1900; 1901).
—Philosophical Exercises on Hume's *Treatise on Human Nature* (seminar, 1899).
—Philosophical Exercises in connection with Spinoza's *Ethica* (seminar, 1900).
—The Philosophy of Kant (1900/1901).

III. 1901–1916   The Years at Göttingen

1901   (September) Appointment as Extraordinarius Professor.
1902   J. Daubert's first visit to Husserl in Göttingen: discussion on the *Logische Untersuchungen*. As a result of this

	meeting relations between Th. Lipps's students in Munich and Husserl begin.
1904	(May) Visit to Munich: meeting with Th. Lipps and his students (J. Daubert, A. Pfänder, etc.).
1905	(March) Visit to W. Dilthey in Berlin. In a letter of 1929 to G. Misch, Husserl wrote "that a few discussions in 1905 with Dilthey in Berlin (not his writings) provided an impulse which led from the Husserl of the *Logische Untersuchungen* to the one of the *Ideen*."
1906	Appointment as Ordinarius Professor.
1906	(December) Visit by the poet Hugo von Hofmannsthal to Husserl.
1907	Visit to Franz Brentano in Florence.
1907	(Summer term) Foundation of the "Göttinger Philosophische Gesellschaft" by Th. Conrad.
1909	(October) Visit by P. Natorp to Husserl.
1910	(January) Husserl agrees with H. Rickert to collaborate as editor of the newly founded journal *Logos*.
1911	"Philosophy as Rigorous Science" in *Logos*, volume 1 (1910/11).
1911	Correspondence between Dilthey and Husserl in connection with the *Logos* paper.
1913	*Ideen zu einer reinen Phänomenologie und phänomenologischen Philosophie*. First book: General Introduction to Pure Phenomenology. The work was published in *Jahrbuch für Philosophie und phänomenologische Forschung*, volume I, founded in 1912 by Husserl as chief editor together with Moritz Geiger, Alexander Pfänder, Adolf Reinach, and Max Scheler.
1913	Visit by K. Jaspers to Husserl.
1914	Participation in the 6th Congress for Experimental Psychology in Göttingen (15–18 April).
1916	(5 January) Appointment to Freiburg as successor of, and on recommendation by, Heinrich Rickert, beginning 1 April.
1916	(8 March) Husserl's son Wolfgang is killed near Verdun.

Topics of Husserl's Teaching at Göttingen:

—On Free Will (lectures, 1901/02; 1903; 1904/05).
—Logic and Theory of Knowledge (lectures, 1901/02).
—Epistemological Exercises in connection with Berkeley's *A Treatise*

Concerning the Principles of Human Knowledge (seminar, 1901/02; 1907).

—General History of Philosophy from the Most Ancient Times through the Nineteenth Century (lectures each summer term between 1902 and 1915).

—Fundamental Questions of Ethics (lectures, 1902; 1908/09).

—Philosophical Exercises on Kant's *Kritik der reinen Vernunft* (seminar, 1902; 1909/10; 1911/12).

—Logic (lectures, 1902/03).

—General Theory of Knowledge (lectures, 1902/03).

—Philosophical Exercises in connection with David Hume's *Treatise on Human Nature* (seminar, 1902/03; 1904/05; 1907/08; 1910/11).

—The Philosophy of the Renaissance (lectures, 1903).

—Philosophical Exercises on Fichte's *Bestimmung des Menschen* (seminar, 1903).

—History of Modern Philosophy from Kant through the Present (lectures, 1903/04).

—History of Education (lectures, 1903/04; 1909/10; 1913/14; 1915/16).

—Philosophical Exercises on Kant's *Kritik der praktischen Vernunft* (seminar, 1903/04).

—Philosophical Exercises on Modern Texts about the Philosophy of Nature by Scientists (first, on E. Mach's *Analyse der Empfindungen*). (seminar, 1903/04, 1911).

—Main Topics of the Descriptive Psychology of Knowledge (lectures, 1904).

—Public Philosophical Exercises in connection with Locke's and Leibniz's *Versuch über den menschlichen Verstand* (seminar, 1904).

—Main Topics from the Phenomenology and Theory of Knowledge (lectures and exercises, 1904/05).

—Theory of Judgement (lectures, 1905; 1912).

—Exercises in the History of Philosophy in relation to Modern Texts (seminar, 1905).

—Philosophical Exercises as an Introduction to the Main Problems of the Philosophy of Mathematics (seminar, 1905).

—Kant and Post-Kantian Philosophy (lectures, 1905/06; 1907/08; 1909/10; 1911/12).

—Philosophical Exercises on Kant's Theory of Experience, according to *Kritik der reinen Vernunft* and *Prolegomena* (seminar, 1905/06).

—Philosophical Exercises on Kant's Doctrine of Principles, according to *Grundlegung zur Metaphysik der Sitten* and *Kritik der praktischen Vernunft* (seminar, 1906; 1909; 1914).

—Introduction to Logic and the Critique of Knowledge (lectures, 1906/07).

—Philosophical Exercises on Selected Problems of Phenomenology and the Critique of Knowledge (seminar, 1906/07).

—Main Topics from the Phenomenology and Critique of Reason (lectures, 1907).

—Discussions on Fundamental Questions of Logic and Critique of Reason (seminar, 1907/08).

—Introduction to the Theory of Science (lectures, 1908).

—Philosophical Exercises on Fundamental Problems of the Theory of Meaning and Judgement (seminar, 1908).

—Old and New Logic (lectures, 1908/09).

—Philosophical Exercises in connection with D. Hume's *Enquiry Concerning the Principles of Morals* (seminar, 1908/09).

—Introduction to the Phenomenology of Knowledge (lectures, 1909).

—Logic as Theory of Knowledge (lectures, 1910/11).

—Fundamental Problems of Phenomenology (lectures, 1910/11).

—Fundamental Problems of Ethics and Theory of Value (lectures, 1911; 1914).

—Outline of the General Theory of Consciousness (lectures and exercises, 1911/12).

—Philosophical Exercises on Lotze's Theory of Knowledge (in connection with the Third Book of Lotze's *Logik*) (seminar, 1912).

—Logic and Introduction to the Theory of Science (lectures, 1912/13; 1914/15).

—Exercises belonging to Metaphysics and Theory of Science on Nature and Spirit (seminar, 1912/13).

—Nature and Spirit (lectures, 1913).

—Exercises on the Ideas "Natural Science" and "Human Science [*Geisteswissenschaft*]" (seminar, 1913).

—Kant and the Philosophy of Modern Times (lectures, 1913/14).

—Philosophical Exercises, partly in connection with Descartes's *Meditationes*, partly in connection with Locke's *Essay Concerning Human Understanding* (seminar, 1913/14).

—Phenomenological Exercises (seminar, 1913/14).

—Selected Phenomenological Problems (seminar, 1914).

—Philosophical Exercises in connection with Hume's *Treatise* (seminar, 1914/15).

—Selected Phenomenological Problems (as an Introduction to Phenomenology) (lectures, 1915).

—Exercises on Fichte's *Bestimmung des Menschen* (seminar, 1915).

—Philosophical Exercises on Nature and Spirit (seminar, 1915/16).

IV. <u>1916–1928</u> As Ordinarius Professor in Freiburg

1917	(April) Husserl's son Gerhart lies wounded in the military hospital at Speyer.
1917	(3 May) Inaugural lecture "Die reine Phänomenologie, ihr Forschungsgebiet und ihre Methode" ("Pure Phenomenology, its Research Domain and its Method").
1917	(July) Death of Husserl's mother.
1917	(8–17 November) Three public lectures on Fichte's ideal of humanity as a part of the University Courses for war participants (repetition 14–16 January 1918; repetition on 6, 7 and 9 November 1918 for the Academic Staff of the Philosophical Faculty).
1918/19	Foundation of the "Freiburger Phänomenologische Gesellschaft."
1919	Publication of Husserl's *Erinnerungen an Brentano*.
1919	(October) Husserl signs Romain Rolland's appeal "Für die Unabhängigkeit des Geistes" ("For the Independence of the Spirit") sent out by the League for the Advancement of Humanity.
1922	(June) Public Lectures at the University College in London: "Phänomenologische Methode und Phänomenologische Philosophie"; stay in Cambridge at the home of G. Dawes Hicks; meeting with J. Ward, G. F. Stout, G. E. Moore.
1922	(December) Election as "corresponding member" of the Aristotelian Society.
1923	Publication of "Erneuerung. Ihr Problem und ihre Methode" ("Renewal. Its Problem and its Method") in the Japanese journal *Kaizo*.
1924	Publication of the two other *Kaizo* papers: "Die Methode der Wesensforschung" ("The Method of Eidetic Inquiry") and "Erneuerung als individualethisches Problem" ("Renewal as Problem of the Ethics of the Individual").
1924–25	R. Carnap attends Husserl's advanced seminar.
1924	(September) First visit of Dorion Cairns to Husserl.
1925	Publication of a meditation "Über die Reden Gotamo Buddhos" ("On Buddha's Teachings") on the occasion of Karl Eugen Neumann's translation into German.
1926	(8 April) Heidegger presents Husserl with the dedication of *Sein und Zeit*.

1927–28	Work with Heidegger on the *Encyclopaedia Britannica* article on Phenomenology.
1928	Publication of Husserl's "Vorlesungen zur Phänomenologie des inneren Zeitbewusstseins" ("Lectures on Internal Time-Consciousness") by Heidegger in volume 9 of the *Jahrbuch*.
1928	(31 March) Emeritus professor.

Topics of Husserl's Teaching in Freiburg:

—Introduction to Philosophy (lectures, 1916; 1918; 1919/20; 1922/ 23).

—Exercises in connection with Descartes's *Meditationes* (seminar, 1916).

—Exercises on Selected Phenomenological Problems (seminar, 1916).

—General History of Philosophy (lectures, 1916/17; 1918/19).

—Exercises in connection with Berkeley's *A Treatise Concerning the Principles of Human Knowledge* (seminar, 1916/17).

—Problems of the Theory of Judgement (seminar, 1916/17).

—Introduction to Phenomenology (lectures, 1917; 1926/27).

—Kant's Transcendental Philosophy (lectures, 1917).

—Phenomenological Exercises (Philosophical Exercises in connection with Kant's transcendental aesthetics) (seminar, 1917).

—Logic and General Theory of Science (lectures, 1917/18).

—Fundamental Problems of the Theory of Judgement (seminar, 1917/18).

—Exercises on Fichte's *Bestimmung des Menschen* (seminar, 1918).

—Exercises on Kant's Transcendental Philosophy (seminar, 1918/19).

—Nature and Spirit (lectures, 1919; 1921/22; 1927).

—Fundamental Problems of Ethics in Philosophical Exercises (seminar, 1919).

—Philosophical Exercises on Transcendental Aesthetics and Transcendental Idealism (seminar, 1919/20).

—Introduction to Ethics (lectures, 1920; 1924).

—On Appearance and Sense (seminar, 1920).

—Logic (lectures, 1920/21; 1925/26).

—Phenomenology of Abstraction (seminar, 1920/21).

—Phenomenology of Time-Consciousness (seminar, 1920/21).

—History of Modern Philosophy (lectures, 1921; 1922; 1924/25; 1926; 1927/28).

—Phenomenological Exercises in connection with D. Hume's *Treatise on Human Nature*, Book I (seminar, 1921; 1926/27).

—Phenomenological Exercises (seminar, 1921/22; 1922; 1922/23; 1923; 1923/24; 1924; 1926; 1927/28).

—Selected Phenomenological Problems (lectures, 1923).

—First Philosophy (lectures, 1923/24).

—Phenomenological Exercises on Berkeley's *A Treatise Concerning the Principles of Human Knowledge* (seminar, 1924/25).

—Introduction to Phenomenological Psychology (lectures, 1925).

—Exercises in the Analysis and Description of Purely Mental Acts and Products (in connection with the lectures on phenomenological psychology) (seminar, 1925).

—Selected Logical Problems (seminar, 1925/26).

—Phenomenological Exercises (on Kant) (seminar, 1927).

Ⅴ. **1928–1938 As Emeritus Professor**

1928	(April) Trip to Berlin on the occasion of the 80th birthday of C. Stumpf.
1928	(April) Public Lectures in Amsterdam: "Phänomenologie und Psychologie. Transzendentale Phänomenologie"; Husserl is introduced to the mathematician L. E. J. Brouwer and to Leo Schestow on visit from Paris.
1928	(April) Husserl is asked by the Ministry of Public Worship and Education to hold the professorial chair of philosophy during the summer term 1928, Heidegger's appointment as his successor being only possible from 1 October.
1928	(August) Ludwig Landgrebe receives a grant in order to continue working for Husserl; Eugen Fink takes over his post and thus begins his collaboration with Husserl.
1928/29	Writing of *Formale und transzendentale Logik* in a few months.
1929	(February) Public Lectures in Paris; Husserl is introduced to L. Lévy Bruhl, E. Meyerson, A. Koyré, J. Hering, and E. Levinas.
1929	(8 April) Presentation of the *Festschrift* on the occasion of Husserl's 70th birthday by Heidegger.
1929	(July) Publication of *Formale und transzendentale Logik* in volume 10 of the *Jahrbuch* and at the same time as offprint.
1929	(Summer term) H. Marcuse and wife study with Husserl.
1929/30	Husserl withdraws his lecture announcement.
1930	Publication of "Nachwort zu meinen 'Ideen zu einer

	reinen Phänomenologie und phänomenologischen Philosophie,' " in volume 11 of the *Jahrbuch*.
1931	(June) Lecture tour in Germany: Husserl talks at the Kant Society in Frankfurt, Berlin (to an audience of 1,600 people) and Halle on "Phänomenologie und Anthropologie."
1933	(6 April) Suspension by decree Nr. A 7642; (20 July) annulment of the decree.
1933	(November) Husserl is offered a chair at the University of Southern California in Los Angeles.
1934	(Around 1 August) Husserl is invited by the Prague Congress to take a position in a letter regarding the present task of philosophy; (30 August) Husserl writes letter to the Prague Congress of Philosophers.
1934	(October) Plan of Archives for Husserl's manuscripts.
1935	(March) Negotiations with Prague in view of delivery of Husserl's manuscripts; L. Landgrebe arrives in Freiburg to establish a detailed inventory (see Note on Husserl's *Nachlass*, below).
1935	(7 May) Public Lecture before the Kulturbund in Vienna: "Die Philosophie in der Krisis der europäischen Menschheit" (repetition on 10 May).
1935	(November) Public Lectures in Prague on "Die Krisis der europäischen Wissenschaften und die Psychologie."
1936	(15 January) Withdrawal of teaching licence as of the end of 1935.
1936	(24 January) Dispatch to Prague of first part of *Krisis* for print in the first issue of the new journal *Philosophia*, edited by A. Liebert in Belgrade.
1936	(25 January) The Ministry of the Reich for Science, Education and Popular Education compels Husserl to withdraw from the philosophical organization founded by Liebert in Belgrade.
1937	(8 June) Rejection by the Ministry of the Reich of Husserl's request to be allowed to participate in the 9th International Congress of Philosophy in Paris.
1938	(27 April) Husserl dies at the age of 79 years.

Topics of Husserl's Teaching as Emeritus Professor:

—Introduction to Phenomenological Psychology (lectures, 1928).
—Phenomenological-Psychological Exercises (seminar, 1928).

—Phenomenology of Empathy (lectures and exercises, 1928/29).
—Selected Phenomenological Problems (lectures and exercises, 1929).

Note on Husserl's *Nachlass*

Husserl published relatively little, but he has written a great deal, so that his philosophical *Nachlass* consists of more than 40,000 handwritten pages, mostly written in shorthand (Gabelsberg system). This large amount of manuscripts is essentially due to the fact that Husserl reflected on problems in writing. Thus his *Nachlass* manuscripts are for the most part not written for readers; they are rather "monologues," in which Husserl strove for a solution of philosophical problems. In addition, there are to be found in the *Nachlass* manuscripts of lecture courses, public lectures and, to a small extent, of preparatory work for publications.

Husserl would have liked to publish more of his philosophical thoughts. Time and again he formed plans for publications, but only rarely he was able to realize them (see "E. Husserl. Persönliche Aufzeichnungen," edited by Walter Biemel. *Philosophy and Phenomenological Research* 16, no. 3 (March 1956), pp. 293–302; see also the introductions by the editor of *Husserliana,* volumes XIV and XV). This inability of Husserl's may well have been caused, on the one hand, by his strong self-critical intellect, which again and again made him call into question results he had reached; on the other hand, however, it may have resulted from the analytical style of his way of practicing philosophy and from the difficulty of systematizing the abundance of particular analyses into a coherent whole. As a consequence of this failing of his plans for publications, the thought of his *Nachlass* took on more and more importance for Husserl himself in the later years. Thus already in a letter of 1922 he writes to Paul Natorp: "I am in a much worse situation than you are, since the bulk of my work is stuck in my manuscripts. I almost curse my inability to come to an end, and that the universal systematic thoughts came to me in part so late, only now. These are the thoughts which, required by all my particular investigations up to now, also require all of them to be revised. Everything is at the stage of re-crystallization! Perhaps I am working, with all humanly possible exertion of forces, solely for my *Nachlass*" (see *Husserliana* XIV, p. xix.) Beginning in spring of 1932, Husserl worked directly in view of his *Nachlass* (see *Husserliana* XV, introduction of the editor, pp. lxii and lxvii f.), and in 1935/36, he let Eugen Fink and Ludwig Landgrebe classify it systematically and append it with suitable signatures (see "Note sur les Archives Husserl à Louvain," in *Problèmes actuels de la phénoménologie* [1952], p. 156, note; see also *Husserl-Chronik*, p. 473 [entry of 8 February 1936]). This systematic classification of 1935 forms still the basis of today's grouping of Husserl's *Nachlass* at the Husserl Archives in Louvain (Belgium) (see below).

After Husserl's death on 27 April 1938 there were no opportunities for editing and publishing his *Nachlass* within Germany governed by the National Socialists and it was even threatened by destruction. Hence, the *Nachlass* was brought abroad the same year, namely to the University of Louvain in Belgium. The merit of this preservation is due mainly to the Reverend Father Hermann Leo Van Breda (see H. L. Van Breda, "Le sauvetage de l'héritage husserlien," in *Husserl et la pensée moderne*). Under his care, and with the help of Husserl's former assistants, Eugen Fink and Ludwig Landgrebe, the Husserl Archives has been set up in Louvain. There, Husserl's *Nachlass* is classified according to the following scheme:

A. Mundane Phenomenology
    I.   Logic and Formal Ontology (41 bundles of manuscripts)
    II.   Formal Ethics, Philosophy of Law (1)
    III.   Ontology (Eidetics and its Methodology) (13)
    IV.   Theory of Science (22)
    V.   Intentional Anthropology (Person and Surrounding-
            World) (26)
    VI.   Psychology (Doctrine of Intentionality) (36)
    VII.   Theory of World Apperception (31)

B. The Reduction
    I.   Paths to the Reduction (38)
    II.   The Reduction itself and its Methodology (23)
    III.   Preliminary Transcendental Intentional Analysis (12)
    IV.   Historical and Systematic Self-characterization of
            Phenomenology (12)

C. Time-Constitution as Formal Constitution (17)

D. Primordial Constitution ("*Urkonstitution*") (18)

E. Intersubjective Constitution
    I.   Constitutional Basic Doctrine of the Immediate
            Experience of the Other (7)

II.   Constitution of the Mediate Experience of the Other (Full Sociality) (3)

III.   Transcendental Anthropology (Transcendental Theology, etc.) (11)

F. Lecture Courses and Public Lectures
     I.   Lecture Courses and Parts from Lectures (44)
     II.   Public Lectures with Appendices (7)
     III.   Manuscripts of Published Treatises with Later Appendices (1)
     IV.   Loose Sheets (4)

K. Autographs, not Included in the Critical Inventory of 1935
     I.   Manuscripts earlier than 1910 (69)
     II.   Manuscripts from 1910–1930 (5)
     III.   Manuscripts later than 1930—to the problems of *Krisis* (33)
     IX–X. Copies of Husserl's Marginal Notes in Books of his Library

L. The Bernau Manuscripts
     I.   (21 bundles)
     II.   (21 bundles)

M. Copies of Husserl's Manuscripts in Running Hand or Typescript, Carried Out by Husserl's Assistants Earlier than 1938
     I.   Lecture Courses (4)
     II.   Public Lectures (3)
     III.   Sketches for Publications (17)

N. Transcriptions

P. Manuscripts by Other Authors

Q. Husserl's Notes from Lecture Courses by His Teachers

R. Letters
     I.   Letters by Husserl
     II.   Letters to Husserl
     III.   Letters about Husserl
     X.   Letters by Malvine Husserl (later than 1938)

X. Archival Material

Groups A, B, C, D, and E were put together according to systematic aspects in 1935/36 (see above). However, this systematic arrangement is only a very global one; for the individual bundles of Husserl's manuscripts, as they existed already prior to this arrangement, were no more analyzed and divided up in detail, but only classified as wholes and according to their overall titles. Group F was put together in 1935/36. Group K consists of those manuscripts, mostly written in shorthand, which Van Breda found in Freiburg in 1938 but which had not been included in the classification of 1935/36. The manuscripts of group L were handed over for editing to Eugen Fink by Husserl, probably in 1929 (?) and they were transmitted to the Husserl Archives in February 1969.

After years of preparatory work (transcribing the Gabelsberg shorthand, cataloguing, etc.), which was also continued in Louvain during the years of the war, publication of the *Nachlass* in the series *Husserliana, Edmund Husserl Collected Works*, could be started in 1950. Up to now (1991), twenty-eight volumes at least have been published by the Husserl Archives in Louvain, partly in collaboration with the Husserl Archives in Köln (Germany) and Freiburg (Germany). The edition is guided by the following principles: (1) Each Husserlian text which is published is critically accounted for in detail, such that the reader is able to get full insight into the textual basis of the manuscript. Dates of the origin of the manuscripts are indicated as precisely as possible. All the modifications (additions, corrections, etc.) made by Husserl himself, insofar as they are of any relevance, are marked as such; possible stylistic changes by the editor are again marked as such. (2) Texts to be published are arranged either according to Husserl's own plans (Husserl's own publications and lecture courses) or in view of a particular theme (passive synthesis, intersubjectivity, intuitional presentations). (3) The aim is not to publish Husserl's philosophical *Nachlass* completely, but rather only those texts which are important regarding their theme or in relation to the development of Husserl's thinking. (4) The sequence of the individual volumes is to a large extent accidental. No detailed complete plan for the *Husserliana* has been established in advance. The reason for this is that prior to such a plan a most precise sifting of the manuscripts and an objective and chronological penetration and division of the *Nachlass* would have been required, so that the beginning of the publication would have been delayed for decades. The archival grouping of the manuscripts (see above) could not serve as basis for the publication, since objectively and chronologically heterogeneous texts are often put together in the individual bundles of manuscripts, whereas the manuscript sheets of a uniform text are often scattered in various bundles of different groups of manuscripts.

Even today, after twenty-eight volumes in *Husserliana* have been published, important texts are still to be expected from the *Nachlass*. The emphasis of publications thus far has been, for clear reasons, on those texts that were written by Husserl for readers. Only a few volumes have been dedicated to the "monologues" (*"Forschungsmanuskripte"*), which are difficult to approach but which make up the bulk of the *Nachlass* and in which Husserl's creative thinking can be followed so to speak *in statu nascendi*. Especially from Husserl's late period (after *Cartesianische Meditationen* [1929]) there is still not much accessible (the only volume hitherto published from the abundance of "Forschungsmanuskripte" of the time between *Cartesianische Meditationen* [1929] and Husserl's work for the *Krisis* [since 1935] is volume XV of the *Husserliana*, *Zur Phänomenologie der Intersubjektivität* [1929–1935]). But there is still much to be made accessible from earlier periods, for instance the manuscripts on acts of feeling and willing as well as more of Husserl's ethics.

Copies of the transcriptions of Husserl's manuscripts (work on the transcriptions from the Gabelsberg shorthand is still not completed) can also be found outside Louvain in the Husserl Archives at the Universities of Köln and Freiburg im Breisgau (Germany), at the New School for Social Research in New York City, at Duquesne University in Pittsburgh, and at the École Normale Supérieure in Paris.

Notes

Chapter 1

1. A comparison with *Ideas I* (§§ 119–22, 158), *Formal and Transcendental Logic* (§ 27) and *Experience and Judgement* (§ 96), shows that Husserl continued even later to adhere firmly to the essential insights of the *Philosophy of Arithmetic* regarding the concept of number.
   [*Translator's note*: It will be our policy henceforth to cite all works of Husserl according to the editions and translations noted in the Bibliography. We shall abbreviate the titles of these works following a schema indicated in the Bibliography. The citation will thus include the abbreviated title followed first by the volume, part, section, chapter, paragraph or page number, then, where appropriate, by an abbreviated reference to the translator (again, as indicated in the Bibliography) and page number of the English translation. As long as a particular work continues to be cited without interruption we shall omit repeated reference to the title. In those cases where reference is made to a text included in a *Husserliana* edition (*Hu*) or found among the manuscripts (*Ms.*) but previously untranslated, we shall simply cite the German text without additional comment. Where English translations are available, the titles of the works of Husserl will be cited and abbreviated according to a translated form of the title. In cases where the pagination from the German text cited is noted in the margin of the English translation, we shall cite the German text alone. The reader may consult the Bibliography for an indication of the texts falling under this category. For the sake of greater consistency within our text, unless otherwise indicated the translations of all quotations will be our own, even in those cases where previous English translations are available. We shall, as a matter of course, *translate* the titles to all works of Husserl referred to in the text and the notes, even those not yet translated into English. In the case of the works of others, the original title will be cited except where English translations are already available.]
2. G. Frege, "Rezension von: E. G. Husserl, Philosophie der Arithmetik. I," *Zeitschrift für Philosophie und philosophische Kritik*. N. F. 103 (1894), 316; or, *Kleine Schriften*, ed. I. Angelelli (Darmstadt, 1967), 181; trans. E. W. Kluge in *Mind* 81 (July 1972), 321–37. Hereafter cited as "Frege."

3. As against such a view, cf. D. Willard, "Concerning Husserl's View of Number," *The Southwestern Journal of Philosophy* 5, no. 3 (1974), 97f., where we read the following: "Frege, far from directing a 'crushing attack' upon *Philosophie der Arithmetik*, did not even understand the view of number which the book expresses."

4. As a rule, the emphases within the quotations are those of the author of the text being cited. Even where this is not the case, however, no express indication will be given.

5. See R. Sokolowski, *The Formation of Husserl's Concept of Constitution* (The Hague, 1964), 15ff. See also J. Ph. Miller, *Numbers in Presence and Absence: A Study of Husserl's Philosophy of Mathematics* (The Hague/Boston/London, 1982), 38ff. In his careful and convincing argument, Miller questions the validity of de Boer's assertion that the *Phil. of Arith.* shows no evidence yet of a properly phenomenological understanding of the concept of origin and constitution. (See Th. de Boer, *The Development of Husserl's Thought* [The Hague/Boston/London, 1978], 72, 119ff.)

6. Husserl himself admitted that the *Logical Investigations* do not succeed in giving a fully satisfactory analysis of categorial intuition. Later, Husserl discarded in particular the view that the representative content of categorial intuition must be understood as a "psychical bond." It is not difficult to recognize a legacy from the *Phil. of Arith.* and its view of the formation of the categorial concept of number in this doctrine of a psychical bond that lies at the basis of categorial apperception.

7. E. Husserl, "[Rezension von] Schröder, Ernst, *Vorlesungen über die Algebra der Logik . . . ,*" newly published in *AR*, 3–43; trans. Dallas Willard in *The Personalist* 59 (April 1978), 115–43.

We are unable here to enter into the central concern of the *Schröder-Review*, namely the connection between extensional and intensional logic, as well as the contrast in principle between a logic of deductive thinking and progressive cognition and the inferential calculus with its automatic and technical manipulation of signs. Husserl says the following:

> Far from being a theory of pure deductions, it [the calculus] is much rather an art of rendering such deductions superfluous. It is nothing other than a technique for handling signs. . . . Here, as in the case of all the disciplines of the calculus, the difficult questions concerning the essence and logical legitimacy of the method of reckoning are inevitable. This is all the more so inasmuch as the *cognitive worth* of the results of those disciplines is first and foremost dependent upon the answer to these questions. . . . But the logic of this algebraic [logical] calculus does not fall within the purview of the researcher who takes it as a deductive logic, especially since the *mental operations* which he presupposes do not themselves belong to the domain of pure deductions over which he has exclusive command. The logical calculus is thus a calculus of pure deductions. It is not, however, the logic of these deductions. [*AR*, 7f.]

8. Cf. Frege's letter to Husserl of 24 May 1891, in G. Frege, *Philosophical and Mathematical Correspondence*, ed. G. Gabriel, trans. Hans Kaal (Oxford, 1976), 63. Concerning the history of the interaction between Husserl's and Frege's thinking, see especially, J. N. Mohanty, "Husserl and Frege: A New Look at their Relationship," *Research in Phenomenology* 4 (1974), 51–62; also in *Readings on Edmund Husserl's Logical Investigations*, ed. J. N. Mohanty (The Hague, 1976), 22–32.

9. See Miller, *Numbers in Presence and Absence*, 19ff.

10. Husserl himself refers to the kinship of these analyses with those of gestalt-psychology. In particular, he refers to Chr. Ehrenfels's theory of "gestalt-qualities" and their common dependence upon E. Mach (*PA*, fn., 210f.).

11. "Because early on we worked upon the continuous apprehension of particulars in respect of the most various sets, these characteristics [scl. figural moments] had necessarily . . . to associate themselves with the concept of the set and thus to erect bridges for the immediate recognition of such an initially uniform sensuous intuition as a set" (*PA*, 203).

12. "The symbolism of numbers (in particular our ordinary decadic system) is thus not merely a method for marking already given concepts. It is much rather a way of constructing new *concepts* and *designating* them with this construction" (*PA*, 234).

13. In particular, we may mention R. Avenarius, A. Bain, H. Cornelius, Th. Elsenhans, B. Erdmann, A. Höfler and A. Meinong, Th. Lipps, E. Mach, Chr. Sigwart, and W. Wundt.

14. This is an essential but frequently overlooked distinction between the respective critiques which Husserl and Frege (cf. esp. *Die Grundlagen der Arithmetik* [Breslau, 1884]) directed at logical psychologism.

15. *PPL*, v / F, 41.

16. Cf. the "Selbstanzeige" to the *Prolegomena* (*Hu* XVIII, 261f.).

17. This holds not only for normative logic but for every normative science, especially for ethics. The distinction merely sketched here between practical and normative precepts, as well as the system of the hierarchical dependencies among values within the framework of an "axiology," plays an essential role in Husserl's still unpublished investigations of the ethical problematic. Cf. A. Roth, *Edmund Husserls ethische Untersuchungen* (The Hague, 1960). Cf. also M. Scheler, *Der Formalismus in der Ethik und die materiale Wertethik*, 5th ed. (Bern and Munich, 1966), esp. 99f.

18. "Just as every law which arises out of experience and induction from individual matters of fact is a law *for* matters of fact, so conversely, every law for matters of fact is a law arising from experience and induction. In consequence . . . assertions of existential content are inseparable from it" (74 / F, 107).

19. *PPL*, §§ 44–48; cf. also 119 / F, 141f., 132 / F, 150f.; 150f. / F, 164f.

20. *PPL*, 128 / F, 148f.; 142 / F, 158f.; 119 / F, 141f.

21. Cf. *PPL*, 139f. / F, 156f.; 122 / F, 144; 162 / F, 173f.; 179 / F, 186.

22. Cf. *PPL*, 122 / F, 144; 143 / F, 159f.; 75 / F, 108f.
23. In a subsequent self-interpretation (1903), Husserl points emphatically to the influence which *Lotze's* interpretation of the Platonic theory of ideas had exercised upon his concept of the ideal being of logical objects. He makes clear that it was Lotze's *Logic* which first opened his eyes to *Bolzano's* doctrine of "propositions in themselves." Though these had previously "appeared [to him] to be merely mythical entities hovering being being and non-being," Lotze had taught him to understand their *"ideal being or validity."* (Cf. [Husserl's review of] Melchior Palagyi, "Der Streit der Psychologisten und Formalisten in der modernen Logik," reprinted in *AR*, 156f.) The early critics of the *Prolegomena*, who characterized Husserl's conception of pure logic as "Platonism," were thus on the right path. As with many later interpreters, as well, they merely tended not to notice that with Husserl it was a matter not of an ontologically, but of a *logically* inspired Platonism. According to the teaching of the *Prolegomena*, the ideal being of logical meanings and laws is not in the proper sense "objective" being, but rather absolute being of logical validity. These logical generalities (species) achieve the status of "ideal objects" only when they come to be investigated thematically in pure-logical apophantics.
24. *LI* II/1 (I), A, 101 / B, 100f. / F, 330. Cf. also *PPL*, 128ff. / F, 148ff.; 101 / F, 128; *LI* II/1 (I), 103 / F, 332f.; *LI* II/1 (II), 106 / F, 337; *AR*, 290f.
25. *LI* II/1 (I), § 30, A, 99 / B, 98 / F, 328; § 31, 99 / F, 329; *LI* II/1 (V), A, 392 / B, 417 / F, 590.
26. *AR*, 292; cf. also *PPL* 101 / F, 128.
27. *PPL*, 101 / F, 128. Cf. also the analogous deliberations at 128f. / F, 148f.; 186f. / F, 191f.; 74f. / F, 107f.
28. *PPL*, 129 / F, 149f.; cf. also 101 / F, 128; 183ff. / F, 189ff.; *AR*, 292.
29. In order to escape psychologism, it is not sufficient to contrast the comprehension of the ideal with that of the real (cf. *PPL*, 128 / F, 148). Over and above this is required a nonempirical description of ideation, a description which refrains from taking ideation as a real fact, a psychological matter of fact.
30. "Entwurf einer 'Vorrede' zu den 'Logischen Untersuchungen' " (1913), *Tijdschrift voor Filosofie* 1 (1939), 329.
31. *PPL*, §§ 67–69 and *FTL* §§ 13f. and 28ff. Our interpretation will be based upon *FTL* only in such respects as the latter surpasses the *Prolegomena*.
32. Cf. *FTL*, §§ 13 and 22; *PPL*, § 67; *LI*, II/1 (IV), § 14, A, 319 / B (significantly expanded), 339 / F, 526. Regarding Husserl's notion of a pure-logical grammar, cf. esp., J. M. Edie, *Speaking and Meaning. The Phenomenology of Language* (Bloomington and London, 1976), 45–71 and 202–11. This work not only provides a careful interpretation of Husserl's discussions, particularly in the fourth *LI* and in *FTL*, but also deals com-

prehensively with the voluminous secondary literature and confronts Husserl's theory of pure grammar with Chomsky's doctrine of linguistic depth-structures and "linguistic competence."

33. Cf. *PPL*, § 68 and *FTL*, §§ 14ff.

34. Cf. also *LI* II/2 (VI), §§ 30–35, which are devoted to this logic of "compatibility and incompatibility." Regarding the central methodological function of Husserl's logic of "wholes and parts" (*LI* [III]) for the *LI* in their entirety, cf. R. Sokolowski, "The Logic of Parts and Wholes in Husserl's *Logical Investigations*," *Philosophy and Phenomenological Research* 28 (1967–68), 537–53; also published in *Readings on Edmund Husserl's "Logical Investigations,"* ed. J. N. Mohanty (The Hague, 1976), 94–111.

35. *PPL*, §§ 69f.; cf. also *FTL*, §§ 28 and 35f. The three "tasks" or "stages" of pure logic are determined in the same way in the *Prolegomena* and in the *Formal and Transcendental Logic*: (1) Pure doctrine of the forms of "significations" (or "judgements"); (2) "logic of consequence"; (3) "theory of deductive systems." However, the *Prolegomena* and *FTL* differ in their determination of the formal logic of possible truth. In the earlier work, the formal logic of possible truth was still identified with the formal logic of consequence, whereas in the later work there is a clear distinction between a formal logic of consequence and a formal logic of truth. When Husserl claims that the "threefold stratification" of formal logic that first appeared in *FTL* is an essential advancement beyond the previous logic and the *Prolegomena* (*FTL*, §§ 22, 70a), he, of course, could not have meant the previously mentioned determination of the three "tasks" or "stages" of pure logic. The "threefold stratification" is rather a consequence of the separation of a formal logic of consequence from a formal logic of truth, and results in the following division of formal logic as apophantic analysis: (1) "Theory of the forms of judgement"; (2) "theory of consequence"; (3) "theory of truth" (§ 70a). Unfortunately, Husserl neglected in the *FTL* to determine more precisely the relationship between the three "stages" of logic and the threefold stratification of logic. The omission has very much affected a correct understanding of *Formal and Transcendental Logic*. See G. Heffernan, *Isagoge in die phänomenologische Apophantic Eine Einführung in die phänomenologische Urteilslogik* (Dordrecht/Boston/London, 1989).

36. *FTL*, §§ 37–46; cf. also §§ 25, 27. The corresponding passages of the *Prolegomena* are to be found in § 67, 244 / F, 237; § 68, A, 246 / B, 245f. / F, 238f.; § 70.

37. In earlier texts, Husserl calls this material ontology an *a priori* ontology of the real "or an *a priori* metaphysics." It explores "the basic categories in which the real as such can be grasped in respect of its essence. Thus, a group of inquiries must be possible which simply ponder everything without which reality as such cannot be thought. The entire *a priori* doctrine of the time, *a priori* phoronomy, and pure geometry would belong to this group" (*LE*, 101).

38. Cf. esp. §§ 24 and 52. Regarding the relation of logic and mathematics in *FTL*, and, in general, regarding the entire first part of *FTL*, usually neglected by the secondary literature, cf. the essay by R. Sokolowski, "Logic and Mathematics in Husserl's *Formal and Transcendental Logic*," in *Explorations in Phenomenology*, ed. D. Carr and E. S. Casey (The Hague, 1973); also published in R. Sokolowski, *Husserlian Meditations: How Words Present Things* (Evanston, 1974), 271–89.

Chapter 2

1. Cf. D. Cairns, *Conversations with Husserl and Fink* (The Hague, 1975), the conversation of 23 June 1932.
2. Cf. esp. *EP* I, where Husserl presents a "Critical History of Ideas." Some impulses for Husserl's deepened interest in skeptical argumentations surely emanated from the work of R. Richter, *Der Skeptizismus in der Philosophie*, of which the first volume appeared in 1904. Husserl received a copy of this book from the author (cf. K. Schuhmann, *Husserl-Chronik*, 81) and submitted it to a careful reading; indications are also to be found in his copy of the second volume (1908), that Husserl read this work as well (e.g., regarding Hume). One finds already in the *Prolegomena to Pure Logic* (1900) a discussion of the concept of skepticism.
3. In this regard, see especially I. Kern, *Husserl und Kant*, § 18; also the introduction of R. Boehm to *Hu* VIII.
4. We see here the possibility "of an introduction to transcendental phenomenology and phenomenological philosophy by way of the history of ideas" (*EP* II, 3), which could well constitute a fourth type of way (cf. *EP* I; *CES*, parts I and II).
5. Cf. Kern, *Husserl und Kant*, 306.
6. Husserl's study of Kant's writings was inspired in important ways by Natorp's interpretation of Kant and by Natorp's conception of philosophical psychology. Cf. ibid., § 17, p. 194.
7. Cf. ibid., 193.
8. Cf. chapters 1 and 9, regarding Husserl's doctrine of the formal and material ontologies and the ontology of the lifeworld as ultimately fundamental to all else.
9. Concerning an "eidetic science," cf. below, § 2.
10. Concerning "intentionality," cf. below, chapter 3, § 1.
11. Cf., e.g., *PP*, 344, 616; in general, the writings from the 1920s: *EP* II; *PP* (main text and essays). Also instructive is the attempt of 1929 at a reworking of *Ideas* I in the direction of a path through psychology to transcendental phenomenology instead of the "Cartesian" path which, having been more prominent in 1913, elicited considerable opposition from Husserl's contemporaries (cf. the new edition of *Ideen* I, 2d half-volume, 1976, ed. K. Schuhmann).

12. Cf. *Id* III. P. Natorp's *Allgemeine Psychologie* of 1912 would presumably constitute a further example.

13. Cf. the *Logos* article of 1911; from the period of the *Crisis*, cf., e.g., *CES*, appendix XXVIII, with the famous but often misunderstood sentence, "Philosophy as science . . . the dream is over" (*CES*, 508ff.).

14. Regarding Husserl's overall conception of philosophy, cf. below, chapter 10.

15. *LE*, 220f. (1906); cf. the "Freiburger Antrittsvorlesung" (1917), *AV*, 78.

16. Cf. *Ms. F I 17*, 26a (1909); "Freiburger Antrittsvorlesung," *AV*, 78f.

17. "Freiburger Antrittsvorlesung," *AV*, 78f.; *IP*, 47; *CES*, 181 / C, 177f.

18. "Freiburger Antrittsvorlesung," *AV*, 79.

19. Ibid. Cf. also *LE* (1906/07); *F I 17* (1909); *F I 4* (1912); *Id* I, part 1.

20. "Freiburger Antrittsvorlesung," 376.

21. Cf., e.g., *PP*, 71, 76; *Id* I, § 7; *EJ*, 87a; *AV*, 13ff.; "Freiburger Antrittsvorlesung," *AV*, 79.

22. Cf. esp. *EJ*, §§ 86–91; or the nearly identical text in *PP*, § 9. Cf. also the critical discussions of the method of viewing essences in W. Stegmüller, *Philosophie der Gegenwart* , vol. 1 (1976), 70ff.; E. Tugendhat, *Der Wahrheitsbegriff bei Husserl und Heidegger* (1967), 137–63; I. Kern, *Idee und Methode der Philosophie* (Berlin, 1975), § 41f.

23. Cf. the citation in Kern, *Husserl and Kant*, 116. As over against this, every empirical generalization outside the boundaries of pure phantasy would always yield only "common characteristics and generalities in respect of empirical extensions," "empirical necessities," or "presumptive" necessities (cf. *EJ*, §§ 86, 97c; *PP*, 79).

24. These lines, reminiscent of Plato's *Parmenides*, seem to express a deep Husserlian conviction. Even if he never conceived of any kind of "hypostatization" of his *eide*, we nevertheless find this universalization of the cidetic as such to be worthy of critical consideration (cf. Kern, *Idee und Methode* § 50).

25. In a manuscript stemming from the 1930s Husserl writes the following with respect to his "standing up for a universal ontology . . . as a universal *a priori* science of being [*das Seiende*] as such":

> The thought which guided me was this, that what mathematics accomplishes for natural science must be possible for all the factual sciences; and, stated universally, the totality of what factually is [*das tatsächlich Seiende*], in its arrangement into universal regions of being [*Seinsregionen*], can become a genuine, that is, a "rational" science, just as physics has become and continues to become a rational physics after beginning as a merely descriptive-empirical discipline, only by way of a return to eidetic universality, to the eidetic possibilities such as can be governed, precisely, in a purely rational fashion in eidetic universality, [to the eidetic possibilities] one of which is pregiven as matter-of-factuality of nature. [*Ms. B I 32*, 32]

26. Cf. *EP* I, 364 (ca. 1908); *LI*, § 64. Regarding Husserl's critique of the

Kantian *a priori*, cf. the discussions in T. Seebohm (1962); I. Kern (1964); E. Tugendhat (1967), 163ff.; and E. Marbach (1974), §§ 34f.

27. "Freiburger Antrittsvorlesung," *AV*, 79f.

28. Ibid.; cf. *Id* I, Introduction; *DR*, 141f.

29. Regarding the mathematical "there is," cf. *EJ*, 450 / C&A, 370f. It is a question here of a " 'there is' in the characteristic modification of the *a priori*," a question of an "it is *a priori* possible that there is" (§ 96c).

30. Regarding the special case of the "*eidos* 'transcendental ego'—*factum* 'ego,' " cf. below, chapter 10.

Supplementary Readings for Chapter 2

For § 1:

Boehm, R. *Vom Gesichtspunkt der Phänomenologie, Husserl-Studien.* Den Haag, 1968. §§ 5 and 7.

Kern, I. *Husserl und Kant: Eine Untersuchung über Husserls Verhältnis zu Kant und zum Neukantianismus.* Den Haag, 1964. Esp. § 18.

Marbach, E. *Das Problem des Ich in der Phänomenologie Husserls.* Den Haag, 1974. Chapter 2.

For § 2:

Kern, I. *Husserl und Kant.* Especially §§ 9a, 11c.

Kern, I. *Idee und Methode der Philosophie.* Berlin, 1975. Part 3, chapter 2.

Tugendhat, E. *Der Wahrheitsbegriff bei Husserl und Heidegger.* Berlin, 1967. Esp. §§ 7, 9c.

Chapter 3

1. Husserl still uses the expression "primary memory" in *Ideas I* (*Id* I, 145 / G, 216).

2. One ought not confuse this consciousness of the tones or tone-phases which have just sounded and faded away, with the phenomenon of "resonance." The resonance of a tone comes to consciousness in a primordial impression (*PITC*, 31 / C, 53).

3. Cf. *PITC*, 43, 69, 109f. / C, 65f., 93f., 146ff.; *APS*, 326f., 110f., 277ff.

4. *PITC*, 22 / C, 42 (the text very likely belongs to the period prior to 1904/05; see the note in the critical apparatus, *Hu* X, 407).

5. *PITC*, 72 / C, 97 (from 1907); appendix V. The original manuscript of this appendix could be discovered in the Husserl Archives. On the basis of its contents, however—and more can be said in this regard than has been mentioned here—the text gives evidence of stemming from an early period (ca. 1905).

6. The editor, R. Boehm, dates it "not before the end of 1908 and probably not before 1911" (*Hu* X, 391).

7. We have amended the text cited here. As it stands in *Husserliana* X it fails

to make good sense: " . . . namely, to that 'before' which is (we may not say: 'was') for the 'before.' "

Supplementary Readings for Chapter 3

For § 1:
Dreyfus, H., ed. *Husserl, Intentionality and Cognitive Science*. Cambridge (Mass.) and London, 1982.

For § 2:
Bernet, R. "Is the Present ever Present? Phenomenology and the Metaphysics of Presence." In *Husserl and Contemporary Thought. Research in Phenomenology*, vol. 12, 1982. 85–112.
Brough, J. B. "The Emergence of an Absolute Consciousness in Husserl's Early Writings on Time-Consciousness." In *Husserl: Expositions and Appraisals*. Edited by F. A. Elliston and P. McCormick. Notre Dame and London, 1977. 83–100.
Eigler, G. *Metaphysische Voraussetzungen in Husserls Zeitanalysen*. Meisenheim/ Glan, 1961.
Held, K. *Lebendige Gegenwart. Die Frage nach der Seinsweise des transzendentalen Ich bei Edmund Husserl, entwickelt am Leitfaden der Zeitproblematik*. Den Haag, 1966.
Sokolowski, R. *Husserlian Meditations: How Words Present Things*. Evanston, 1974. 138–68.

Chapter 4

1. Concerning the terminological designation of the representational sensations as "images," cf. *DR*, § 57: "In the most general sense, the case remains that which we have ascribed to those appearances in which images function as representational contents (and it is only for the sake of their representational function that we call them 'images' in respect of the objects represented)."

Supplementary Readings for Chapter 4

Asemissen, H. U. *Strukturanalytische Probleme der Wahrnehmung in der Phänomenologie Husserls: Kantstudien. Ergänzungshefte 73*. Köln, 1957.
Bernet, R. "Endlichkeit und Unendlichkeit in Husserls Phänomenologie der Wahrnehmung." *Tijdschrift voor Filosofie* 40, (1978[a]). 251–69.
Bernet, R. "Zur Teleologie der Erkenntnis: Eine Antwort an Rudolf Boehm." *Tijdschrift voor Filosofie* 40 (1978[b]). 662–68.
Claesges, U. *Edmund Husserls Theorie der Raumkonstitution*. Den Haag, 1964.

Gurwitsch, A. "Beitrag zur phänomenologischen Theorie der Wahrnehmung." *Zeitschrift für philosophische Forschung* 13 (1959). 419–37.

Rang, B. "Repräsentation und Selbstgegebenheit. Die Aporie der Phänomenologie der Wahrnehmung in den Frühschriften Husserls." *Phänomenologische Forschungen* 1 (1975). 105–37.

Chapter 5

1. Cf. also, e.g., "Psychological Studies Concerning Elementary Logic" (1894), newly edited by B. Rang in *Hu* XXII, 92ff.; in the same volume can be found texts from the 1890s stemming from the literary remains, especially "Intuition and Representation, Intention and Fulfillment" (1893), 269ff.

2. Concerning these matters, cf., e.g., the introduction to the sixth of the *Logical Investigations*; the beginning of his lectures from 1904–5 bearing the title, reminiscent of the *Logical Investigations*, "Principle Matters of Concern [*Hauptstücke*] [Drawn] from Phenomenology and [the] Theory of Cognition," cited in the editor's introduction by R. Boehm, *Hu* X, xv; further, the diary entry of September 1906, also cited in the aforementioned editor's introduction, *Hu* X, xiii f.

3. For historical information, cf. the editor's introduction by E. Marbach, *Hu* XXIII, xliii ff.

4. Cf. the citations in *Hu* X, xv f. and *Hu* XXIII, xliv; cf. also, e.g., E. Husserl, "Reminiscences on Franz Brentano" (Munich, 1919), 153 and 157. Large portions of Franz Brentano's lectures, "Ausgewählte Fragen aus Psychologie und Ästhetik," have been edited by Frau F. Mayer-Hillebrand and incorporated as the first part of the volume, F. Brentano, *Grundzüge der Ästhetik* (Bern, 1959); cf. the editor's remarks on 225, as well as her foreword, esp. xiv.

5. See F. Brentano, *Grundzüge der Ästhetik*, 86; cited hereafter as "Brentano."

6. Cf., e.g., *LI* II/1 (V), § 14. This early doctrine of Husserl's is seated in an empiricistically influenced theory of consciousness. This theory assumes present, experienced *contents*—sensations and phantasms—within consciousness (however they may have arisen). According to the character of the act or the "mode of consciousness," these contents experience diverse sorts of *apprehension*, interpretation, apperception, corresponding with which we have a perceptual appearance, a phantasial appearance, a pictorial appearance, and so on (cf. *LI* II/1 (V), § 14). In the present setting, an adequate discussion of this content-apprehension–schema would lead us too far afield. (For a discussion of this matter, cf. *Hu* X, editor's introduction; and R. Sokolowski, *The Formation of Husserl's Concept of Constitution* [The Hague, 1970].) We shall merely remark that, by way of his deepened analysis of the consciousness of intuitive presentation, Husserl

broke through to a decisive revision of this doctrine of apperception. The results of this revision will come into play in our further portrayal (cf. *Hu* XXIII, Einl. d. Hrsg., and esp. nos. 8 and 9).

7. The frequent terminological vacillations in Husserl's manuscripts must also be left out of the present discussion. As far as possible, we try to employ the designations which Husserl himself ultimately preferred.

8. Moreover, these two moments also come more or less expressly into play in ordinary usage. On the one hand, the English word "imagination" contains the moment of intuitiveness in the sense of "picturing by means of an image" (*imag*ination, image). On the other hand, the expressions "mere imagination" and "mere semblance" indicate that we have a consciousness of unreality in respect of what is presented in consciousness; that is, we "imagine" to ourselves that it is so, do not *posit* it as reality, do not "believe" in it (cf. *PBE*, e.g., no. 1, § 8).

9. Besides the positing presentation (perception) Husserl attempts now and again to speak of nonpositing presentation. As an ostensible example of this he brings forward consciousness of the picture-object [*Bildobjektbewußtsein*] (cf., e.g., *Id* I, § 111; *PBE*, e.g., no. 13 and passim).

10. Other act-qualities would be, for example, the wish, the will, the feeling, and so on. The entire problem coheres extremely closely with Brentano's classification of "psychical phenomena." Concerning this discussion, see, e.g., E. Tugendhat (1967), 41f.; and chap. 3, § 1 above.

11. A critical discussion of this universalization of neutralization can be found in I. Kern (1975), 146ff. Notably, Husserl himself seems at times to have thought neutralization impossible in the case of perception or primordial doxa. Cf. *PBE*, e.g., no. 15j (1912); cf. also *LI*, 455f.

12. With the "extension of the reduction to intersubjectivity" a certain intentional-analytical understanding of our experience of the other is already presupposed. On the other hand, according to Husserl, an actual intentional understanding of our experience of the other can no doubt only be obtained on the methodological basis of the phenomenological reduction.

13. Husserl employs the terms "primordinal" and "primordial" interchangeably to characterize the sphere of ownness [*Eigenheitssphäre*]. We shall render both words by the contrived word "primordinal" in order to distinguish them from "*ursprünglich*," which we have translated primarily as "primordial," though in some instances as "original." The latter word, however, we reserve for the most part in order to render Husserl's term "original."

14. Appresentation="a co-presentation [*Mitgegenwärtigung*] of that which can not be presented primordially [*ursprünglich nicht zu Gegenwärtigendes*]" (*PI* II, 513).

15. In a number of texts Husserl makes this similarity problematical. Cf. *PI* I, no. 9; *PI* II, no. 33; apps. LXX, LXXI, LXXII, etc.

16. The corresponding passage in the *Cartesian Meditations* seems to me to be corrupt (144, lines 13–20). Husserl's original manuscript of this text is no

longer extant. There remains only a transcript and a partial revision from the hand of Husserl's assistant at that time, Eugen Fink.

Supplementary Readings for Chapter 5

For § 1:

Conrad, T. *Zur Wesenslehre des psychischen Lebens und Erlebens.* Den Haag, 1968.

Fink, E. "Vergegenwärtigung und Bild: Beiträge zur Phänomenologie der Unwirklichkeit" (1930). *Studien zur Phänomenologie, 1930–1939.* Den Haag, 1966.

Kunz, H. *Die anthropologische Bedeutung der Phantasie. Erster Teil: Die psychologische Analyse und Theorie der Phantasie.* Basel, 1946.

Sokolowski, R. *Presence and Absence. A Philosophical Investigation of Language and Being.* Bloomington, 1978.

For § 2:

Franck, D. *Chair et Corps. Sur la phénoménologie de Husserl.* Paris, 1981.

Schütz, A. "Das Problem der transzendentalen Intersubjektivität bei Husserl." In *Gesammelte Aufsätze III, Studien zur phänomenologischen Philosophie.* Den Haag, 1971.

Theunissen, M. *Der Andere. Studien zur Sozialontologie der Gegenwart.* Berlin, 1965.

Waldenfels, B. *Das Zwischenreich des Dialogs. Sozialphilosophische Untersuclungen in Anschluss an Edmund Husserl.* Den Haag, 1971.

Supplementary Readings for Chapter 6

Atwell, J. E. "Husserl on Signification and Object." *American Philosophical Quarterly* 6 (1969). Also in *Readings on Edmund Husserl's Logical Investigations.* Edited by J. N. Mohanty. The Hague, 1977. 83–93.

Bernet, R. "Zur Teleologie der Erkenntnis: Eine Antwort an Rudolf Boehm."*Tijdschrift voor Filosofie* 40 (1978). 662–68.

———. "Bedeutung und intentionales Bewußtsein: Husserls Begriff des Bedeutungsphänomens." *Studien zur Sprachphänomenologie, Phänomenologische Forschungen* 8 (1979). 31–64.

———. "Logik und Phänomenologie in Husserls Lehre von der Wahrheit." *Tijdschrift voor Filosofie* 43 (1981). 35–89.

Derrida, J. *La voix et le phénomène: Introduction au problème du signe dans la phénoménologie de Husserl.* Paris, 1967.

———. *De la grammatologie.* Paris, 1967.

———. *Marges de la philosophie.* Paris, 1972.

Husserl, E. *Briefe an Roman Ingarden. Mit Erläuterungen und Erinnerungen an Husserl.* Edited by R. Ingarden. Den Haag, 1968.

Ströker, E. "Husserls Evidenzprinzip: Sinn und Grenzen einer methodischen Norm der Phänomenologie als Wissenschaft." *Zeitschrift für philosophische Forschung* 32 (1978), 3–30.

Tugendhat, E. *Der Wahrheitsbegriff bei Husserl und Heidegger.* Berlin, 1967.
———. *Vorlesungen zur Einführung in die sprachanalytische Philosophie.* Frankfurt am Main, 1976.
Twardowski, K. *Zur Lehre vom Inhalt und Gegenstand der Vorstellungen: Eine psychologische Untersuchung.* Wien, 1894.

Chapter 7

1. On the other hand, from the point of view of this genetic phenomenology, Husserl can wrest a valid facet from the psychological-genetic considerations of his *Philosophy of Arithmetic.*
2. The influence of Marburg neo-Kantian Paul Natorp would appear to have been significant for Husserl's conception of a genetic phenomenology.
3. A letter of 29 June 1918, cited by I. Kern, *Husserl und Kant,* 346f.
4. Cf. *Ms. B IV 6,* 5a; certain beginnings of genetic considerations reach back as far as the first draft of *Ideas II* (1912): cf. *Ms. F III 1,* 11 a/b (cited by E. Marbach, *Das Problem des Ich . . .* , 306). At the time of their formulation, however, these beginnings were still understood in a merely psychological manner.
5. This "history" of consciousness (the history of all possible apperceptions)

   > has nothing to do with the exhibition of a factual genesis for factual apperceptions or for factual types in a factual stream of consciousness or even in the consciousness of all factual human beings . . . ; rather, every configuration of apperceptions is an eidetic configuration with a genesis in accordance with eidetic laws, so that the idea of such an apperception entails that it can be submitted to a "genetic analysis." It is not the necessary coming-to-be of the occasional, isolated apperception (if it is thought of as a fact), that is given; rather, the only thing given with the genesis of the essence is the mode of genesis in which some or another apperception of this type had originally to have arisen within an individual stream of consciousness. [*APS,* 339]

6. In 1910 Husserl still regarded the laws of association as made up of merely "approximate rules," not eidetic laws (cf. *PI* I, 83).
7. Husserl could scarcely make a similar assertion with regard to ideal objects, mathematical concepts, let us say, insofar as these can be given "adequately" (not in appearances). Hence, static phenomenology would be "more realistic" vis-à-vis ideal objects than vis-à-vis nature.

Important Texts Concerning Genetic Phenomenology

Concerning the Phenomenology of Intersubjectivity. Vol. 1. *Hu* XIII. App. XLV.
Analyses Concerning Passive Synthesis. Hu XI. 336ff.
Concerning the Phenomenology of Intersubjectivity. Vol. 2. *Hu* XIV. App. I.

Formal and Transcendental Logic. Hu XVII. §§ 85 ff.; app. II.
Cartesian Meditations. Hu I. §§ 37–39.
Concerning the Phenomenology of Intersubjectivity. Vol. 3. *Hu* XV. No. 35.
The Crisis of the European Sciences and Transcendental Phenomenology. Hu VI.
App. III.

Supplementary Readings for Chapter 7

Holenstein, E. *Phänomenologie der Assoziation.* Den Haag, 1972.
Welton, D. *The Origins of Meaning.* The Hague/Boston/Lancaster, 1983.

Chapter 8

1. Essential thoughts of Husserl regarding the concept of the personal "I"
   find their expression especially in connection with, or with respect to, his
   problematic concerning intersubjectivity (cf. *PI* I, II, III).

Supplementary Readings for Chapter 8

Brand, G. *Welt, Ich und Zeit, nach unveröffentlichten Manuskripten Edmund Husserls.* Den Haag, 1955.
Gurwitsch, A. "Phänomenologie der Thematik und des reinen Ich: Studien über Beziehungen von Gestalttheorie und Phänomenologie." *Psychologische Forschungen* 12 (1929).
Held, K. *Lebendige Gegenwart: Die Frage nach der Seinsweise des transzendentalen Ich bei Edmund Husserl, entwickelt am Leitfaden der Zeitproblematik.* Den Haag, 1966.
Marbach, E. *Das Problem des Ich in der Phänomenologie Husserls.* Den Haag, 1974.
Sartre, J. P. *La transcendance de l'ego.* Paris, 1965.

Chapter 9

1. See *Id* II, 375; *Ms. D 13 I*, 173a (ca. 1918); *Ms A IV 22*, transcr., 70
   (1920).
2. This concept, borrowed from Richard Avenarius, can be found as early as
   the lectures on "Basic Problems of Phenomenology" in 1910/11 (*PI* I,
   125).
3. For example, in the essay, *Philosophy as a Strict Science*, from 1911, and in
   the treatise, *Ideas*, from 1913.
4. Cf. above, fn. 3; cf. also, Husserl's judgements concerning Avenarius in
   the *Prolegomena*, 192ff., and in the *Crisis*, 198 / C, 195.

5. The same sense is expressed in "Nature and Spirit," from 1927. There Husserl says the following: "Is not science itself then a function of life, and not of a contingent, individual life and a contingent present; but rather of one of the greatest products of historical intention and accomplished labor in millennia? Is it not itself a part of the one lifeworld?" (*Ms. F I 32*, 108b).
6. Cf. Husserl's letter to Hugo von Hofmannsthal, published in *Sprache und Politik* (Festgabe für Dolf Sternberger) (Heidelberg 1967), 111–14.

Supplementary Readings for Chapter 9

Carr, David. "The Lifeworld Revisited: Husserl and Some Recent Interpreters." In *Interpreting Husserl: Critical and Comparative Studies*. Den Haag, 1987. 227–46.
———. "Husserl's Problematic Concept of the Life-World." In *Husserl: Expositions and Appraisals*. Edited by F. A. Elliston and P. McCormick. Notre Dame, 1977. 202–12.
Claesges, U. "Zweideutigkeiten in Husserls Lebenswelt-Begriff." In *Perspektiven transzendental-phänomenologischer Forschlung*. Edited by U. Claesges and K. Held. Den Haag, 1972. 227–67.
Janssen, P. *Geshichte und Lebenswelt*. Den Haag, 1970.
Strökcr, E., cd. *Lebenswelt und Wissenschaft in der Philosophic Edmund Husserls*. Frankfurt, 1979.

Chapter 10

1. In a similar spirit, as early as the lectures on "Basic Problems in Ethics and the Theory of Value" from the summer semester of 1911, Husserl says the following:

   > If we give the name metaphysics to the science that is related to factual Being, insofar as this science wants, in satisfying the highest interests, to be absolute science, then it is clear that metaphysics is nothing other than the continuation of all actual sciences of nature and spirit, as the consummation, the completion, the philosophizing of these sciences, and this in accordance with the principles developed in the pure [=*a priori*] philosophical disciplines, in accordance with the ideas and ideals given shape to in these disciplines in a pure fashion. [*Ms. F I 14*]

2. In the *Paris Lectures*, Husserl says almost word for word the same thing (*CM*, 39). Cf. also *EP* II, 506, where Husserl says the following: "History is the great fact of absolute Being; and the ultimate questions, the ultimate metaphysical and teleological questions, are one with the questions regarding the absolute meaning of history."
3. Cf. I. Kern, *Husserl und Kant*, 300–303.

4. Cf. the text in *Ms. D 17*, 21a (May 1934), which is published in *Philosophical Essays in Memory of Edmund Husserl*, ed. M. Farber (Cambridge, Mass., 1940 [2d ed. 1970]), 323, where we read the following: "The *ego* lives and precedes all actual and possible Being, and [this means] Being in every sense, whether real or irreal."

5. A somewhat more detailed view of the relationship between primary and secondary philosophy can be found in I. Kern, *Idee und Methode der Philosophie*, 333ff.

Bibliography

N.B. The following list includes only the published works of Edmund Husserl referred to within the present study. Each listing is followed by a bracketed notation indicating (1) the abbreviation employed to refer to the work in question; (2) if translated, the abbreviation employed to refer to the translator of that work; (3) if published in the *Husserliana* series, a Roman numeral designating the corresponding *Husserliana* volume; (4) where appropriate, either the sign "g.p." indicating that the pagination of the German edition being cited is noted in the margins of the English translation (where this information is not provided in the English translation, we shall make no notation at all), or the sign "n.t.," indicating that the work has not been translated. The order of the works listed is determined by the sequence of the corresponding *Husserliana* editions. Works not published in the *Husserliana* series have been placed toward the end of the list following the order of their original appearance (first edition).

Gesammelte Werke. Auf Grund des Nachlasses veröffentlicht in Gemeinschaft mit dem Husserl-Archiv an der Universität Köln vom Husserl-Archiv (Louvain) unter Leitung von H. L. van Breda. Den Haag, 1950–1975. *Husserliana (Hu),* Bände I–XVIII.

Gesammelte Werke. Auf Grund des Nachlasses veröffentlicht vom Husserl-Archiv (Louvain) in Verbindung mit Rudolf Boehm unter Leitung von Samuel IJsseling. Den Haag, 1976–. *Husserliana (Hu),* Band III, Halbbände 1 u. 2 (Neuausgabe); Bände XXI–XXVIII.

Cartesian Meditations: An Introduction to Phenomenology. Translated by D. Cairns. The Hague, 1977. [*CM* / C / *Hu* I / g.p.].

The Paris Lectures. Translated by P. Koestenbaum. The Hague, 1967. [*PL* / K / *Hu* I / g.p.].

The Idea of Phenomenology. Translated by W. P. Alston and G. Nakhnikian. The Hague, 1964. [*IP* / A&G / *Hu* II / g.p.].

Ideas: A General Introduction to Pure Phenomenology. Translated by W.R.B. Gibson. London and New York, 1931. [*Id* I/ G / *Hu* III].

Ideas Pertaining to a Pure Phenomenology and to a Phenomenological Philosophy [*Ideen zu einer reinen Phänomenologie und einer phänomenologischen*

Philosophie]. Book I, *General Introduction to Pure Phenomenology*. Translated by F. Kersten. The Hague and Boston, 1982. [*Id* I / *Hu* III / g.p. All references to *Ideen I* cite the pagination of the Gibson translation; however, the Kersten translation is to be preferred as a rendering of the original.]

Ideas Pertaining to a Pure Phenomenology and to a Phenomenological Philosophy. Book II, *Phenomenological Investigations Concerning Constitution* [*Phänomenologische Untersuchungen zur Konstitution*]. [*Id* II / *Hu* IV / n.t.].

Ideas Pertaining to a Pure Phenomenology and to a Phenomenological Philosophy. Book III, *Phenomenology and the Foundations of the Sciences*. Translated by T. Klein and W. Pohl. The Hague, 1980. [*Id* III / *K&P* / *Hu* V / g.p.].

The Crisis of the European Sciences and Transcendental Phenomenology: An Introduction to Phenomenological Philosophy. Translated by D. Carr. Evanston, 1970. [*CES* / C / *Hu* VI].

First Philosophy [*Erste Philosophie*]. 2 vols. [*EP* I, II / *Hu* VII, VIII / n.t.].

Phenomenological Psychology. Translated by J. Scanlon. The Hague, 1977. [*PP* / S / *Hu* IX / g.p.].

The Phenomenology of Internal Time-Consciousness. Translated by J. S. Churchill. Bloomington, 1964. [*PITC* / C / *Hu* X. All references to *PITC* cite the pagination of *Hu* X].

Analyses Concerning Passive Synthesis [*Analysen zur passiven Synthesis*]. [*APS* / *Hu* XI / n.t.].

Philosophy of Arithmetic [*Philosophie der Arithmetik*]. [*PA* / Hu XII / n.t.].

Concerning the Phenomenology of Intersubjectivity [*Zur Phänomenologie der Intersubjektivität*]. 3 vols. [*PI* I, II, III / *Hu* XIII, XIV, XV / n.t.].

Thing and Space [*Ding und Raum*]. [*DR* / *Hu* XVI / n.t.].

Formal and Transcendental Logic. Translated by D. Cairns. The Hague, 1969. [*FTL* / C / *Hu* XVII / g.p.].

Prolegomena to Pure Logic. In Vol. 1 of *Logical Investigations*. Translated by J. N. Findlay. London and New York, 1977. [*PPL* or *LI* I / F / *Hu* XVIII (*LU* I; see below)].

Essays and Reviews [*Aufsätze und Rezensionen*]. [*AR* / *Hu* XXII / n.t.].

Phantasy, Picture-Consciousness, Memory [*Phantasie, Bildbewußtsein, Erinnerung*]. [*PBE* / *Hu* XXIII / n.t.].

Introduction to Logic and the Theory of Knowledge [*Einleitung in die Logik und Erkenntnistheorie*]. [*LE* / *Hu* XXIV / n.t.].

Lectures on the Theory of Meaning [*Vorlesungen über Bedeutungslehre*]. [*VBL* / *Hu* XXVI / n.t.].

Essays and Lectures [*Aufsätze und Vorträge*] (1922–1937). [*AV* / *Hu* XXVII / n.t.].

Logische Untersuchungen (Band I: *Prolegomena zur reinen Logik*; Band II, 1: *Untersuchungen zur Phänomenologie und Theorie der Erkenntnis*; Band II, 2: *Elemente einer phänomenologischen Aufklärung der Erkenntnis*). Halle, 1928 [Vierte Auflage (Unveränderter Abdruck der zweiten umgearbeiteten Auflage)]. [*LU* I, II/1, II/2].

Logical Investigations. 2d ed. 2 vols. Translated by J. N. Findlay. London and
  New York, 1977. [*LI* I, II/2 / F / *LU* I (*Hu* XVIII; see above), II/1,
  II/2].
Philosophie als strenge Wissenschaft. Herausgegeben von W. Szilasi. Frankfurt
  am Main, 1965. [*PSW*; originally published in *Logos* 1 (1910/11); the
  pagination from *Logos* is noted in the Szilasi text].
Philosophy as a Strict Science. Translated by Q. Lauer, in *Phenomenology and the
  Crisis of Philosophy.* New York, 1965. [*PSS* / L / *PSW*].
Erfahrung und Urteil: Untersuchungen zu Genealogie der Logik. Redigiert und
  herausgegeben von L. Landgrebe. Hamburg, 1954 (Zweite unver-
  änderte Auflage). [*EU*].
Experience and Judgement: Investigations in a Genealogy of Logic. Translated by
  J. S. Churchill and K. Ameriks. Evanston, 1973. [*EJ*/ C&A/ *EU*].